RALPH FIENNES

THE UNAUTHORISED BIOGRAPHY

BY

YORK MEMBERY

Freelance journalist and writer York Membery is the author of an acclaimed biography of the new 007, Pierce Brosnan. A former show business writer on the *Daily Mirror* and *Daily Express*, he has contributed to *The Times*, *GQ*, *Reader's Digest*, *Mail on Sunday* and many other publications. This is his fourth book.

In Memory of my Father

First published in Great Britain in 1997 by
Chameleon Books
an imprint of Andre Deutsch Ltd
106 Great Russell Street
London
WC1B 3LJ
www.vci.co.uk

Andre Deutsch is a subsidiary of VCI plc

Typeset in North Wales by
Derek Doyle & Associates, Mold, Flintshire.
Printed and bound by
WBC Book Manufacturers Ltd, Bridgend.

ISBN 0 2339 9290 1

Contents

Acknowledgements

My thanks to Kim Kent, Juliet Hickman, Andrew Galt, Simon Morrissey, David and Justine Scouller, Toby Chetwynd-Talbot, Todd Brewster, Kathryn Worth, Mike Flowers, Susan Engel, Glyn Evans, Hugh Davies, John McCloud, Hugh Cruttwell, Sally Fairall, Anne Stammers, Estelle Kohler, Bill Homewood, Jim Driscoll, Duncan Davies, Tania Wade, Angela Turnbull, Henry Fitzherbert, Sean O'Brien, Stephen Hayward, Mary Walsh, Frances Tobin, Caroline Rippier, Steve Clark, Louise Johncox, Fiachra Gibbons, Sylvester Morand, Bob Diamond, David Humphrey, Steve Hughes, Ann Williams, Jim Thomas, Luke Jennings and Sue Longstaffe, as well as to Cathy O'Neill, Gareth Negus and David Rustidge at the Coliseum Theatre, Oldham, Elizabeth Pettitt at Flintshire Public Records Office, Rhodri Owen and Catherine Squires at the BBC, Sarah Bathena at Homes Associates, Brenda Molson at the Society of Film Distributors, and to all those people who spoke to me but wish to remain anonymous.

I am also indebted to the library staff at News International, Mirror Group Newspapers, the *Guardian*, Eastern Counties Newspapers, the Shakespeare Centre, Stratford-upon-Avon, and the Academy of Motion Picture Arts and Sciences, Los Angeles, as well as to the staff at Westminster Reference Library, the Theatre Museum Study Room, the Family Records Centre, London, the Suffolk Record Office and Bantry Library for their assistance. Finally, I would like to thank Virgin Trains, RyanAir, Acton Lodge, Southwold, Suffolk, and the Atlanta Guesthouse, Bantry, for help with travel and accommodation during the researching of the book.

In addition, the following publications proved a rich source of information and I am grateful to them: *Daily Express, Daily Mail, Daily Mirror, Daily Telegraph, Daily Star, East Anglian Daily Times, Eastern Daily Press, Empire, Evening Standard, Harpers Bazaar, Financial Times, Girl About Town, GQ, Hello!, High Life, Hollywood Reporter, Independent, Independent on Sunday, Jewish Chronicle, Los Angeles Times, Lowestoft Journal, Mail on Sunday, Manchester Evening News, National Enquirer, New York Times, New Yorker, Observer, OK!, Oldham Evening Chronicle, Première, Preview, Punch, Salisbury Journal, San Francisco Chronicle, Stage, Sun, Sunday Telegraph, Sunday Times, Times, Time Out, TV Times, Vanity Fair* and *Variety.*

Preface

It was a chilly March evening. Within days the winners of the 1997 Academy Award would be announced at the Hollywood Oscar ceremony in Los Angeles. Five thousand miles away from this star-studded event, a crowd was gathering outside a former Salvation Army citadel in a nondescript side street in Islington, north London.

Despite its reputation as the home of the chattering classes Islington is, in reality, like much of London – a patchwork quilt of rags and riches, smart town houses and shabby council flats existing in uneasy proximity.

It's hard to believe that 'merry Islington' – as it was once known – used to be a spa resort which the well-to-do visited for its semi-rural charms and clean air. Today, it has fewer green spaces than any other London borough and you can feel the dirt in the air. However, the cosmopolitan district has caught the imagination of the capital's bright young things, who add a certain glamour to its grubby streets.

That night the crowd outside the Almeida, that citadel-turned theatre, was made up of students, well-dressed young couples, and a surprising number of smartly-dressed suburban types more likely to be seen in the West End on a Saturday night than in an Islington back street, as well as a smattering of local fashionable twenty-some-things.

A loud speaker crackled to life, and the audience quietened momentarily with the announcement that the next performance of *Ivanov* would commence in ten minutes.

A solitary lamp glowed on the dimly lit stage as theatregoers began to file into the auditorium, squeezing onto the theatre's notoriously cramped bench seats. Any of them looking up at the stage would have noticed an unobtrusive moustachioed figure in an overcoat, sitting at a small table, reading a book.

'Is that one of the actors?' a voice in the audience sheepishly enquired. 'No, it's probably an extra,' answered another knowingly. Neither suggestion quite rang true. As the seconds ticked by, the more alert theatregoers started to nudge each other, whispering: 'You don't think that's ... him?'

Unthinkable as it was to most of the audience that the play's leading actor would take to the stage ten minutes before the play had even begun, it slowly dawned on them that here, before them, sat the man being hailed as the most exciting British actor of his generation. As desired as Brando, as private as Alec Guinness, as English as David Niven, as magnificent a screen and stage presence as Laurence Olivier.

Ralph Fiennes' latest film *The English Patient*, which had already grossed more than $50 million in America and received a dozen Oscar nominations, was yet to be released in Britain, and already the excitement surrounding the movie had turned him into the show business world's man of the moment.

Many critics felt he was in with a real chance of winning the Best Actor award – having already been nominated for Best Supporting Actor three years earlier. The nomination seemed to be more than just a passing nod in his direction from the luminaries of Tinseltown; it seemed a recognition of both his power as an actor and of his burgeoning superstar status. And the hopes of the British film industry – indeed of Britain itself – were resting on his slender shoulders.

Following his Oscar nomination, tickets for *Ivanov* became the nearest thing to gold dust. The very idea that an Oscar-nominated actor would be treading the boards in a fringe theatre the weekend before the ceremony sounded decidedly quaint, at the very least – if not bordering on insanity – to America's sharp-suited movie executives. The idea that an Oscar-nominated actor would do so for a paltry £250 a week (before tax) was beyond belief. You could almost hear them choking on their salads.

It was impossible to imagine fellow Oscar nominee Tom Cruise performing in a theatre for £25,000, let alone £250 a week.

Most Oscar nominees were taking things decidedly easy that

weekend. They were likely to be found topping up their tans by their Malibu swimming pool, visiting the gym in the hope of shedding a few surplus pounds or perhaps making a last frenzied attempt to curry favour with Academy Award judges in a bid to land one of the movie world's febrilely and reverently prized statuettes.

None other than Fiennes, you could be certain, were to be found working in cramped conditions for the sort of money most self-respecting Hollywood stars routinely spent on getting their hair cut at an exclusive Beverly Hills salon.

Just why would an actor who was already a member of the million-dollar-a-movie club want to put himself through such an ordeal? Was it because he was so obsessed with his craft that he felt a need to prove himself in front of a theatre audience? Was it out of sheer perversity, as some cynics thought? Or out of a desire to wrong-foot the pundits and put two fingers up to the show business world's men-in-suits whose only interest was in generating ever-bigger profits?

It's this very unorthodoxy which helps to make Ralph Fiennes so fascinating a figure in an age when the bottom line, more than ever before, is what matters in today's film business, regardless of the quality of the end product.

Yet, it is probably true to say that for all the pseudo-psychological babble that has been written about him in the media, few people know the real Ralph Fiennes.

He's a man of undoubted contradictions who's sought out the spotlight and chosen a career in that highest profile of businesses – show business. Yet he appears as reluctant as Queen Victoria to smile for photographers, regards the most benign questions as 'intrusive' and has been accused of converting shyness into an art form.

He's a man who is quietly spoken in person but has the capacity to dominate stage or screen, transforming himself into as monstrous a villain as Amon Goeth in *Schindler's List* or as complex a romantic hero as Count Laszlo de Almasy in *The English Patient*. He's also a man whose private life is to say the least, complicated.

Having risen through the ranks of the Royal Shakespeare Company to almost instant screen triumph, he appears to have it all – fame, money, success and acclaim – and no shortage of women offering him a respite from the pressures of stardom. Yet he never truly seems happy. Just who is the moody, seemingly unfathomable man behind those famously intense eyes?

CHAPTER ONE

A Question of Breeding

The Swinging Sixties never quite reached Suffolk. Some feel that the East Anglian county's allure is that, in many respects, it preserves a distance from the rest of Britain without becoming totally isolated. Virtually untouched by the Industrial Revolution, it is still, even now one of the quietest, least densely populated corners of England.

If anything, the north Suffolk village of Wangford, which is dissected by the A12, is even more remote. The nearest towns of any size are Lowestoft, 15 miles to the north, and Ipswich, about 35 miles south, although the charming little seaside town of Southwold lies a couple of miles to the east. As for London, it may be just over 100 miles away but it might as well be ten times as far. 'One child in my class then hadn't been as far as Southwold, let alone London,' recalls Anne Stammers, a former teacher at Wangford Infant School.

The village takes its name from a stream called the Wang, a tributary of the River Blyth. Large parts of the surrounding area belong to the Earl of Stradbroke, whose family has owned land in the district since 1533. The present Earl – dubbed the 'Aussie Earl' because he lives down under – is still lord of the manor of Wangford as well as of the nearby manors of Henham and Reydon.

The village, which has about 500 inhabitants, dates back to at least 1160 A.D. when a priory was founded on the site of the present church. And by the 1870s Wangford had six public houses, five boot makers, a wheelwright and a couple of saddle-makers. All that remains today are a couple of pubs and a post office/general store.

1

Some homes were still without electricity as late as 1960. Farms were labour intensive and relied on human brawn and horse-drawn ploughs – and the population was made up almost entirely of farmers, farm labourers and their respective families. 'There was no middle class to speak of,' says Stammers. 'And it was still a time when some parents were reluctant to let their children go to grammar school for fear of them getting above themselves.'

In 1960 Mark Twisleton-Wykeham-Fiennes became a tenant farmer at Elms Farm, Wangford. A former pupil at Britain's most prestigious public school, Eton – where the fees now exceed £13,000 a year – he came from one of Britain's most distinguished ancestral lines.

His family had owned land in England since the days of Ingelram Fiennes, who lived around 100 A.D. and had inherited manors at Martock, Wendover and Carshalton through his marriage to Sybil de Tingries, heiress to the Duke of Ponthieu. His son, Enguerrand Fiennes, married the daughter of King Alexander of Scotland. While a cousin, who was killed in the Crusades, donated his heart to the citizens of London, along with a burial plot which is known as Finsbury Square.

Other ancestors included Jeahna Fiennes, one of the five famous 'Burghers of Calais'; Roger Fiennes, a constable of the Tower of London; James Fiennes, 1st Lord Saye and Sele, born in 1395, who became Lord High Treasurer; and William Fiennes, 2nd Lord Saye and Sele, who inherited Broughton Castle, near Banbury, through a timely marriage.

The list went on: Nathaniel Fiennes was a colonel in Oliver Cromwell's roundhead army; Celia Fiennes was a famous travel writer immortalized in a nursery rhyme – 'Ride a cock horse to Banbury Cross to see a Fiennes (fine) lady upon a white horse'; Gregory Twisleton Fiennes, 14th Baron Saye and Sele, lived to be 'the oldest Whig in the House of Lords'; while Frederick Fiennes, 16th Baron Saye and Sele, was related to Jane Austen and restored the old family name: Twisleton-Wykeham-Fiennes.

In addition, there was Eustace Twisleton-Wykeham-Fiennes who became private secretary to Winston Churchill, and was later made Baronet of Banbury and Governor of the Seychelles.

Mark's own father was the industrialist Sir Maurice Fiennes, knighted for his part in securing Britain's biggest-ever export order in the 1950s. Born Maurice Alberic Twisleton-Wykeham-Fiennes in 1907, he was educated at Repton and then went into engineering. Appointed managing director of Sheffield-based Davy and United Engineering in 1945, he helped make it the biggest firm of its type in the Commonwealth, employing over 2,000 people. He went on to become president of the Iron and Steel Institute and an adviser to the United Nations and World Bank. Following his death in 1994 his obituary appeared in *The Times*. Mark's mother was the daughter of a major in the Dragoon Guards.

Becoming a tenant farmer has never been easy. 'It's usually down to the old boy network,' according to John Holmes of White House Farm, just outside Wangford. But in 1960 the adjoining 350-acre Elms Farm, part of the Henham Estate, was put out to tender.

'Relatives of mine ran the farm and showed more than forty people around,' reveals Kim Kent, who served as parish council chairman for seventeen years. 'But the Earl, who owned the farm, was still trying to marry off one of his daughters. And I've a strong suspicion that the prospect of having an eligible bachelor like Mark around tipped the odds in his favour – even though the Earl had received several higher bids. As I understand it, Mark was told that if he raised his bid slightly, to about £650 an acre, his bid for the farm would be accepted.'

After leaving Eton, Mark Fiennes had worked on sheep farms in Australia and Texas. With the benefit of his livestock experience he grassed down the land, bought 500 head of sheep and set about making a success of the farm. It was no nine-to-five job, though. 'There's always something to do and working fifteen-hour days isn't uncommon,' says Holmes, who became friends with Mark.

However, there were compensations. Farm labour was cheap and in plentiful supply – and the broad shoulders of burly local workers performed most of the heavy physical work.

One of the biggest attractions of being a tenant farmer was getting to live in a grand house for next-to-nothing. Many of Suffolk's farm-houses look more like manor houses than houses for farmers. The Elms Farm residence is no exception. Even the most gushing, superlative-laden estate agent advertisement would be hard pressed to do justice to the magnificent twenty-two room property.

Dating back to 1500, it has a two-acre garden at the rear and looks out over a pretty farmyard pond. The red brick façade frontage, featuring eight windows, extends more than 50ft from left to right. The rear of the house has an equally impressive mock Georgian façade complete with pillars. Inside there are seven bedrooms, two bathrooms, a sitting-room, a dining-room, a drawing-room and a breakfast-room in addition to a boot-room, a laundry room, a box-room, various storerooms and even a cellar. Mark's mother supplied a set of heavy, Paris-made silk curtains which still hang in the house today.

It was without doubt the grandest house in Wangford – and was to be Ralph's home for the first seven years of his life. Here was a boy who was, effectively, to the manor born. Today, his childhood home is conservatively estimated to be worth £300,000 – although a similar property in London would certainly top the £1 million mark.

It was a vast house for one man living on his own. But at least Mark was spared the job of cleaning this country palace. A woman from the village would 'come round to do his cooking, ironing and cleaning', says Kent, leaving Mark to devote his energies to the 3500-acre farm. It wasn't a bad life for a single man in his twenties.

Ironically, the Earl's bid to play Cupid ended in failure because, in 1960, Mark met Jini, the woman who would become his wife. She, too, had breeding, as the old-fashioned saying goes.

Born in Chichester, West Sussex, on 24 February 1938, Jennifer Anne Mary Alleyne Lash – or Jini – was the daughter of an army officer, Henry, who served in India and then Burma under General Slim. Her mother, Joan, was from Irish Catholic stock and an uncle, Bill, was the Bishop of Bombay. As a child, Jini moved to India with her parents where the family lived like royalty, pampered by devoted servants.

In 1947, they returned to England, settling in a house called Bridge End, situated in Churt, a prosperous, leafy Surrey village with an air of mock Tudor respectability. In fact, the sort of place in which relics of the Raj lived out the twilight of their lives after fulfilling their imperial duties. Before long, Jini's father was known universally as 'The Brigadier'.

His spirited, strong-headed daughter was sent to the Convent of the Sacred Heart in Tunbridge Wells where she is remembered as 'anarchic', and left after faring poorly in her O-levels.

Things were no easier at Bridge End where she enjoyed a difficult relationship with her mother. Screaming matches with her parents became a common occurrence and, at 16 years old, she left home for good. Living alone in London, Jini suffered intense mood swings and on one occasion took an overdose of sleeping pills. She was found unconscious on the Brompton Road and hospitalized and was then subsequently seen by a succession of psychiatrists who diagnosed her 'a malignant hysteric'.

In a bid to find her feet, she went to live with an old family friend, Iris Birtwhistle, in the village of Walberswick, Suffolk – close to Southwold but linked to the outside world by just one narrow road. Long a magnet for the bohemian-minded, it features an unlikely number of artists and sculptors among its 300 residents. It also became home to the late actress Ann Todd, who starred in *The Seventh Veil*, following her retirement. Relishing its privacy, she would often be seen cycling around the village.

The 'formidable' Birtwhistle was 'a patron of the arts with influential friends', according to one former neighbour. She had an extensive library, had been acquainted with Virginia Woolf and introduced Jini to Dodie Smith, author of *The Hundred and One Dalmatians*. Most importantly, Birtwhistle took the highly-strung young woman under her wing, encouraging her to write her first novel at the age of 21, and helped to get it published.

The book, *The Burial*, was written in the throes of mental turmoil and, perhaps not surprisingly, dwelt on themes such as alienation and breakdown – experience of which on one occasion resulted in Jini being briefly admitted to a mental hospital. The novel was not a success – but, with the support of Birtwhistle, Jini determined to pursue her writing career.

Despite her often fragile state of mind, she stood out in the sedate Suffolk countryside, riding around on a motor-scooter, alternately clad in beatnik outfits or twinset-and-pearls. One day Birtwhistle introduced her to Fiennes, half-jokingly describing him as 'a rough diamond'. He was certainly the sort of man to sweep a girl off her feet. 'Mark was quite a personality,' reveals Kent. 'I liked him enormously despite his touch of arrogance.' A touch of arrogance that, in all probability, only served to heighten his attraction to the opposite sex.

It was a case of love at first sight for Fiennes. 'Jini was sitting on a sofa in the library, on a cold November evening, her feet curled up under her as she always sat, and I thought, *that's it*, I didn't need to look or think any more about it,' he recalls. 'It was completely extraordinary.' He invited her to tea at his farm and she turned up on her moped. 'She came in, and almost the first thing she said was, "You don't want to be frightened of this writing bit. All I want is to have six children".'

They married eighteen months later, on 14 April 1962, at St Benet's Minster in nearby Beccles. He was 28, she was 24. The marriage certificate records Mark's full name as Mark Twisleton-Wykeham-Fiennes. Intriguingly, it states Jini's residence as 90 Eaton Square, London – one of the capital's most exclusive addresses.

Within weeks of the marriage, Jini was pregnant – and she gave birth to a baby boy at Ipswich and East Anglia General Hospital on 22 December 1962. 'It was a difficult birth,' says one family friend.

It was the year of the Cuban missile crisis, in which Kennedy and Kruschev played real-life poker with the world's future. It was also the year when Cliff Richard topped the charts with 'The Young Ones' and the Beatles had their first hit. It was the year *Lawrence of Arabia* won the Best Film award at the Oscars; *Juke Box Jury, Dixon of Dock Green* and *The Avengers* were showing on television; Marilyn Monroe died; and sixty people were killed by London's infamous pea-soup fog. In sleepy Suffolk it was reported that a 'mysterious object' had been spotted in the sky.

A brand new Moris Minor cost £245. A Dansette record player – apparently 'in tune with teenagers' – would set one back £1. And a Moulinex food mixer – 'sure to be a hit with mum' – was only ten shillings.

The child's full name was Ralph Nathaniel Twisleton-Wykeham Fiennes – though in the course of time he would shorten it to Ralph Fiennes (pronounced 'Rafe Fines').

It was not a common or garden name to be sure, but it was no more unusual a name than given to many an illustrious ancestor or even his second cousin – the Eton-educated, aristocratic explorer Ranulph Fiennes. However, in the years ahead some people would assume this his insistence on being called 'Rafe' was a snobbish attempt at one-upmanship. According to the author Hammond

Innes, also called Ralph, 'it's a cheap affectation used by the middle classes. No-one calls me "Rafe". If they did it would be over my dead body'.

In fact, it was Innes, not Fiennes, who was wrong, according to Leslie Dunkling, author of the *Guinness Book of Names*.

He explains that the name Ralph has evolved through a number of incarnations – Radolphus in Roman times, Raedwulf in ninth and tenth century Norse and Old English, and then, in the eighteenth and nineteenth centuries, the version 'Ralph' emerged, spelt as nowadays. At that time the correct pronunciation, accepted by everyone, was 'Rafe'. Dunkling suggests that, since it has always been a relatively uncommon boy's name, it has been more often encountered in print, rather than heard in 'normal' conversation. As it is one of the many words in the English language in which spelling and pronunciation differ (like 'debt' and 'Thames') it is easy to see how the contretemps over the 'correct' pronunciation has come about.

Within eight years, Jini had indeed had the six children she had told Mark she wanted. Ralph was swiftly followed by Martha, Magnus, Sophie and twins Joseph and Jacob. Jini and Mark had also adopted Michael, a 10-year-old foster-child, after seeing an advert in *The Times* which stipulated that the would-be parents must have 'a house full of books'. Life was hectic at the Fiennes household, as Holmes, a frequent visitor, recalls, 'They were a lively bunch but that was only to be expected with a family of that size.'

For the first time, Jini's life acquired the purpose it had up to that point lacked – and she found her place in the world. 'The family,' says Mark, 'became everything.' And daughter Sophie says, 'I think she gained enormous confidence in herself through being mistress of this empire. It made her fearless.' Indeed, she was 'hardly able to contain her enthusiasm to enlarge it,' as one friend puts it.

Life for the Fiennes children revolved around the small area of Suffolk in which they lived, encompassing Wangford, Southwold, Blythburgh and Walberswick.

It was an area of gently rolling countryside, typical of southern England. But the closer you got to the coast, the lower-lying the land and the bigger the sky. Some of the land was still marshy but much had been reclaimed, allowing cattle to graze in dyke-lined fields. It was a peaceful enough scene – but one that could, as every East Anglian knew, easily be shattered.

For the entire region had been fighting a losing battle with the sea for centuries and, just a few miles south of Wangford, the ancient East Anglian capital of Dunwich had been wholly swallowed up. The great flood of 1953 had killed forty-six people in Suffolk, including five in Southwold alone. The sea had never reached Wangford but the perpetual danger of flooding helps explain why much of the area still has a strong sense of community – long since vanished from much of Britain.

Travelling to Wangford, Southwold and Reydon (a suburb of Southwold) is like stepping back in time. Life moves at a snail's pace and the shops shut at 5p.m. sharp. Even today a storekeeper will let a customer out of the back door if it's raining, and householders leave magazines for sale at 10p on their window sill with a note telling passers-by to put the money through the letterbox.

In many ways, life in Suffolk for Ralph and his siblings was idyllic. They had a huge garden in which to play. Mark further enhanced it by erecting a swing and a treehouse. The air was fresh, there was plenty of food, the surrounding countryside offered endless opportunity for adventure and the seaside could be reached in ten minutes. 'It was a very happy time in my life,' says Ralph.

There was also the thrill of living on a working farm. Lambing took place in the spring, shearing took place in the early summer and the sheep were dipped in the autumn. 'I remember watching my father help a cow give birth,' says Ralph. 'He covered his hands with a special oil, put his hand inside and then pulled out this calf. It was wonderful to watch. I also remember being excited by seeing a crop-spraying plane come down.'

The winters were usually the quietest time of the year, and this gave Mark Fiennes time to indulge in the hobby that would soon become his livelihood – photography.

'My father used to get me up very early and I would go into the dark-room and watch him develop film,' says Fiennes. 'Occasionally I would go for a walk with him and then go to the dark-room. In hindsight, he was giving me his time, one to one. The rest of the day was taken up with work. I just remember damp English mornings. They're so still and quiet and no one's around. I could hear the birds cooing. That's one of the sounds that haunts me.'

Jealousy was apparently unheard of amongst the Fiennes children. 'I was never aware of it,' says Ralph's younger brother, Joe. 'From the earliest crayon drawings, our mother recognized each of our merits and encouraged our particular aspirations. It was never a case of "isn't this other person wonderful?" '

Jini also nurtured Ralph's passion for the arts, giving him, when he was 7 years old, a Pollocks toy theatre, with cardboard characters operated by wires.

He found a ready audience in Jini, and his brothers and sisters. 'Ralph had to play all the parts,' says his sister Martha. 'And we had to sit down in front of and watch three-hour-long plays – like long versions of *Treasure Island* or *The Corsica Brothers*. But to be fair, he did it brilliantly.'

His mother also helped bring out Ralph's nascent love of the lime-light – and he soon displayed a burning enthusiasm for singing, more than once jumping up in front of the family to sing the theme to *Rawhide*.

'My father had an album of Frankie Lane singing Western cowboy songs like 'Gunfight at the OK Corral' and 'Rawhide' was the opening song,' says Fiennes with a flicker of embarrassment. 'We had a mono record player with a big speaker and for years I was convinced that Frankie Lane was inside the speaker.'

However, life wasn't the remorselessly blissful picture the family have sometimes painted. There were tensions – usually triggered by Jini's temperamental behaviour. If playing the matriarchal head of the household went a long way towards healing her own psychological wounds, anything that threatened the family's stability could easily make them suppurate again. 'There would always be this awful tripwire of her own anxiety,' remembers Ralph. 'Any little circumstance could trip her into a sense of desperation.'

There was a brittleness in Jini's temperament which Dodie Smith was aware of – and she was quick to judge and slap people down.

Kim Kent, a regular visitor to Elms Farm, viewed Jini with ambivalence. 'She suffered these tremendous mood swings and always struck me as being somewhat neurotic,' he says. 'She would suddenly get the urge to paint the wall of a room red, blue or green – and when I moved into the house the drawing room was painted a deep blue and half the rooms were a weird yellow. The whole house was decorated most unusually.

'She was a very effusive sort of woman and she could really be quite embarrassing at times. She'd make eyes at you – and you knew it didn't mean anything but it always made me feel rather awkward. Sometimes Mark would get terribly fed up with her eccentricities. But he was very patient. In my opinion, Jini had him tied in knots. She always got her way – he really spoilt her. I think he'd always been around domineering women and didn't quite know how to handle them.'

Young Ralph's introduction to school also proved traumatic. He attended Reydon Infant School, a modern new school in a quiet cul-de-sac with sixty pupils.

'He was in my class for two years,' says Anne Stammers. 'I'll always remember him because he would turn up in what looked like Harrods cast-offs and a smart leather briefcase while the rest of the class had plastic satchels and club book clothes. Sometimes he'd wear a Harris tweed-type coat. It definitely gave him a more upper-class appearance. He was also very well spoken. The difference, I suppose, was one of breeding.'

Ralph's background – his 'breeding' – helped make him an irresistible target for bullies. And even though the school day only lasted from nine o'clock in the morning until three in the afternoon, sometimes it must have seemed all too long.

'He was a little posher than everyone else,' recalls classmate Edgar Martin. 'He was also very quiet and, as a result, the other lads were always ganging up on him. I was a big lad and didn't like what was going on so I told the rest of them to "bugger off". I was always getting into fights with my brothers but I don't think Ralph came from that kind of home. He was scared of some of the kids.

'We became chums. You could say I was his best friend – in fact, his only friend. I think he was quite lonely. I used to go over to play at his house. His parents had a big garden with a paddling pool and a swing. I'll always remember going to a birthday party of his because there was a Punch and Judy show. I'd only ever had ice cream and jelly on my birthdays. I was really impressed.'

The fear of being picked upon helps explain why, having been invited to a birthday party, he would invariably politely ask the hostess if he could play on his own with a jigsaw puzzle rather than join in party games with the other children. 'I was obsessed with animals and loved doing jigsaw puzzles of animals, particularly African animals,' says Ralph. 'But the other mothers would get very irritated that my mother wouldn't force me to join in the silly party games.'

His sister Martha comments, half-jokingly, 'My mother used to joke that it was such a relief when I came along because I was a social, busy, normal child in comparison.'

Despite a few difficulties at school, Ralph's early years were largely happy. He was part of a large, loving family and there was a reassuring air of permanence and stability about life at Elms Farm. Unfortunately it was not to last.

In the increasingly classless Britain of the 1960s and 1970s, it was becoming as easy for the well-bred to sink in the world as it was for the lowly-born to rise. This was the predicament the Fiennes family found themselves in when Mark was unable to make a success of the farm.

'He was a damn good chap with sheep and cattle but simply wasn't an arable farmer,' says Kim Kent. 'Rearing livestock wasn't the most productive way to farm the local land. And, as I understand it, money had become tight and Mark decided to try to make a go of the photography. Farming can be a tough business.'

It was the first of a number of moves they would make but the entire family, especially Ralph, would always have fond memories of life at Elms Farm. Despite this, they have never returned to their magnificent former house. 'I suppose they prefer to remember things as they were,' says Kent. 'I can appreciate their feelings.'

CHAPTER TWO

Irish Interlude

If living in Suffolk could be reasonably compared with stepping back in time, living on the Sheep's Head Peninsula was akin to moving to the edge of the world. In 1971 Ralph's mother, Jini, who always thought of herself as Irish, travelled to County Cork with her husband, on a photographic assignment.

'They fell in love with it,' remembers Sophie. 'She just decided that she didn't want to bring up her children in England but there, on the south-west coast of Ireland. I can remember her saying, "I knew that you would understand when you read the brothers Grimm – you would understand the archetypes that occur in painting and writing, because those are still alive and kicking there".'

On a darker note, it was also the beginning of what Sophie describes as 'a gradual process of downscaling', with the family living off what Mark made from photography and the proceeds of buying houses cheaply, renovating them and selling them.

County Cork takes its name from Corcaigh – the Irish for 'marshy place'. As well as being Ireland's biggest county, covering nearly 3,000 square miles, it is almost its most southerly. About half of the population of 400,000 live in Cork City in the eastern part of the county.

As you head west, the countryside becomes increasingly empty but ever more rugged and breathtakingly beautiful. Where Suffolk is flat, West Cork is dramatic and awe-inspiring. The air, sweeping in off the Atlantic, has the freshness of the sea.

Even now, communications are poor. There is one A-road heading west from Cork. And the further west you go the narrower, more winding and pot-holed are the roads. The journey time to Bantry by car is anything from ninety minutes to two hours – depending on whether or not you get stuck behind a tractor which invariably seems to be stuck in second gear. The buses are patchy and rail links non-existent.

However, travelling to the Sheep Head's Peninsula – where the Fiennes moved *en famille* – is even more of an endurance test, with just one main road linking the peninsula to the mainland.

This sliver of land – which, for the record, looks nothing like a sheep's head – juts, with the thrust of an ET-like finger, into the Atlantic. It is bounded to the north by the vast expanse of Bantry Bay and to the south by Dunmanus Bay.

About three miles wide at its broadest extremity, it tapers to a point 15 miles west of the mainland. The area to the north might be more mountainous but the peninsula's rocky, ragged spine, reaching as high as 1,000 ft in places, is every bit as dramatic in its own way.

The peninsula has a population of just 300, roughly a third of whom live in the main settlement, Kilcrohane, which is situated halfway along its length – a village with two pubs, a church, a post office/general store and a two-room primary school.

Most of the population live on the south side of the peninsula, because the climate is kinder and the terrain less mountainous; the Fiennes too were attracted to this area.

Even today it is possible to take the road to Kilcrohane (which shares its name with a sixth century hermit) and not pass another car, let alone person. It's the sort of place where people still feel it unnecessary to lock their cars or houses, and frail old ladies fearlessly accept lifts from complete strangers who offer to take them to Mass.

Not for nothing does a popular local postcard show a small herd of cows ambling along a lane beside a caption reading 'Rush Hour Ireland'. As one Welsh photographer says, having lived on the peninsula for more than a decade, 'The word hurry doesn't exist in the local vocabulary. It's a totally stress-free environment compared with most of the western world.'

It is easy to be seduced by such a place. Anyone with a love for nature could not fail to be moved by the sea, the hills and the peninsula's rugged beauty. On a summer's day, as you watch the sun set over Bantry Bay, you could be forgiven for thinking you had stumbled upon an earthly paradise. The calm of the place may have enhanced the profundity in Ralph's nature, later reflected in the depth of his performances.

The only visible reminder of the outside, imperfect world is the memorial, on the road from Kilcrohane to the mainland, to the 329 people who died in 1985 when an Air India plane crashed into the sea off the coast, the suspected victim of a terrorist bomb.

But if you dig into the past, you soon realize the area has seen more than its fair share of misery down the years.

The very emptiness of the place, which so appeals to tourists, is the legacy of the great famine of the 1840s caused by the repeated failure of the potato crop. And even today, Bantry, which lies 15 miles north-east of Kilcrohane, has yet to attain its pre-famine size, its population having shrunk from an 1830 high of 4,000 to under 3,000.

'There is not a house from Bantry to Schull (lying south of the Sheep's Head Peninsula) that does not contain the sick, dead or dying,' said an eyewitness account at the time. 'The latter lay where they die – their relatives too feeble to remove them and the strong afraid to handle unshrouded and uncoffined bodies.'

Thousands subsequently left for America, Britain and the colonies in a bid to escape their wretched, starvation-threatened existence.

If Mark and Jini Fiennes had come from a humbler background, one suspects that while they may still have fallen in love with the area, they would have realized that moving there was impractical. Studying its tragic history, and asking just why it was so empty, might have led them to the same conclusion.

However, the couple tended to embrace challenges with an unusual degree of confidence. So when the chance arose to buy a one-and-a-quarter-acre plot of land on the water's edge, Mark Fiennes moved quickly and sealed the deal. One-acre plots of land on the peninsula could be bought for as little as £1,000 in the 1970s – a snip at the price.

Having purchased the land, Mark drew up plans for a split-level bungalow with the help of an English builder, Wally Webb. The two men then set to work turning Mark and Jini's dream into reality. 'My father was brilliant with his hands,' recalls Ralph.

Within a year he and the family were able to move into the beautiful, whitewashed, six-bedroom house with its spacious kitchen, roomy lounge and sunny roof terrace, which looked out across Dunmanus Bay and to the hills beyond, dominated by the 1,400 ft tall Mount Gabriel.

It was a magical spot. There wasn't a house to be seen for miles around. The blue-green sea was cleaner than most of the water surrounding the British Isles. And the only sounds to be heard on a summer's day were the sea lapping the shore, the cries of the seagulls, swans and smaller land-based birds, and the joyous laughter of the Fiennes brood echoing around the bay.

Having purchased boiler suits for the children – from Harrods, naturally – Jini would send Ralph and the others to a nearby hilltop and tell them to draw what they could see. That might not be seen as the actions of a responsible mother today, but this was Ireland. Besides, Jini had never had time for convention.

'When Ralph was in his boiler suit he was allowed to do anything,' recalls one neighbour. 'He and his brothers and sisters enjoyed a lot more freedom than most of the kids in Kilcrohane.'

At the time, few outsiders lived on the peninsula. But contrary to what one might imagine, the locals did not adopt a 'them and us' attitude towards the newcomers.

'They're country folk,' says one British migrant. 'The sort of people who call a spade a spade. If you're civil and friendly, and treat them with respect, they'll welcome you with open arms. On the other hand, if you adopt airs and graces, look down your noses at them, and make no attempt to fit in, they'll turn their back on you.'

There is no doubt in which category the Fiennes family belonged in the eyes of local people. 'They fitted in perfectly and got involved in village life,' says Frances Tobin, a teacher at the local primary school for nearly forty years and choir-mistress at Kilcrohane's Catholic Church.

'They were a very musical family. All the children sang in the choir. They, along with Mark and Jini, would turn up at Sunday mass as regular as clockwork. I remember Ralph had a lovely voice and even then some of the little girls at the church couldn't keep their

15

eyes off him. But I could see why – he was both handsome and charming.' The family also took part in folk music dances, carnivals and fêtes.

At first, all went well. Mark – who hung a sign saying 'Mark Fiennes: Photographer' at the end of the narrow, winding lane that led to their Irish hideaway – made money from selling photographs of vanishing rural Irish life to his London contacts and, sometimes, out of the back of the family car.

While the children, in a typically unusual arrangement, were taught at home by their mother – affectionately dubbed 'Gipsy Jin' by her brood because of what Mark calls 'the almost psychic way she had with gypsies and tinkers'.

Ralph explains: 'My mother got permission to teach us herself for a period. Everyone always thinks life must have been chaotic and hippyish but in fact it was incredibly disciplined. She always treated us as individuals and found separate time for us which was no mean feat. It worked because we adored her and respected her and really cared about her opinion.'

Life on the Sheep's Head Peninsula must have seemed every bit as idyllic as life in Suffolk: whereas before, Ralph and his siblings had had fields and forests on their doorstep, they now had a semi-tamed wilderness outside their front door, bounded by the sea and the mountains.

'It was all about adventure, about the wild wind and sea, to an impressionable four-year-old like me,' says Ralph's younger brother, Joseph. 'It was a wonderful dream come true.' Fiennes, however, sheds light on the flip side of being a member of a large family, recalling that everyone did things *'en masse'* – a *mélange* of children, friends, animals and endless queues for the bath.

Few local people of Ralph's generation have clear memories of him, for while the younger children were later sent to Kilcrohane primary school, he was too old to attend. His parents duly found him a place at the prestigious Newtown School in Waterford, the ancient county town 125 miles to the east – founded by the Danes in the ninth century and now most famous for its glass.

A mixed, multi-denominational establishment, this Quaker boarding school of 330 pupils (which celebrates its bicentenary in 1998) prides itself on being one of the region's leading educational institutions, and pupils are drawn from as far away as Great Britain. Even though Ralph has frequently stressed the fragile state of the family's finances, Mark and Jini somehow managed to find the fees – now £4,500 a year.

'The school prided itself on its relaxed atmosphere,' according to one of Ralph's classmates. Ties and blazers did not have to be worn, the uniform – if it can be so described – consisted of navy corduroy trousers and jumpers. Notable former pupils include the singer Sinead O'Connor and the historian Roy Foster.

Life on the Sheep's Head Peninsula might have been a largely stress-free existence. But as time went by, Mark and Jini duly discovered – as we all must, sooner or later – that there is no such thing as an earthly paradise. 'There was a real struggle between the dream and the reality,' admits Joseph.

The peninsula's population had been declining ever since the 1840s – largely because it was remote, isolated and the only real employment opportunities were in farming or fishing. Otherwise, youngsters were obliged to do what they had been doing for decades, heading for cities such as Dublin or Cork, or crossing the water to England or America.

That's why most of those – with the exception of the Fiennes family – who had moved to the Sheep's Head tended to be retired couples with a steady income who did not need to scavenge for work.

With six hungry children, not to mention Ralph's school fees, Mark and Jini eventually accepted that they needed a steadier, more reliable source of income. The only option was to return to England. 'They left very suddenly,' recalls a neighbour. 'One minute, Ralph and the rest of them were going about their business as usual, the next they had gone.'

The decision to move again upset Fiennes, who enjoyed life at Newtown School. 'I was very, very distressed,' he says. 'From then on I don't think I ever considered that any school would be permanent, that any friendships would be permanent. I would always move on; there would always be change.'

The Fiennes family had an endearingly bohemian, carefree upbringing. And yet the constant displacement of a travelling tribe cannot but have an effect on its children. 'It helped me know that nothing is forever' says Ralph, which is both a brave and a sad sentiment. How can one trust love, friendships or, indeed, success if your philosophy is one of transience?

Interestingly, many actors are the products of mobile homes. The children of soldiers, diplomats and hippies they learn to readjust, to assimilate and recreate with each new production as they once did at each new school.

The depressing outcome to the family's Irish adventure inevitably raises the question of whether Mark and Jini were rash to move to the edge of the world in the first place. Yet who can predict the future? Ironically, if they had hung on to the property they would now be sitting on a valuable nest-egg – maybe their timing was simply wrong.

CHAPTER THREE

In the Shadow of the Spire

The family's next stop was Salisbury, the historic Wiltshire city dating back nearly 800 years to the decision to construct the Cathedral of St Mary's. Built between 1220 and 1258, the place of worship is a supreme example of medieval architecture. Its treasures include an original *Magna Carta* sealed at Runnymede in 1215, along with Europe's oldest working clock, dating back to 1386.

The city, which still looks from a distance much as it did in John Constable's day, has something of the air of an olde world theme park. It's the sort of genteel place where teashops outnumber taverns, you're afraid to drop a cigarette end for fear of soiling the streets and every other building (be it the Guildhall, St Anne's Gate or the Church of St Thomas à Becket) seems to be a historic monument.

Tourism is big business and coach-loads of foreign visitors pump millions of pounds into the local economy every year, ensuring this bastion of middle England remains among the most prosperous places in the land – and helping to explain why it was one of the few places to remain true blue in the 1997 general election.

Once again, Mark and Jini enrolled Ralph in a top-notch school – Bishop Wordsworth's, a boys-only, rugby-playing grammar school, lying in the shadow of the cathedral's 404ft-high spire (the tallest in the land), and founded by John Wordsworth in 1890 shortly after he became Bishop of Salisbury.

It originally set great store by the Victorian values of Christianity, duty and responsibility and its Latin motto – *Veritas in caritate* (Truth in a Caring Society) – reflected the high standards it set both itself and its pupils.

Of course, by the 1970s the empire was long gone, but the school was still pursuing its mission to turn out a better breed of pupil, as can be seen from a contemporary prospectus which stated its aim was 'to provide an education founded on Christian ideas of regard for truth, knowledge, service and fellowship – and to educate a young man to use his gifts to the full so that he can take his place in the world with confidence, and lead a happy and useful life'.

Unlike many state schools, boys were required to wear a uniform consisting of navy-blue blazers, white shirt, blue tie and flannels right up until the sixth form. Jeans were banned and the dress code warned, 'Socks of vivid colours are not acceptable.' In a throwback to the past, boys still addressed each other by their surnames.

The school competed with public schools on the sports field, reaching the final of a national rugby competition in 1991 and proving itself a fertile breeding ground for a number of first-class rugby players including Richard Hill.

Architecturally, Bishop Wordsworth's is nowadays something of a hotch-potch consisting of a core of Victorian buildings, various post-war additions and a series of temporary classroom blocks erected to meet the growth in pupil numbers.

However, the 'proto-public school' ethos, as one teacher puts it, has stood Bishop Wordsworth's in good stead. At the present time, competition for entry is as stiff as it was in Ralph's day, with three applicants for every place. Ninety per cent of pupils go on to higher education and it was ranked the twenty-third best state school in 1995, reason enough to see why it's regarded as 'the envy of many of its fee-paying rivals'.

Celebrated old boys – 'Old Wordsworthians' – include BBC news-reader Andrew Harvey, concert pianist Hamish Milne, Mervyn Alexander and the Roman Catholic Bishop of Clifton. But in Ralph's day the school was probably most famous for its William Golding connection. The author taught there for fifteen years, retiring in 1961, and the boys at the school are thought to have inspired his famous book *Lord of the Flies*.

There were four houses, each named after a bishop of Salisbury –

Osmund, Jewel, Mortimer and Poore. Ralphe was in Poore. Staff remember him as a well-read, articulate, serious-minded and usually courteous boy.

He studied English, History and Art at A-level but was by no means an academic. 'He was good at class discussion but less good at discursive essays,' remembers John Cox, who doubled up as Ralph's English and Drama teacher. 'His reading was more responsive. He was better at empathizing than analyzing.'

Nor did he excel on the sports field. 'One of the strengths of the school was rugby but Ralph wasn't much of a games player,' says Glyn Evans, who taught Ralph general studies in the sixth form and was headmaster from 1974 to 1992. Shuddering at the memory, Fiennes still talks about the indignity of being made to play rugby at school and 'having some instructor yell at you to get in line so you can kick a ball'.

However, he was something of a keep fit fanatic, according to his peers, proud of the fact that he could do more press-ups than anyone else in his class. He also took karate lessons. 'He used to practice doing karate chops on classroom desks until his knuckles were blue,' recalls fellow pupil Andrew Galt.

Thanks to its location in a prosperous part of the country, far from any urban sprawl, Bishop Wordsworth's, according to Evans, was largely spared the problems of bad behaviour and bullying common at inner city schools.

While Ralph was at Bishop Wordsworth's he never experienced the sort of bullying he suffered in Suffolk, but his early years at this school were not easy ones. Arriving later than most other pupils, he was cast as the outsider. 'It was inevitable he would have a bit of trouble adapting to a new school,' says classmate Toby Chetwynd-Talbot, who went on to become one of Ralph's closest friends. While a pupil at the South Wiltshire Girls' School says, 'When I first met him, I got the impression he was a bit of a hanger-on.'

As a result, he tended to keep himself to himself. 'My overriding memory of Ralph is of somebody who was rather shy,' says fellow pupil David Scouller. And Ralph's sister, Sophie, agrees that he was something of 'a loner' in those early days. While John Cox says:

'There was a sense of apartness about him, an independence of mind.' And cornered by crowds he could become 'melancholic and wistful'.

His name and speech (traditional received diction) also caused him problems. 'He was very posh when he first arrived and we took the piss out of him, especially when we discovered his full name was Ralph Twisleton-Wykeham-Fiennes,' says one classmate. 'But he usually laughed it off. A lot of people assumed he'd come from public school and his family had fallen on hard times.'

But Andrew Galt says, 'I think he was more sensitive about his family background than he let on. I remember asking him what his dad did and he told me he was a photographer. But he never ever elaborated. He was guarded about his private life even then.' With his exalted ancestry, and triple-barrelled name, he was perhaps reluctant to admit that the family finances were as dependent on his father's skills as a handyman as his photographic eye.

From an early age he also showed a fascination for two characters immortalized in the movies. 'He was obsessed with Lawrence of Arabia who was killed in a motor-bike crash in Dorset, not that far from Salisbury,' says another classmate. 'And he was always going on about James Bond. I think he saw himself in the James Bond or Lawrence of Arabia mould.'

In fact, Ralph had the numbers '007' scrawled in felt tip on the side of his Hush Puppy shoes. 'He really wanted to be James Bond and whenever we saw him coming we'd start whistling the 007 theme tune,' reveals fellow pupil Todd Brewster.

The teenager was also something of a 'non-conformist in the classroom', according to teachers. 'He was a sparky, stubborn lad who liked to challenge the accepted view and did a few daft things,' admits deputy headmaster Joe Newman. Teachers are, however, always reluctant to reveal anything which might harm the standing of the school or a famous ex-pupil.

Former classmates shed more light on 'Ralph the Prankster'. 'He was always up for a laugh and for taking the mickey out of teachers,' says Galt. Another classmate commenting on his 'non-conformity in the classroom' says, 'In class, he was never frightened to speak his mind and would say the first thing which came into his head.'

One famous incident occurred in a French lesson when the

teacher, who had reached the end of his tether, asked pupils if they wanted to step into his shoes. 'I will, sir,' said Ralph calling his bluff and walking to the front of the classroom – to the surprise of both teacher and pupils. But the best moment was yet to come.

'He turned to the teacher and asked him a question,' reveals a source. 'The teacher couldn't answer so Ralph calmly went up to him and tapped him on the head with the chalky dustboard cleaner. I don't know who was more shocked, us or the teacher.'

Another incident occurred during a geography field trip to Wales with pupils from the South Wiltshire Girls' School. One night a pillow fight broke out in the youth hostel dormitory where the boys were sleeping. Suddenly, a reputedly bisexual games mistress from the girls' school appeared at the door.

'Ralph was standing bollock-naked in front of her,' recalls Galt. 'But he held a macho pose and made no attempt to cover himself up. She started telling us off. Then Ralph coolly told her, "Would you mind taking your hand off my knob". Everyone burst out laughing, the games teacher was lost for words and turned on her heel. But as she opened the door she slipped on the mat and fell, ending up in a crumpled heap at the bottom of the stairs. It was hilarious.'

However, Joe Newman insists, 'I certainly never had cause to cane Ralph. In my experience, the cane didn't solve a lot of problems and was only to be used for the most outrageous anti-social behaviour that went way beyond the realms of what was reasonable.' If hitting a French teacher on the head didn't constitute outrageous behaviour, though, what did?

Of course, playing pranks was a surefire way to win peer approval, something Fiennes – 'never the most popular of pupils,' according to one classmate – readily appreciated. His ability to mimic movie characters like Bond won him further Brownie points. 'He was very good at impersonating people,' says Chetwynd-Talbot. 'I'll never forget the time he took off a Nazi officer.' A prophetic act in view of the SS commandant he would play in *Schindler's List* – and an indication of where his true talents might lie.

There were two areas where Ralph did make a positive mark at Bishop Wordsworth's – in art and amateur dramatics.

The art department lay in a leafy, secluded garden. Thick shrubs and bushes ran along an ancient wall at one end, helping to give it a country-like tranquillity, while the cathedral's graceful spire looked down on the peaceful scene. Then, as now, boys – among them Fiennes – could be found sitting outside with paper and charcoals, sketching the spire and surrounding scenery.

'Art was by far and away his best subject,' says Duncan Davies, the department head who taught Ralph. 'His observational skills were very high and he could draw very well. He also had a good visual recall. Coming from a creative, artistic family and having a father who was a photographer, in some ways it was only natural that he would possess an artist's eye.

'I remember Ralph did a particularly interesting series of drawings in the sixth form. I had set the class a project to be inspired by an idol of their choice. His subject was Lawrence of Arabia and he went on to produce some striking images of smashed motor-cycles and camels, reflecting key moments in his hero's life.'

The school also had a strong dramatic tradition, dating back to 1893 when selected scenes from *A Midsummer Night's Dream* were staged before a specially invited audience including the Mayor. The school's founder, Bishop Wordsworth, had a passion for the theatre and was the inspiration behind this production, which took place on a miniature stage complete with scenery, footlights and a curtain. He even helped rehearse pupils for their roles.

The 1893 Christmas production extravaganza included scenes from *Julius Ceasar*, a short cantata and a lively humorous debate.

In 1928 the Bishop's Players were founded, and with the building of the school hall in 1933, the amateur dramatics society gained a well-equipped stage on which to perform plays. Subsequent productions were suitably traditional and canonical and included Shakespeare's *Hamlet* and *Macbeth*, Marlowe's *Dr Faustus*, Chekhov's *On the High Road* and George Bernard Shaw's *Androcles and the Lion*.

Budding thespian Ralph appeared in an end of year revue, *The Seven Ages of Man*, but his real stage debut would come in the school's 1979 production of Shakespeare's great tragedy, *King Lear*. Like a budding film star whose crucial debut scenes end up on the cutting room floor, Ralph only got to appear in the first act, in his minor role as King of France.

But having tasted the limelight, he did not look back, going on to play leading parts in two more school plays – Robert Bolt's *A Man For All Seasons* in February 1980 and Shakespeare's *Love's Labour's Lost* in November 1980.

A co-production with the local girls' grammar school, *A Man for All Seasons*, focused on the events leading up to the execution of Sir Thomas More, Lord Chancellor to Henry VIII, in 1535. First staged in London in 1960 with Paul Scofield in the title role, Bolt's play explored the conflict between More's duty to the king and the promptings of his conscience, which would not allow him to recognize the annulment of Henry's marriage or the Act of Supremacy.

The school magazine – predictably well-disposed to the production – praised Andrew Torrance for playing More with 'grace, poise and serenity' and Fiennes for 'playing the part of the scheming bully, Thomas Cromwell, with eloquence and force – providing a realistic insight into the dark corridors of ambition'. Even then, it seemed, Ralph was drawn to the darker side of a character's persona.

In the accompanying programme, Ralph revealed that his interests included 'cinema, the theatre and physical exercise' and his ambition – common enough in boys of his age but surprising given his later choice of career – was to win 'a commission in the Army'. There was, however, a long and proud tradition of military service on his father's side of the family: his second cousin, the flamboyant Ranulph Fiennes, served in the army before becoming famous for his daredevil exploits, and his maternal grandfather had been a brigadier.

In the autumn of 1980, Ralph trod the boards again, this time in a co-production of Shakespeare's *Love's Labour's Lost*, the story of Ferdinand, the King of Navarre and his lords – Berowne, Dumain and Longaville – who have taken a vow to study, fast and live apart from women. But the arrival of the Princess of France and her attendant ladies obliges them to disregard their vows. Before long, the king is in love with the princess and his lords with her ladies – and the courting proceeds with much merriment.

Having been impressed by Ralph's Cromwell, drama teacher John Cox had no hesitation in casting Ralph in the role of Berowne.

Fellow pupil David Scouller, who played the King of Navarre, says jokingly, 'Worryingly, I was above him in the cast list but it was quite evident which of us had the talent.'

The play was rehearsed during breaks and after school. However, Cox says, 'It's a verbally complex play and we had to work fast because several pupils lived some way from the school, restricting the rehearsal times available.' Pupils' parents and teachers' wives helped make the costumes.

The play was performed at an assembly hall at the South Wilts Girls' school, holding about 350 people, in November 1980 and was duly hailed by the school magazine as 'a lively, flowing production'.

'It went surprisingly well, although surviving the ordeal was my main preoccupation,' recalls Scouller. 'No one forgot their lines and nothing went disastrously wrong. Looking back, I don't think it was a particularly outstanding production. But Ralph was very good. Having said that, we weren't falling at his feet.'

The magazine once again singled out Fiennes for praise, calling his performance 'outstanding' – praise that Justine Reilly, a friend of Ralph's younger sister, Martha – feels was fully justified. 'I remember the veins in his neck standing out during one of his soliloquies,' she says. 'He seemed to take the entire production more seriously than the rest of the cast. I got the impression he'd taken the text home and tirelessly read it again and again.'

The teachers were also impressed. 'In my 40 years as a teacher I've only seen three boys and girls I thought had it in them to be successful actors,' says Glyn Evans. 'Ralph, without doubt, was the best of them. He had a concentrated absorption in the part he was playing that you rarely find in school plays. Even then he seemed drawn to playing introspective characters – rather like some of the other parts he's played in his career.'

The director, John Cox, was also delighted with the way things had gone. 'It was a very mixed cast and Ralph stood out,' he says. 'But he didn't try to outshine the weaker players. He was a good ensemble player – a team player as well as an individual actor – and that was a vital factor in the play's success.'

After the play's third and final performance, the cast 'got uproariously drunk', says Scouller, now an army officer who admits that he's never since trodden the boards. A rare instance, if the teaching staff are to be believed, of Bishop Wordsworth's pupils behaving badly.

By now, Ralph's family were living at 46 Rectory Road in Salisbury – a large, three-storey Victorian family house just around the corner from the picturesque Queen Elizabeth Gardens, where in the summer ducks sun themselves on the banks of the meandering River Avon. A former rectory, the six-bedroom, bay-windowed property was big enough even for the Fiennes clan. It was just five minutes' walk from the city centre, and ten minutes' walk from Ralph's school.

Once occupied by a retired naval commander, the house – valued at £180,000 to £200,000 by local estate agents – is now home to barrister David Bartlett and his family.

Life there was nomadic and crowded, 'like a mini-commune', says one friend. Jini, to all intents and purposes the head of the household, would laugh and weep with equal ease. There would be visits from a disparate range of relatives – a Communist aunt, an uncle who was a monk, and another who had become an archimandrite in the Greek Orthodox Church.

'They were a very literary family, bordering on the intellectual,' says a classmate of Ralph's, Simon Morrissey. Another old friend describes the Fiennes family as 'the sort that novelists perpetually struggle to invent'. Indeed, there were echoes of those eccentric, bohemian upper middle class households that so often feature in novels. The family in question might not be rich; but they certainly aren't poor. They somehow muddle along oblivious to the perils of the outside world. And whenever a crisis looms, something comes up – perhaps a rich relative pops his clogs – and everything comes up smelling of roses.

Justine Reilly – who has since married Ralph's *Love's Labour's Lost* co-star David Scouller – says: 'His entire family seemed so sophisticated to a country girl like me. It was such a cultured, artistic environment to grow up in – quite unlike the average family. They even used to go up to parties in London which really impressed me. We didn't even know anyone in London.'

The actor's sister, Martha, herself admits that her parents were 'like out of another age'. Today, Mark and Jini would be viewed as new-age hippies, with their penchant for what one friend calls 'moving houses as casually as their peers bought Volvos'.

But Jini – who Toby Chetwynd-Talbot recalls as being 'as mad as a hatter but in the nicest possible way' – consciously sought to recreate the warm, supportive, family atmosphere that she felt had been witheld from her as a child.

Despite being the oldest child, Ralph, who shared a room with his younger brother Magnus, shrank from being leader of the brood. 'My sister Martha was a year younger but there was never much differentiation,' he says. 'If anything, we were equals. But all of us were so bunched-up, age-wise, that people used to refer to us as one – the Fiennes children. We used to rebel against that; we all wanted to stake our own territories.'

Words such as 'reticent' and 'quiet' repeatedly crop up when people talk about the teenage Ralph. 'He was terribly nice but always struck me as very shy and distant,' says Justine Reilly, who lived down the road. 'You couldn't get an awful lot out of him. He wasn't very good at letting people in, and was picky about his friends.' Perhaps this was a legacy of being what one friend calls 'always the new boy, always the outsider'.

Not that Mark Fiennes thinks his itinerant upbringing did him any harm. 'We did move a lot,' he admits. 'I could not feed, clothe and educate six children by photography. I did up houses, and when they were finished we had to move on so that we could sell them for a profit. I don't think the children suffered. Variety is the spice of life.'

While close friends, like Chetwynd-Talbot, say, 'Ralph might have appeared shy but he opened up when you got to know him'. And despite his initial difficulties in adjusting to life in Salisbury, another classmate insists that 'by the sixth form, Ralph was pretty confident'.

His knowledge of who was hot and who was not in the fast-changing British music scene of the time was one of the things that boosted his standing in the eyes of his peers.

The first record he bought was David Bowie's *Ziggy Stardust* but after going through what he calls a brief 'Bowie phase', Ralph was caught up in the excitement of the punk rock explosion of the late

1970s – even if it did take a bit of time to reach sleepy Salisbury.

He was a fan of new wave acts such as Iggy Pop, spending hours playing his album *Transformer*, and Patti Smith. But his favourite band, without doubt, were the Stranglers – the controversial rockers best known for songs like 'No More Heroes', 'Something Better Change' and 'Bring on the Nubiles'. 'I was obsessed with the first Stranglers album, *Rattus Norvegicus*,' admits Ralph. 'I just loved its aggression and its blatant, pulsating bass sound.'

Inspired by the album's artwork, he even drew a big, black rat on his bedroom wall. Most parents would have been horrified at the thought of their children behaving in such a way, but not the forward-thinking Fiennes parents. 'They were so proud of him,' moans one old friend. 'If I'd painted a picture of a rat on my bedroom wall, I'd have been thrown out of the house.'

'I was a mental punk,' says Ralph, who travelled to Southampton and Bournemouth to see the Stranglers in concert and was soon wearing punk-style drainpipe jeans. 'Although sartorially it didn't go very far. I took my jeans in extremely tightly and my mother cut my hair extremely badly to make it look really crap.'

However, as Chetwynd-Talbot, now an advertising copywriter in New Zealand, points out: 'It was hard to be a punk in Salisbury and, while we entered into the spirit of the thing, Ralph never became a fully-fledged punk rocker and certainly never went in for the Mohican look.'

His sister Martha, for one, was grateful. 'I remember Ralph wearing a lot of army-surplus stuff and a great coat and cutting his hair very short because he wanted to look mean. But it never really worked because he's got quite a sensitive face.'

For a while he also went out with a punk rocker – albeit one who was a pupil at nearby Godolphin, the girls' public school which counts the author Jilly Cooper among its ex-pupils. 'I really looked the part with my torn fishnet stockings, mad black hair and safety pins,' says Sally Fairall. 'I was always more of a punk than Ralph.'

The teenage Fiennes, regardless of his sartorial endeavours, became increasingly aware that his chiselled good looks, refined voice and aristocratic air were stirring the interest of the opposite sex.

'Like 007, he was definitely a bit of a charmer,' says Brewster, now a psychiatric nurse. 'He cut a dashing figure and most of the girls seemed to find him appealing,' adds Chetwynd-Talbot. While another classmate complains that his sister's girlfriends 'were always talking about bloody Ralph'.

Besides massaging his ego, such attention helped give him the confidence needed to strut the stage in school plays.

In 1979, his parents moved to London, initially making for Putney where his grandfather, Sir Maurice, lived. It was an essential career move if Mark Fiennes was to fulfil his dream of becoming a success-ful photographer, and not have to rely on renovating properties to top up the family's finances – along with Jini's 'peanuts' from her part-time job as a sales assistant at the Everyman Bookshop.

In a sense, Ralph admired his father's ability to make money from doing up houses. He asserted, 'My father could increase the value of a property just by giving it a garden and improving the interior infrastructure.' But there was a downside to earning one's living this way as Ralph recognized: 'The moves were always exciting, but though it all sounds rather wonderful in hindsight, it was full of strain and we had to move into rented accommodation while a house was being prepared.'

Neighbours recall how, on the day of their next move, Jini chalked the words 'The Fiennes are off to London' on the side of their removal lorry – a typically playful gesture.

It was decided that, rather than disrupt Ralph's schooling again, it might be best if he stayed in Salisbury until he had completed his A-levels. No one minded too much about exams. Jini, a poor speller, thought qualifications meant little and had none herself. While Mark thought university should only be attended if one was academically gifted, not because one came from a certain background. But Ralph wanted to go to art college, and getting good grades in his A-levels would clearly help him achieve this objective. It was a mark of the independence Jini and Mark granted their children, a mark of their lack of possessiveness.

Ann Driscoll, a colleague of Jini's at the Everyman Bookshop, offered to let Ralph stay with her family. The plan had an obvious appeal to the independently-minded Ralph. It would allow him to stay in Salisbury, which he now thought of as home. Moreover, it would allow him real privacy for the first time in his life.

He consequently spent the best part of two years living with Ann, her husband Jim and their son James (about ten years Ralph's junior), at their three-storey Victorian house in Wyndham Road, Salisbury, about fifteen minutes' walk from his old Rectory Road home.

'Ralph spent a lot of time sketching with a pencil in his top-floor room at the back of the house,' reminisces Jim Driscoll, a building consultant. 'He liked drawing hands. Once he sketched a birthday card for my wife. He struck me as quite intense, someone who knew what they wanted to do with their life. He wasn't a pubby person.

'We went along to see him in a couple of school plays. I could see there was something special about him even then and I was particularly impressed by his performance in *Love's Labour's Lost*. In a way, we became surrogate parents and he became a second son to my wife.'

The decision to stay in Salisbury certainly paid off academically. For Ralph went on to get a '1' in his three A-level art papers – still-life drawing, figure-drawing and composition – guaranteeing him an A-grade. 'He couldn't have done better,' says Davies. 'Going to art college was a natural progression', in his art teacher's words – and if he had any desire to be a professional actor he didn't let on just yet.

While the Driscolls had great affection for the quiet, studious teenager who spent many an hour drawing in his room, they only saw one side of him. Classmates such as Toby Chetwynd-Talbot, Simon Stone and Simon Morrissey – not to mention their friends from Godolphin and the South Wilts Girls' School – got to see a very different side of him during his final years in the cathedral city.

'I first met Ralph at a party at Bishop Wordsworth's,' says Sally Fairall. 'A bunch of guys at the school had formed a band and were playing in the assembly hall. There were soft drinks on sale but some of the boys had smuggled in alcohol.

'We were part of a gang that used to hang around together. I went out with him for a term – he was skinnier than he is now – and then started seeing someone else. That was the way it was then. We'd often end up getting drunk. The boys would usually drink snakebite and the girls bottles of Pils lager. We also smoked a bit of dope but drugs hadn't really hit Salisbury.'

Another member of the crowd recalls, 'We spent a lot of time at local tea shops like Snell's. The boys would sit at one table and the girls at another and we'd both pretend to ignore the other group entirely though we were secretly watching each others' every move. Us girls all thought Ralph looked gorgeous.'

At weekends, Fiennes and his friends would often end up going back to the country houses owned by the girls' parents for 'wild, raucous parties invariably centring on drink,' according to Simon Morrissey. 'We'd consume as much Watneys beer as we could with the intention of getting as pissed as possible. Most of us were obsessed with the opposite sex and there would always be a room where various teenage fumblings would go on. Being at Bishop Wordsworth's, it was our only opportunity to get close to girls.'

Ralph was every bit as interested in girls as his pals but despite his good looks he didn't necessarily 'get his wicked way', according to a female member of the gang. 'He made a pass at several of my friends, including one called Judith. They ended up sleeping in the same bed one night and he turned round and snogged her but she wouldn't let him go any further. Another friend, Siobhan, simply turned him down when he asked her out.'

She adds, 'I remember him as being a bit lewd. Sometimes I felt there was a lascivious, almost lecherous quality, about the way he looked at you. Some of the boys he hung around with were pretty filthy and were involved in a lot of saucy stuff. I heard they got up to all sort of sexual pranks and seemed to know a lot about each other's private parts.'

However, it should be stressed that Ralph never had any homo-sexual leanings – despite a fondness for singing Tom Robinson's queer anthem, 'Glad to be Gay'. 'I remember going to discos and everyone, even these aggressively hetro guys, innocently singing along,' he says. 'None of us really appreciated the song's signifi-cance.'

One point on which Ralph's friends agree is that he never had any difficulty attracting the opposite sex.

'A few of us went to a quiz at the South Wilts Girls' School one evening,' recalls Galt. 'Having been to single sex schools all our lives, most of us were a bit nervy of girls. So afterwards we sat around on our own drinking lemonade and eating sandwiches. Someone noticed Ralph had disappeared so we set off in search of him – and found him in a room virtually holding court surrounded by lovely young women!'

He also went out with some of the best-looking girls in Salisbury, among them lawyer's daughter Andrea Phillips, and bragged that one of his conquests had given him 'a blowjob' on the bus to Tisbury. 'He told me himself,' recalls Galt.

The real importance of all these stories is that they reveal an unusual and perhaps unexpected aspect of Ralph's character. As a contemporary points out, 'Nowadays, Ralph has such an aesthetic image that you get the impression he has little or no interest in sex. That's something I find hard to believe having known him in his youth.'

Despite his popularity with girls, Ralph is un-nostalgic about his 'misspent' early life. 'I wouldn't care to relive my adolescence,' he says. 'It's that period of inadequacy and sexual awakening. You know your parents know it's happening to you and you bring girls home and they're talking about them and it's just horrible.'

But while adolescence in some ways proved especially difficult for so private a person, his good looks and adaptability helped him to play the game, as they had before and would again.

CHAPTER FOUR

Art for Art's Sake

Founded by a group of local artists in 1891, the Chelsea School of Art has since acquired a reputation as a leader in its field. 'It's the sort of place where ambitious young artists always want to study,' says one education expert. Its image combines artistic integrity with glamour.

Past students include the actor Dirk Bogarde, comic Alexei Sayle and pop star Mike Flowers, sculptors Mark Batten, Liz Frink and Ossip Zadkine, and artists Edward Burra, Anish Kapoor and Christopher Ofili. Its equally distinguished teaching staff have included sculptor Henry Moore and artist Graham Sutherland (famous, in particular, for his controversial portrait of Winston Churchill).

The college is based in the King's Road, Chelsea – a historical location and home down the years to actors like Laurence Olivier and Michael Caine, writers Boris Karloff and Tom Stoppard, and rock stars Mick Jagger and Eric Clapton. In 1981 – when Ralph arrived – the area had more of a 'youth scene' than it does today. It was an era when punks, rockers and new romantics were in full evidence and in full regalia.

There were about four applicants for every place at Chelsea Art School (now renamed the Chelsea College of Art and Design). Applicants were expected to have at least five O-levels or equivalent qualifications and were selected following an interview in which they were expected to produce a showcase of their work.

However, gaining entry was not difficult if you had the requisite 'correct' background, according to Flowers who studied fine art at Chelsea from 1978–81 – more than ten years before scoring a festive hit with his easy listening version of the Oasis song 'Wonderwall'.

'It had a not-undeserved reputation at the time for being a finishing school for little rich girls before they went on to marry someone even richer,' Flowers says. 'It seemed to attract a lot of bohemian upper-crust types who smoked roll-ups and liked going around with holes in their jumpers. Looking back, it was made up of a lot of pretentious people using public money to "discover themselves".'

Despite being drawn to acting, Fiennes enrolled at art college at his mother's urging, his interest in joining the army having flagged earlier.

It seemed the only sensible option. Art had been his best subject at Bishop Wordsworth's. And it was considerably tougher to get into drama school. Besides, he still wasn't sure if he wanted to pursue a career in the notoriously competitive world of acting. Going to art school was a convenient stop-gap measure – as it is for countless others who have not yet chosen their path in life.

Chelsea Art School, having seen his collection of charcoal drawings, readily offered the serious-minded, intelligent youngster from Salisbury a place on its foundation course – a one-year run-up to a three-year degree – which provided a thorough grounding in design, painting and sculpture. The fees were £595 a term.

If, as Fiennes did, students wanted to specialize in one discipline at the expense of another, the staff were glad to acquiesce. 'Ralph was supposed to do some design work but I don't remember him doing any,' says his former tutor Hugh Davies. 'He was clearly interested in painting and it wasn't the school's policy to encourage someone to do something that was going to waste their time.'

Belying its name, the Chelsea School of Art had several sites in west London and most of Ralph's time was spent at the Fine Art Faculty in Bagley's Lane, Fulham. One day a week was spent studying the history of art – mainly twentieth century painting – and the remaining four days painting in a communal studio divided up between students. 'I was very impressed by a charcoal drawing Ralph made of a cow's back, showing its vertebrae in great detail,' says Davies. 'He was a good draughtsman.'

Ralph also revealed a talent for life-drawing. 'One of his paintings showing the back of a reclining nude was particularly good,' says Davies. 'He was a good colourist and had a real feel for the materials he was using. All his work involved painting people or objects. As I recall, he did nothing abstract. It was very English and very fluid – but not in the least pedantic.

'But he was also interested in the process of transferring an image to a canvas or a blank sheet of paper. He was intrigued by the process of making a painting and how the painting depicted something. He took an intellectual approach to the subject of fine art.'

According to Davies, students often found themselves on the receiving end of some pretty severe criticism. He says, 'There were regular tutorials in which the course tutors would spread a student's work over the floor and then discuss his or her progress. It was a very public form of critical appraisal in which having a thick skin was a distinct advantage. Our view was if you're going to get your arse kicked – and every young artist is – you may as well get used to it early.'

However, the syllabus was hardly intensive. 'You could get away with doing very little work,' says Flowers. 'And most people spent a lot more time worrying about painting than actually getting down to it.' The studious and hard-working Fiennes was no exception. 'He took it all terribly seriously and would agonize about his work,' says Davies. 'I think he fancied himself as a tortured soul.'

A classmate echoes this view: 'Ralph was as accomplished an artist as anyone in our year but he sometimes seemed more interested in the idea of being an artist than in actually *being* an artist. Nobody was really surprised when he dropped out.'

In his spare time Ralph, who found digs near Clapham Common at a time when a room cost as little as £8 a week, would occasionally drink with fellow students in a then-scruffy Fulham pub, the Queen Elizabeth, go to art galleries, visit his parents and now and then return to Salisbury to see friends.

Contrary to popular belief life at art school wasn't one long party. 'I thought art school would be all about sex and drugs and wild parties but I couldn't have been more wrong,' says Flowers. 'While there was a bohemian atmosphere about the place, a lot of the students were quietly eccentric and seemed happier reading a book than hanging out in nightclubs.'

And Fiennes seems to have been among the more conservative students, favouring jeans or corduroys with a casual jacket, his flirtation with punk just a memory. 'He was fairly reserved,' says one contemporary. 'He got on well with other students but you also got the impression that he liked his own space.'

Fiennes, who had matured into a lean, handsome, sensitive-looking young man, attracted an inordinate amount of interest from female students at Chelsea Art School. 'He was obviously good looking and had no shortage of female admirers,' reveals a former student. 'If he'd wanted to, he could have put it about a bit.'

Little more than a term and a half into the foundation course, though, Ralph began to question whether he might, after all, be better cut out for acting. 'I knew it was all wrong,' he says. 'I had this definite longing – a call, a push, call it what you will – to be an actor.'

Recalls Davies: 'I remember taking the piss out of him sometimes because I knew he was contemplating a career in acting. "Hallo, dear boy",' I'd sometimes joke. Then one day he asked if we could talk and he said he was unsure whether he should pursue art or acting.

'I told him he wouldn't have much trouble getting onto a degree course. He was a good student. He had what it took to be a painter – but, just as importantly, he had the intellectual curiosity you find in an artist. But I told him, "Ralph, you've got to follow your instinct. If acting's what you want to do, do it. It's your life." I was sorry to see him go because I had a lot of time for him.'

Looking back, Fiennes considers the year was far from a waste of time. Indeed, he believes that studying art prepared him psychologically for acting.

'All kinds of linear thinking were knocked out of me, giving me the confidence to say "Actually, if I can think about being a designer, painter or sculptor, I can think about being an actor",' he comments. 'Once there, acting came to me with such clarity. I knew I had to act. It wasn't so much an academic interest – I was never that great at English at school – but more an articulate desire to say those lines and play those parts.' His decision to turn his back on fine art was also influenced by a feeling that – in the words of his sister Martha – he would never 'be an original'.

One person who wasn't surprised by Ralph's move was his old

Bishop Wordsworth's teacher Duncan Davies. 'Several other pupils of mine had gone the same route,' he says. 'It should be remembered that the performing arts are very much an extension of the more traditional arts, providing a creative person with the same sort of opportunity for individual self-expression as painting.'

CHAPTER FIVE

The Voice Beautiful

The Royal Academy of Dramatic Art is arguably the most famous acting school in Britain, if not the world. Founded in 1904 by Sir Herbert Beerbohm, the leading actor-manager of the day, it began life in London's West End before moving to Gower Street. The writer George Bernard Shaw was a great benefactor, and the royalties from *Pygmalion* and his other works helped to fund the academy's subsequent expansion.

A roll-call of ex-students – John Gielgud, Albert Finney, Glenda Jackson, Tom Courtenay, John Hurt, Anthony Hopkins, Jonathan Pryce, Juliet Stevenson, Alan Rickman and Kenneth Branagh among others – reads like a veritable 'Who's Who' of the great and good of the British stage and screen.

Gaining entry to such an establishment is not easy. Thousands apply every year. Candidates have to be 19 or over, and while there is no fixed upper age limit, acceptance over the age of 30 is rare. The vast majority of those applying are weeded out before being auditioned.

Undeterred, Ralph walked into RADA one 1982 day, asked for an application form, sat waiting under the busts in the foyer and was told he would need a postage stamp. As he left for the post office to get one, someone said: 'While you're there you can post these for us – it might bring you luck.' And so it proved.

'Everyone who gets through the initial screening is interviewed and, if they stand out, invited back to audition a short piece in front

39

of a five-member panel,' says Hugh Cruttwell, principal at RADA from 1966–84, and a member of the panel which auditioned Fiennes.

The would-be actor bravely chose to audition with the 'O, what a rogue and peasant slave am I' soliloquy from *Hamlet*. One of Shakespeare's most famous speeches, it had been immortalized by Laurence Olivier, amongst others. But Cruttwell recalls, 'Ralph was very impressive and we all thought he deserved a place.'

The prospectus boasted that RADA's favourable student-staff ratio enabled 'the acquired skills of the actor, both vocal and physical, to be taught at an intensive level' during the seven-term course. It continued, 'Performances take place in a variety of acting spaces. These circumstances combine to enable the student to explore his work from as many angles as possible.' In addition, students benefited from working with visiting directors and actors.

Twenty-two fresh-faced students arrived at RADA on a cold morning in January, 1983, at the start of their first term. A couple were bursting with confidence, a few – including Ralph – were quietly confident, while others were secretly terrified. However, all were conscious they were embarking on a great adventure.

Fourteen were male, 8 female; 2 American, the rest British. The intake was drawn from all walks of life, and had a much greater provincial representation than would have been likely a generation earlier. In hindsight, the 'Class of '83' appears an exceptional year – for not only did it include Fiennes, but also other leading actors of the 1990s such as Iain Glen, Jane Horrocks and Imogen Stubbs.

To begin with, Fiennes came across as 'unusually self-contained'. Kathryn Worth noticed 'an other-world, almost naïve quality' about him while another student, Tania Wade, thought he had 'a delicious innocence.' Hugh Cruttwell's successor as principal, Oliver Neville, describes Ralph as 'reticent' even though he didn't arrive at RADA until the spring of 1984, by which time Fiennes had been a student there for more than a year.

However, Neil 'Dudge' Dudgeon was one individual who did not take to Fiennes. 'I thought he was a total wanker,' he says bluntly. 'The only thing I heard him say the first three weeks was "Um, it's Rafe, actually. It's the correct, Old English pronunciation". I thought "You upper-class git!" '

*

The course was initially structured around daily acting, speech, movement, improvization and fencing classes. Students were exposed to Greek drama, Restoration comedy and Elizabethan verse and told to immerse themselves in their acting and speech lessons. 'It was very intensive,' says Cruttwell. 'I worked them terribly hard – there were high expectations.'

'The Fab Four' – as Fiennes, Glen, Horrocks and Stubbs have since been dubbed – were fast-trackers from day one, according to Worth. 'It was sink or swim,' she says. 'You knew who would find life easy. Their egos were strong; there was an edge to them, to Iain and Imogen in particular.'

One of the guest teachers was Bill Homewood, a former Royal Shakespeare Company actor with many television appearances to his credit. He was the Shakespearian text tutor, teaching Ralph twice a week during his time at the Academy.

'I remember the very first lesson I gave the class because Ralph stood out,' he says. 'He delivered a Shakespearian soliloquy with great passion. It was a committed and brave performance. The group were an erudite, talented lot and I'm sure they didn't sit back and think "we have a star among us", but I immediately noticed his beautiful voice, his concentration and his interpretive intelligence.'

Over the course of the next two-and-a-bit years, Homewood oversaw broad-ranging Shakespeare workshops that involved the students in what he calls 'get-up-on-your-hind-legs-and-perform Shakespeare'.

He formed a particularly close bond with Fiennes because they shared a mutual fascination for Elizabethan verse. 'I believed very strongly that an actor had to work hard to acquire a real familiarity with Elizabethan verse – something Elizabethan actors took for granted,' he says. 'Ralph had a real hunger to study Elizabethan text in detail and worked tremendously hard on verse speaking in order to give himself the freedom he wanted to have with the language.'

But there was surprisingly little emphasis on the 'method acting' that was all the rage at other acting schools such as London's Drama Centre. 'I never heard Stanislavsky mentioned during my years at RADA,' says one ex-student.

41

Echoing these comments, Wade says: 'They didn't strip you down as they did at some schools. And you never had to be a tree or an orange. Instead you did "trust exercises" where you jumped off a piano and the others had to catch you – and you went straight into rehearsing plays. Usually they'd just give you a part and let you get on with it.'

In the second term the emphasis shifted to performance, and during Ralph's two-and-a-bit years as a student he would appear in a total of fifteen RADA productions.

All were staged at the Academy's Vanbrugh Theatre off Tottenham Court Road. Members of the public could see performances for just £1 in the evening or 70p in the afternoon – the one condition being that they became a club member, a bargain at £2 a year. For an outlay of a mere £2.70, anyone could therefore see a play featuring several leading future actors.

Some of Ralph's roles were very minor. For instance, he appeared as a servant in one play and a peasant in another. But he also played more interesting roles – including the treacherous Brutus in *Julius Caesar*, the tragic hero of Chekhov's *Ivanov*, and in his seventh and final term, the fatherly, old-fashioned King of France in Shakespeare's *All's Well That Ends Well*.

His Ivanov was 'highly regarded' according to one student, and confirmed his promise. Tania Wade, who played Ivanov's long-suffering wife, recalls, 'The Ralph I remember was very focused and incredibly passionate about the theatre – I've never seen someone so passionate about the theatre.' While his King of France left a lasting impression on Oliver Neville, who says: 'It's a very difficult part but he did it brilliantly.'

Such productions were staged on a shoestring: as is clear from the programme notes accompanying *Peer Gynt*, one of the plays Ralph appeared in. Every assistance is acknowledged from 'Sally Hanson for the nail varnish' to 'Robin Greene for the lute' and 'Imperial Tobacco for the cigars and cigarettes', to 'Young's the brewer for the barrels'. It was a long way from the bright lights of Broadway and the West End.

Student life at RADA revolved around the classroom, the common room and the canteen where the young thespians wolfed down the sort of food – beans, bangers and chips – which sustained students across the land. Between lessons, Ralph and his classmates would congregate in the common room, 'a horrible little room next to the boys' changing room, with a linoleum floor and a green bench running around it', in the words of one ex-student.

The student common room was to be the scene of numerous good-natured brawls between the so-called 'lads' in the Class of '83. 'They were loud, they'd tell lewd jokes and pretend to hump each other', says one old classmate. 'There was a whole bunch of boys, led by Glen, who indulged in the sort of puerile, testosterone-fuelled antics typical of males of that age.'

While Ralph sometimes got caught up in the physical exuberance, he never became a fully paid-up member of the gang. 'He remained somewhat aloof from them and, in fact, everyone on the course,' adds the classmate. 'But not in a snobby way, more of a dreamy way.'

Not for the first time, Ralph had to put up with some cryptic asides about his name – but he never let it rattle him. 'He'd just smile,' says a source. 'The jibes just passed him by, the lads soon got bored with trying to rile him and turned their attention on someone else.'

In time, though, the lads in the class were to come to revise their opinion of the beautifully spoken student. Partly out of affection and partly out of jealousy, they dubbed him 'The Voice Beautiful'.

Dudgeon was won over the day Fiennes gave him a cassette introducing him to Billie Holiday. 'He turned around quite rapidly in my estimation,' says the actor, who stars in *Common As Muck*, the hit sitcom about binmen. 'We had just seemed to be totally different people who couldn't possibly have anything in common, which was partly about the working-class chip on my shoulder.

'Before long, though, we were spending school breaks together. He said "Oh, you must come down, my mum's got a cottage in Dorset". And not knowing him very well at that stage, I imagined we'd be going to his great big mansion, he'd have his snooty family around and I wouldn't fit in at all. And Ralph said, "No, no, really, it's ever so small. And Mum's there and the twins and my sister." We got there and it was the smallest place you've ever seen. Totally lovely!'

It was also at RADA that Fiennes met Alex Kingston, the woman who was to be the first great love of his life. Born on 11 March 1963, the striking butcher's daughter with the mass of curly hair who was a term below Ralph arrived fresh from Roseberry Grammar School for Girls in Epsom and the National Youth Theatre. She admits that she fell in love with Ralph straight away.

'I wanted to marry him from the moment I met him,' says Kingston. 'I very clumsily showed I really liked him and he did nothing about it for about eight months. It was heart-breaking. The day I acknowledged there was no real chance, he asked me out to supper.'

The romance took off after Ralph's starring role in the student production of *Ivanov* in the summer of 1984, and he and Alex were soon an item, even though in many ways they were chalk and cheese. 'Those who met him and Alex could not avoid being struck by the almost painful contrast,' says one old friend. 'His brooding shyness alongside her garrulousness. It was a classic case of opposites attracting.'

What propelled Kingston into acting was her need for attention – but everyone agreed that the extrovert Alex, brimming with self-confidence, had a positive influence on Fiennes.

Nevertheless Ralph was by no means the heart-throb of his year. In fact, he barely registered on his female classmates' Richter scale of romantic yearnings. 'All the girls fancied Iain Glen,' says Tania Wade, now a mother and part-time actress. 'He was fiery and there was a problematical element of danger about him. He was a bit of a bad boy and you know what twenty-year-old girls are like – they always fall for the sort of guy who is going to end up breaking their hearts.'

Some of the lads on the course, according to another female student, 'would shag anything in sight' but Ralph was 'gentler, softer and somehow more romantic' and, unlike some of his more macho contemporaries, 'never set out to be Mr Sexy'.

In fact, at times, Ralph must have felt particularly misunderstood, as one episode reveals. 'We all had to do a turn on stage and Ralph told a story that was meant to be poignant but had everyone in stitches because they thought the passage he was reading was meant to be funny,' says Kathryn Worth. 'He got tremendous applause but when he came offstage he asked with a perplexed look: "Why was everyone laughing?" '

While Fiennes might have been a 'sweetie' in the eyes of women like Wade and Worth, he was every bit as competitive as the louder, brasher members of the class – and every bit as good, if not better, a student as indicated by his tally of RADA prizes.

The academy had long had a tradition of handing out awards, some worth a considerable amount of money, to the most promising graduating students.

Ralph was already perfecting his own blueprint for stage success, involving painstaking research into a role, followed by however many readings of a play as were necessary to make the lines *his* lines. And, while no recluse, his work – which happened to be his over-riding passion – always came first. Frivolities, like drinking with his classmates at the nearby Marlborough tavern, were low on his list of priorities.

The hard work paid off, and upon graduating with an Honours Diploma in April 1985, he was awarded the Shakespeare Schools Prize, the Bossom diction prize, the Crean and Ware stage-fighting prizes, and a rare triple crown: the Forbes-Robertson, the Emile Littler and the Kendal awards (the last the equivalent of the year's silver medal).

The year's top prize, the Bancroft (equivalent to the gold medal) went to Iain Glen. However, Oliver Neville says, 'I can't possibly forget Ralph. In many ways he was the perfect student. He was a civilized young man with a lovely, light sense of humour but he was also a worker. If you are going to make it in the acting business and not be a flash in the pan, you need to be a worker. He was very thorough and worked on everything: he was probably the best swordsman RADA ever produced and he could play a great range of parts.'

Few had any doubts that Fiennes was destined for success. However, even his biggest fans among the teaching staff would be surprised at the speed of his ascent.

The other members of the 'Fab Four' were also soon on their way. Glen carved out an impressive career as a Shakespearian actor before going on to star in Cameron Mackintosh's West End musical, *Martin Guerre*. Stubbs, now married to former Royal Shakespeare Theatre director Trevor Nunn, starred in the controversial television adaptation of D.H. Lawrence's *The Rainbow* and the TV police drama *Anna Lee*. While Horrocks – perhaps the best known of the four after Fiennes – played the airhead Bubbles in *Absolutely Fabulous*, won acclaim as an anorexic teenager in Mike Leigh's *Life Is Sweet* and hosted a memorable one-off television comedy special, *Never Mind the Horrocks*.

Others, too, have prospered with Claire Hackett appearing in TV series such as *A Touch of Frost*, *The Bill* and *Medics*, Serena Gordon playing a Bond girl in *GoldenEye*, and Peter Gunn, Wayne Foskett and Neil Dudgeon making regular television appearances.

However, not everyone from the class of '83 has been as lucky, for going to RADA does not, in itself, guarantee thespian success. At least four of Ralph's graduation year do not have agents and some have turned their back on the acting world altogether, to all intents and purposes vanishing.

'A lot of people on the course were very sensitive,' says Kathryn Worth, who has since worked in fringe theatre and is a part-time assistant to a casting director. 'It's too painful for some of them to have reality thrust in their faces so they turn their back on the profession. Not everyone can be successful. Acting is a tough business.'

CHAPTER SIX

The Repertory Boot Camp

However famous an actor eventually becomes, the chances are he began his career in the provinces. Fiennes was no exception, first heading for North Wales and then Lancashire – both of which are a long way from London's theatre-land.

Opened in 1976, Theatr Clwyd is built on a hill overlooking the market town of Mold and the Clwydian range of mountains beyond. The view towards Moel Fammau on a summer evening can be breathtaking. The rural backdrop has been known, however, to become a little too prominent – one actress was disturbed mid-soliloquy by a cow, chewing ruminatively, who stuck its head through her dressing room window. More importantly, it has been hailed as the nearest thing Wales has to a national theatre.

Having left RADA a star student, it didn't take him long to find work – and his first professional appearance would be in Theatr Clwyd's Tenth Anniversary Season production of Tom Stoppard's quasi-documentary 1978 West End hit, *Night and Day*. Two rather better known actors – Vanessa Redgrave and future 007 Timothy Dalton – would appear in a Theatr Clwyd production of *Antony and Cleopatra* later that season.

Stoppard's play follows the activities of a motley bunch of journalists who, reporting on a rebellion in a fictitious British African colony, congregate in a large house owned by Carson, a white mining executive. Brash newsman Dick Wagner (Jonathan Burn) and photographer George Guthrie (Keith Barlett) are with the '*Globe*' newspaper, while Jacob Milne (Fiennes) is a freelance 'scab' whose anti-union idealism puts him at odds with Wagner. It is Milne's exclusive interview that has made the *Globe*, not Wagner's piece. To complicate matters, Carson's alcoholic, bored and promiscuous wife, Ruth (Caroline Lagerfelt), has spent a night with Wagner in London but is now attracted to Milne.

A former journalist himself, Stoppard saw the story as an opportunity to set off on a moral safari into the jungles of journalism, sex and politics. And having already produced the play elsewhere, Robertson's intimate knowledge of *Night and Day* allowed him to give the production a precise structure and flesh out Stoppard's characters in all their complexity.

A fellow member of the cast of *Night and Day* recalls Fiennes 'taking the part and play very seriously' but 'happily unwinding over a pint of beer after the curtain had gone down'. Being so far from London, the production got virtually zero coverage in the national press, but the *Stage* congratulated Robertson's production on 'illuminating every nook and cranny of the play' while commenting favourably on Ralph's 'effective support'.

Early in the following year, 1986, Fiennes landed a seasonal contract with the Coliseum Theatre, Oldham – somewhere literally worlds apart from the genteel Salisbury and Suffolk of his youth.

The industrial town of 220,000 people stretches from the outskirts of Manchester to the northern edge of the Peak District National Park. It achieved fame in the nineteenth century as one of the world's leading cotton-spinning towns but was hard hit by the decline in Britain's traditional industrial base in the late twentieth century. Cotton mills still dot the landscape but their tall, red-brick chimneys have long since fallen idle.

Considerable effort has since been made to breathe new life into Oldham – by, for instance, the opening of the impressive new Spindles shopping centre – but with limited success. However, the town boasts some magnificent examples of Victorian architecture and its people have a warmth often lacking in the more prosperous south.

Found in a backstreet between a protective-clothing factory and a reject furniture shop, the Coliseum has always been a cash-strapped, struggling theatre.

It began life in 1887, the brainchild of a circus proprietor, but by the 1900s was staging silent films and variety acts, among them Fred Karno's troupe. With the coming of the Depression, the Coliseum closed. In the 1930s, it reopened, but in 1947 an actor was stabbed on stage during a performance of *Macbeth*. He subsequently died from his injuries and before long the theatre was facing new financial difficulties. But the Coliseum somehow struggled on, with the professional services of Dora Bryan, Bernard Cribbins, Eric Sykes and Thora Hird – not to mention 'half the cast of *Coronation Street*', among them Jean Alexander and Anne Kirkbride.

Today it looks at first sight more like a warehouse than a theatre. Its mustard-coloured walls are dotted with damp patches, the foyer has a musty smell and one ex-employee jokes that you 'need wellington boots to wade down some corridors after heavy rain'. However, the three-tier auditorium, seating 584 people, is surprisingly impressive and the Coliseum won a Theatre of the Year 'people's award' in 1995.

When Fiennes arrived in February 1986 – after a spell 'between jobs' – Britain was in the grip of what the newspapers called 'the big freeze'. Snow and ice had closed roads from Scotland to Sussex and the Coliseum was chillier than usual.

The first play he appeared in was Barry Heath's *Me Mam Sez*. Billed as 'a side-splitting slice of Northern family life,' it was a nostalgic wartime comedy affectionately evoking working class life in Oldham in 1943 – an era when blackouts and air raid sirens reigned supreme; the *Daily Herald* was relegated to toilet paper duties, and Vera Lynn ruled the airwaves.

Former *Coronation Street* actress Judith Barker played a long-suffering Lancashire mum-of-eight living in a crowded two-up, two-down terraced house. She was married to a tyrannical coal miner husband but worshipped her 21-year-old son, Jack (Fiennes) who had had the sense to escape such a life by joining the Navy.

The play, directed by John Retallack, won generally favourable reviews and was a sell-out. Oldham's *Evening Chronicle* described *Me Mam Sez* as 'extremely funny', adding: 'There are some hilarious running jokes, as well as some brilliantly engineered knockabout comedy.' However, it cautioned, 'The play's one fault is that, though it zooms along, it goes nowhere.' It also had reservations about the play's perpetuation of stereotypical images of Northern family life.

The *Guardian* observed that Judith Baxter was the anchor in a cast 'galvanized into milking comic opportunity' and also had praise for the actors playing her three youngest sons. The *Manchester Evening News* critic thought the play itself 'a mite repetitive' but added, 'Should you find the first act over-long, I can promise a hilarious second act scene which is well worth the wait.'

Of Ralph – who in his spare time, according to the programme, enjoyed 'decorating, vegetarian cookery and playing with the Pollocks toy theatre which he had had since he was eight', there was not a mention. However, the *Evening Chronicle* ran a picture story about the actor headlined: 'Ralph's a real Romeo!' alongside a picture of this putative Valentino looking more like a meek school choirboy than a future screen heartthrob.

'I found Ralph very attractive,' reflects Judith Barker, who appeared in several scenes with him, 'not so much for the way he looked but for his personality. He got on with the job and was very good, though he only had a few scenes.'

Less than a week after the last performance of *Me Mam Sez*, Ralph was stepping out in his second Coliseum production, *The Mad Adventures of a Knight*, which opened in March.

Written by a group of authors, including Richard Curtis – who went on to pen *Four Weddings and a Funeral* – it was loosely based on Cervantes's stories of Don Quixote and his faithful companion, Sancho Panza. The Coliseum version, directed by John Retallack, opened with languorous guitar music and several members of the cast relaxing, their sombreros lolling in the heat of the seventeenth century Spanish setting.

It followed the adventures of Don Quixote and Sancho Panza (played by Barry McGinn and Stuart Golland) in the traditional style of the lean, bearded knight and portly squire. But the sly, subversive humour of the long, rambling book was reduced to would-be slapstick comedy. Fiennes played several minor characters – including the Duke and the Double.

Reviews were patchy with few if any critics agreeing with the Coliseum's pronouncement that the production was 'the perfect

Easter outing for all the family'. The *Guardian* complained that 'nothing much happened interminably slowly', adding, 'There can be few things more tedious than watching two men prancing around a stage pretending they are on horseback'.

The *Manchester Evening News* felt 'the story was hard to follow and the audience were unsure whether to laugh or cry'. While the *Evening Chronicle* thought the story was 'exceedingly slow, enjoyable moments were few and far between and it would have a limited appeal to children'. However, unlike the other reviews, this latter newspaper did at least praise Ralph for 'turning in a fine performance'.

Barely had Fiennes and the rest of the cast had time to catch their breath before they were rehearsing their next production, *Cloud Nine*. The first half of this sexual satire, written by Caryl Churchill, was set in Africa in the mid-nineteenth century and focused on Clive, a Victorian colonial officer who was flying the flag and flogging the natives. But, bizarrely, his wife was a man, his son a girl, his daughter a doll and his black manservant white. To confuse matters further, they were joined by a homosexual explorer and a widow with lesbian tendencies. Things got even more complicated in the second half of the play, which was set in London in 1985 – though Clive's wife and children were only 25 years older than they were 125 years earlier.

This time Ralph played two minor characters: Harry Bagley in the first half and a character named Martin, who wears a dress, in the second. Having such small roles proved a blessing in disguise, for the Barry McGinn-directed play – billed by the Coliseum as 'good, unclean fun' – was panned by the critics.

'By the time one of the gay men began to wonder if he's a lesbian, I'd lost my bearings completely,' wrote Brian Hope in the *Manchester Evening News*. 'The cast works hard enough but the show misfires badly. *Cloud Nine* is definitely not my idea of heaven.' The *Evening Chronicle* thought it a play 'from which it is impossible to derive any pleasure. It is very bad, unclean fun, and strictly for adults with minds like children.' While the *Daily Telegraph* described it as 'an evening of unmitigated, pretentious boredom – so lustreless that only embarrassment could excuse the cast's lack of conviction.' Only the *Guardian* could find a kind word for the production, describing 'almost every individual performance as lively or interesting'.

The reviews were so bad that the director wrote to the local newspaper, claiming that *Cloud Nine* was 'one of the best plays written in the last ten years'. But the *Evening Chronicle* retorted, 'Best plays of this type are invariably notable milestones on the road to theatre closures.'

By then, though, Fiennes was only interested in fulfilling his contractual obligations and moving on to his next job at the Open Air Theatre where he would get his teeth into the sort of plum parts he had not got a chance to play at the Coliseum.

Happy though he was to enjoy drinks in the theatre bar after a performance with members of the cast, it has been said that he never made 'a special effort' to get to know his fellow actors. 'Offstage, he was reticent, low-key and you had to make a real effort to have a conversation,' says Barker. While David Rustidge, the theatre's house manager since 1982, found him 'a serious, unassuming young man'. Most weekends Ralph travelled back to London to see Alex. 'They appeared to be very much in love,' says Barker.

Sometimes as he trudged back to his digs through Oldham's invariably dark, rain-sodden streets that winter he must have wondered what on earth he was doing so far from home. And Rustidge himself admits, 'There's something rather incongruous about a big movie star like Ralph Fiennes having started their career at Oldham.'

Yet his repertory boot camp stint would not be in vain. As Ralph observes, 'Doing rep toughens you up. You go through the mill and you can't be precious about it. Your only target is that night's performance. It's great training for an actor.'

CHAPTER SEVEN

Beneath The Stars

In June, 1986, Fiennes made his professional London stage début at Regent's Park Open Air Theatre. Outside performances had taken place in this location since early in the century but the Open Air Theatre itself did not come into being until the 1930s – the product of a collaboration between impresario Sydney Carroll and actor/manager Robert Atkins, who in 1932 staged a bizarre version of *Twelfth Night* in which every character was dressed entirely in black and white.

The following summer saw the advent of the first full season at Queen Mary's Gardens, with its unique lawn-stage surrounded by a vast semi-circular auditorium consisting of deckchairs and slatted park seats. One production of *The Tempest* attracted a 250,000-strong audience – and actresses such as Fay Compton, Vivien Leigh, Deborah Kerr and Jessica Tandy would go on to grace this most charming and unusual theatre.

The Second World War forced Carroll and Atkins to scale down the summer season. But the late 1940s and early 1950s saw a revival in the Open Air Theatre's fortunes, with the appearance of stars like Michael Bentine, Dandy Nicholls and Charles Gray – although the theatre's finances remained precarious.

Just when the future looked at its bleakest, a new management team – led by David Conville and David William – took over and revitalized the theatre. In 1963 the duo formed the Regent's Park-based New Shakespeare Company which has since staged many memorable productions, featuring actors such as Felicity Kendal, Anthony Andrews and Jeremy Irons. Tours of the Middle East, Europe and Asia have even been undertaken.

The first Regent's Park production Ralph appeared in was *Romeo and Juliet* – Shakespeare's first romantic tragedy and one of his best-known works. Playing opposite Fiennes was Sarah Woodward (daughter of *Equaliser* star Edward Woodward) who in 1997 starred opposite Michael Gambon in the acclaimed Richard Wilson-directed West End play, *Tom and Clem*.

The Open Air Theatre production got a controversial overhaul, courtesy of the avant-garde director-designer team of Declan Donellan and Nick Ormerod. The city of Verona was given an Edwardian setting; the men were dressed in boaters, straw hats and blazers or whites, ties and tails; while the women wore long, ornate dresses. But Fiennes admired Donellan and Ormerod for their fresh approach. 'He believed in taking chances,' says a fellow actor.

Donellan was one of the first to spot Ralph's prodigious talent, noting, 'He was a fantastically charismatic player with an electric quality and an extremely big, almost nineteenth-century voice. He was always very direct, and had this faintly crazed element in his eyes which is very attractive – especially to a movie camera. He also had a poetic quality you simply couldn't ignore.'

The play opened on a grey, overcast June evening but, providentially, the rain stayed away. After reading the following day's reviews, however, some of the cast must have wished the critics had stayed away too.

The *Daily Mail* pronounced it 'a brave and interesting attempt' to bring Shakespeare's urban tragedy to the park's pastoral setting. But it disliked the way the actors so seldom left the stage except to change costumes. However, it conceded, 'In Ralph Fiennes we have as romantic and heroic a young blade as any Edwardian Miss would find between the covers of her book'.

But most critics were underwhelmed by Ralph's Romeo and Woodward's Juliet. 'The star-crossed lovers are as much overprivileged brats as tragic victims,' commented *Time Out*. 'Ralph Fiennes's rakish Romeo has the air of a callow youth as much preoccupied by recreational drugs as the fair Rosalie before he succumbs to the intoxicating delights of Juliet.' It concluded: 'An uneven, fitfully beguiling production.'

While *Punch* damned Fiennes as 'more fortune's fool than matinée idol in the making'. And the *Sunday Telegraph* thought the two central roles 'emerged the least satisfactorily', though it added, 'This is more the fault of the director than the stars. Instead of a balcony, Juliet has to make do with standing on a table with a white sheet stretched out below her. Meanwhile Romeo is frantically chasing about the auditorium, bawling out his lines like a flustered commuter looking for the last train to Brighton.'

As for Donellan's other innovations, the critics thought some 'brilliant', others 'exasperatingly obtrusive'. The *Evening Standard* was most struck by the production's brevity, commenting that it could 'lay claim to being one of the speediest versions of the tragedy yet seen.' It too was critical of the leading man, claiming: 'Ralph Fiennes as Romeo occasionally looked more like an accountant in love than an Italian teenager' but approvingly added that 'he met his doom with real pathos'.

The *Financial Times* thought the production lacked 'real passion' and the central love affair was 'a little on the prim side'. While *Today* had trouble with the play's Edwardian setting. 'You half expect them to sing a boating song or start a game of tennis,' it said. The now-defunct newspaper went on to half-jokingly claim that the high point 'came by accident when a duck outside the theatre uttered a loud quack as Romeo was about to kiss Juliet'. Such were the pitfalls of performing Shakespeare in a 'natural' habitat.

Interestingly, Fiennes himself – the last person from whom one would have expected such criticism – agreed with those critics who felt that his performance left something to be desired.

'I wasn't very good,' he admitted afterwards, showing the seriousness with which he viewed the acting process. 'It's a difficult part, Romeo. You've got to be youthful yet you need tremendous acting experience to really pull it off, and it's rare to have both. I was inexperienced. I remember being so frustrated because all the actors had to project the material in a big amphitheatre. It was impossible, really. I wouldn't touch it now in that place. The open-air theatre is great for plays such as *A Midsummer Night's Dream*. But to do any of the tragedies there is technically tough.'

Ironically, the rest of the cast were a lot less tough on Fiennes than he was on himself. 'As far as we were concerned, he did a fair job,' comments one of his co-stars. 'He hadn't been out of RADA long so no one was expecting an Olivier-like performance. But he was by no means a bad Romeo.'

The second Open Air Theatre production that Ralph appeared in was *A Midsummer Night's Dream*. Directed by David Conville and Emma Freud (later to become a television celebrity in her own right), was based on a Toby Robertson reworking of the original. The fairies were dressed as punks in a hearty, boisterous affair that also starred the former 'Carry On' films star Bernard Bresslaw as the buffoonish, donkey-headed weaver, Bottom.

With much of the action taking place at night, the play lent itself beautifully to being staged in the open air. 'Unscripted wildlife noises for once assist rather than detract from the enjoyment,' observed one critic – conveniently ignoring the open-mouthed human wildlife slurping their drinks and munching noisily on their salads.

Reviews were mixed. 'It is energetic, funny and full of good gags even if it does take more than a few liberties with the text,' commented *Today*, the only paper to give the production a resounding thumbs-up. Although the *Sunday Telegraph* conceded that 'it should delight everyone with its inventiveness and high spirits.'

The purists, on the other hand, were offended that liberties had been taken with the text. 'I cannot remember disliking a revival of *A Midsummer Night's Dream* more than this chronically perverse version,' wrote the *Guardian*'s indignant critic.

But most important, surely, as *Punch* pointed out, was that 'the crammed house revelled in the production on a gorgeous summer evening', something the cast were quick to appreciate.

Starring in a Shakespearian season at the Open Air Theatre was an idyllic summer experience for a young actor. 'It was a lot better than being stuck inside a West End theatre,' says a fellow cast member. 'After a performance ended, Ralph and the rest of us would sometimes sit beneath the stars laughing and chatting. It was a lot of fun.'

The predominantly young cast also learnt a lot about their craft that summer, as Fiennes acknowledges: 'Doing Shakespeare taught me that the actor must stop getting in his own way.'

However, an unexpected cloud appeared on the horizon when Jini was diagnosed as suffering from breast cancer. She was 48, Ralph not yet 24. It was a bolt from the blue and left her husband Mark and the children reeling. Jini was still relatively young, though, and like Ralph she had true grit and determination. The last thing she intended to do was succumb to the cruel disease while still in the prime of her life.

The family rallied round in support and her ensuing battle drew her even closer to the children, especially Ralph, with whom she had an especially strong bond.

As well as undergoing conventional cancer treatment, the possibility of impending mortality spurred a new interest in Jini in spirituality and religion. She began to study Tibetan Buddhism and became devoted to the mystical writings of the medieval anchoress, Julian of Norwich, although she never entirely turned her back on the Catholic faith of her youth.

Jini viewed the diagnosis with surprising detachment. 'Cancer,' she wrote – almost poetically, as if it posed not the slightest threat to her well-being – 'is a constellation, you become simply one of the thousands and thousands of stars within it. It is a common everyday disease.' After a certain time period the disease went into remission – and the family wept with relief. It seemed living proof that miracles could happen.

CHAPTER EIGHT

The National

In 1987, Ralph arrived at the prestigious National Theatre. The establishment of a permanent state-subsidized theatre in London, along the lines of the Comédie-Française, had first been mooted in the eighteenth century.

Not until 1908, though, was a committee formed to investigate the possibility, the plan being to throw open the doors in 1916, the tercentenary of Shakespeare's death. A foundation stone was laid in Gower Street in 1914 but the outbreak of the First World War brought the project to a standstill. In 1938 another site, this time in South Kensington, was acquired – and no less a person than George Bernard Shaw laid the foundation stone. However, the outbreak of the Second World War brought further delay.

The scheme was resurrected in 1951 – with a third foundation stone being laid on the South Bank of the River Thames. Ten years later, a National Theatre company under Laurence Olivier was finally established.

Performances took place at the nearby Old Vic until the doors of the vast, purpose-built complex eventually opened in 1976. Designed by Denys Lasdun, it housed three theatres – the Lyttleton, the Olivier and the Cottesloe – as well as numerous rehearsal rooms, workshops and dressing rooms for 150 actors. Ever since, the monolithic concrete building has been controversial. Whatever its architectural failings though, its superb facilities have indisputably enriched the nation's cultural life.

In the 1980s, a number of directors at the National set up their own companies. Among them was Michael Rudman who offered Fiennes a job following an audition. Despite being American-born, Rudman had taken an MA at Oxford and since worked largely in England. Ironically, though, he is best known for his 1984 New York production of Arthur Miller's *Death of a Salesman*, starring Dustin Hoffman.

The first play to be staged by Rudman's new company was Luigi Pirandello's *Six Characters in Search of an Author*. Rehearsals started virtually straight away, and it opened in March at the National's 2,000-seat Olivier theatre.

When Pirandello's play premièred in Rome in 1921 it caused uproar – members of the audience were seen chasing the playwright to his taxi after the show, hurling streams of abuse.

Hugely influential at the time, the play won its author an international reputation as an original and outstanding writer, and its subversive nature 'left its fingerprints' all over modern drama. Yet the fiftieth anniversary of his death the previous year had been met with a resounding silence in Britain. Did the play still have the power to shock?

The Italian dramatist was fascinated by questions such as: 'How real are the emotions expressed by actors in a play?' and 'Can the theatre honestly depict what we really feel – or is the art of playwright merely dedicated to creating illusions?'

His play revolved around a theatre company whose rehearsals are interrupted by the arrival of a fictional husband and wife, stepdaughter, son (played by Fiennes) and two younger children lost in dramatic limbo. They are the outcasts of an unfinished play, desperately wandering around in a theatrical purgatory looking for someone who will allow them to bring their story of trauma and intrigue alive.

As *Six Characters in Search of an Author* unfolds, the tragic quality of the play-within-the-play becomes apparent. First, the father, while visiting a bordello, finds himself about to make love to his own step-daughter. Then the father's angst-ridden recalcitrant son (Fiennes) retreats into Oedipal fury at his aberrant mother's return home with a family of bastard children.

Rudman's version of the original was extensively reworked by

Nicholas Wright – the result being, amongst other things, that the language was more explicit, prompting the *Tablet* to claim, 'This is not a "version". It should be described as "a play by Nicholas Wright, loosely based on the play of the same name by Luigi Pirandello".'

This gave a foretaste of the critical opprobrium Rudman's adaptation would draw from some quarters.

The *Financial Times* thought 'Mr Rudman's fastidiously cramping production denies … the play's sinister, flesh-tingling potential'. The *Observer* accused it of 'never visualizing the crucial debate between reality and illusion'. The *Independent* felt 'the production merely suggested Pirandello was a word-spinning charlatan'. The *Daily Mail* called it 'strangely flat'. And *Time Out* argued that if the National was going to create 'additional layers of obfuscation and actually add to the dust rather than blowing it away', it would be better if the theatre didn't tackle more European masterpieces.

But there was praise too. The *Sunday Telegraph* called Rudman's production 'admirably strenuous and scrupulous', adding, 'He's displayed this work in all its glittering artifice but has also succeeded in finding the darkness at its centre'. The *Daily Express* said, 'This production is littered with outstanding performances. This is theatre at its best.' And the *Guardian* hailed it as 'sensitive and inventive.'

While Ralph was not mentioned, let alone singled out for praise by the press, it didn't take Rudman long to recognize his star quality. Within days of the rehearsals starting, he predicted that his young prodigy – 'who would sometimes get miffed when he felt others weren't working hard enough' – was 'going to go all the way'.

It wasn't his talent that prompted the remark, according to Robert Butler, then working as Rudman's assistant, so much as his dedication, his propensity for sheer hard graft.

By the start of rehearsals, Butler says, 'Most people had got as far as running the highlighter over their lines and looking at the costume designs pinned up on the wall. But Fiennes had read *Six Characters* in four different versions. Unusually, he could talk about the whole play, not just his own part. But there was nothing academic in his approach; he had none of the knowingness of the graduate.'

Butler, who went on to become the *Independent on Sunday*

theatre critic, got to know the young actor well during his year at the National.

'He was a private, willowy figure, rather like a young priest,' he recalls. 'His hair fell either side of his deep-set eyes and he had a quick, anxious smile. He was not one of the boys – a flip remark could get him looking worried – but his shy, polite manner could give way to sudden bursts of earnestness.'

One night in the bar of the Green Room, a traditional theatrical drinking haunt on the other side of the Thames, Fiennes suddenly leant across a table and confessed to Butler how much he'd been 'thinking about God'. Even then, it was becoming apparent that Ralph was not your typical actor.

Soon after *Six Characters in Search of an Author* ended its run, Ralph and the rest of the company began rehearsing their next production – a seven-scene, two-and-a-half-hour play by Irish dramatist Brian Friel based on Ivan Turgenev's 1862 novel, *Fathers and Sons*.

It was the story of two university students, Bazarov (played by Robert Glenister) and his disciple Arkady (Fiennes), who fired with youthful enthusiasm for change, return to the country estate shambolically run by Arcady's father. The students are hell bent on seeing an end to the old order.

The central figure is Bazarov, the anti-hero and professed nihilist who questions all received ideas and rejects art, love and nature. He and Arkady argue like a pair of Jacobean students. But while Bazarov – who has been dubbed 'the first Bolshevik' – holds firm to his belief in the need for violent change, Arkady is seduced by love, liberalism and the family estate.

Rudman's production premièred at the National's Lyttleton Theatre in July 1987. However, if he, Fiennes and the rest of the company were hoping for a positive response from the press, they were to be sorely disappointed.

'The whole thing has an undigested, inconclusive feel, and the first hour is extraordinarily unengaging,' complained the *Listener*. The *Mail on Sunday* called it 'a Chekhov with the head cut off'. The *Observer* branded the play 'an unsatisfactory hybrid'. While the *Independent* lamented that a play that was 'tragic, complex and subtle' was diminished into something 'farcical, simplistic and crass'.

Even the 'morose-looking' scenery was verbally torn apart, one critic likening its 'rickety compound of planks and timbers' to a 'Wild West stockade'.

The *Jewish Chronicle* was slightly more generous, saying, 'A strong, lyrical production and thrilling performances can't compensate for the weakness of the play's structure.' And one publication, *Time Out*, hailed it as 'a fine, solid piece of drama'.

This time Ralph at least got mentioned in several reviews, his performance receiving some accolades.

'Out of the wreckage,' said one critic, 'just two performances skilfully salvage something of Turgenev. Robin Bailey is first-rate as Bazarov's father – and, until Friel foists a character change upon him, Ralph Fiennes excellently captures Arkady's effervescent and soon evaporating young radicalism.'

Further praise came from *Punch* which was impressed by his 'wistful' performance. The *Spectator* thought both Fiennes and Glenister were 'superb'. And the *Financial Times* enthused how 'the gangling, sunny Arkady of Mr Fiennes is transformed into a raging, comic poltroon noisily echoing Bazarov's revolutionary ardour'.

On the other hand, the *Independent* thought Fiennes 'contrives to be at once stilted and hysterical'. And the *Evening Standard* proved itself no friend of the thespian at this stage in his career, commenting, 'Ralph Fiennes, as Arkady, seems gauche and juvenile and a curious inheritor of the mantle of nihilism that he dons when we learn that Bazarov has died in a typhoid epidemic.'

The third and final play Ralph appeared in at the National was Nick Darke's *Ting Tang Mine*. Originally commissioned as a community play, it was about rival Cornish mining villages fighting for work in the economic depression following the Napoleonic Wars. Ralph played the slow, suspicious tin-miner Lisha Ball.

'Villages like Ting Tang and Brigan used to be entirely dependent on the copper mines being open,' explained Darke, who wrote the play in his garden shed at night. 'So when investors decided to shut down a mine, they shut down an entire village. If it wasn't for the miners' strike, *Ting Tang Mine* wouldn't have been written in the form that it is. But I'd hate to think people are coming to see a play about the miners' strike.'

Fiennes himself held no strong political views, according to one

National Theatre contemporary, but 'like most actors, felt a degree of sympathy for the coal miners during the strike'.

Despite Darke's hopes that the two-hour play, which opened at the Cottesloe Theatre in September 1987, would not be seen as overtly political, it was immediately categorized as a 'left-wing' play by right-wing newspapers.

The *Sunday Telegraph* called it 'muddled', *The Times* thought it 'childish and confused' and the *Evening Standard* loftily pronounced, 'The play's didactic purpose is almost as dark as the underground tunnels in which the miners work'. Even the left-leaning *Guardian* felt the play 'could not bridge the gap between docu-drama and socialist fairy-tale'. Few, if any, of the newspapers, had any praise for the actors involved.

It would have been nice for Fiennes if he could have gone out on a high – but 'by the end of the year you felt you had seen what he could do,' according to one highly-placed National source.

With the benefit of hindsight, Rudman says, 'I knew Ralph would go all the way. He had such intensity. He was very strong and had a backbone of steel.' Butler is more circumspect, saying, 'In 1987 there were eight actors in the company as skilful as Fiennes and the company was only one of seven in the building. He had the looks, the voice and the intelligence but so did others. And they didn't all have the same tendency to overdo the emotion; to pull the choke out too far. At times you knew Ralph was acting.'

However, those other eight did not have what one contemporary calls 'Ralph's capacity for success' – his knack for being in the right place at the right time, impressing the right people, and crucially, getting those all important breaks which could make or break a career.

CHAPTER NINE
Stratford

In 1988 Fiennes auditioned for the Royal Shakespeare Company, and was offered a job by artistic director Adrian Noble. During the four seasons he would spend with the RSC he would win his acting spurs and go on to be hailed as 'the new Gielgud', the greatest compliment a young actor could hope for.

Created in 1961 from the company playing at the Shakespeare Memorial Theatre, the RSC embarked on an ambitious programme under its first director, Peter Hall, which included the establishment of a permanent London base – in addition to its traditional Stratford-upon-Avon home. The RSC has since gone from strength to strength: its companies have toured the world; and in 1970, two years after Hall was succeeded by Trevor Nunn as Artistic Director, a Stratford company became the first British theatrical ensemble to visit Japan.

The first RSC play Ralph appeared in was Shakespeare's comedy, *Much Ado About Nothing*, first performed in 1598.

Rehearsals began at the RSC's new rehearsal rooms in Clapham, London, amid the usual clutter of costume designs, cups of cold coffee and scrawled notes. The two-hour, forty-five minute long play, which launched that year's RSC season at Stratford-upon-Avon, was first performed at the 500-seat Royal Shakespeare Theatre on 7 April 1988.

Like so many modern versions of the classics, this Di Trevis-directed production had been updated – but nobody seemed quite certain in which era it was supposed to take place. The *Stage* thought it was set in the 1930s, *Today* in the 1940s, the *Daily Mail* in the 1950s, and the *Bristol Evening Post* in the 1980s. That may have been intentional. As one critic observed, 'Nothing is what it seems. The costumes could come from World War One, the 1940s or a Bermuda beach. The music befits a monastery in one scene, a tea dance the next.'

The opening was arresting, with soldiers abseiling down ropes from an imaginary helicopter – not many of which were in existence in Shakespeare's day. Most critics admired the impressive stage set with its marble patio and tall, curtained archways which offered a smooth transition to the church scenes, the central arch becoming a brightly tessellated chancel banked with candles.

But this version of *Much Ado About Nothing* suffered when measured against memorable past productions starring Donald Sinden and Judi Dench, and Derek Jacobi and Sinead Cusack. The casting was problematic and the acting disturbingly one-dimensional while the production itself meandered aimlessly, showing little of Shakespeare's eye for humour or ear for romantic verse.

The *Daily Mail's* late Jack Tinker summed up most critics' reactions when he reflected, 'There are times when I seriously wonder whether the RSC actually likes Shakespeare and all his works? Instead of helping to marry the starkly contrasting elements of the play into a comprehensible whole, this treatment merely drives them further apart.'

But there was praise. The *Daily Express* thought it a 'very enjoyable *Much Ado* played for broad comedy' though it felt 'the lightly facetious tone proves less than equal to the melodrama.' And the *Stage*, the actors' newspaper, had nothing but praise for newcomer Fiennes. 'He gradually grows in presence as Claudio,' it said, 'suggesting a callow youth sobered by his experience at the end.'

A month later, Ralph stepped out in his second RSC production – a new version of Shakespeare's little-known *King John*, which had not been performed at Stratford for nearly a quarter of a century.

This underrated play tells how John finds his hold on the English throne threatened by a rival claimant, Arthur of Bretagne. To neutralize the threat, he arranges the marriage of a niece to the heir of the French throne, Lewis the Dauphin, (Fiennes). The Pope excommunicates John and authorizes a French attack on England. The attack fails but Arthur becomes John's prisoner – and, when he subsequently leaps to his death, the King inevitably falls under suspicion.

The first reading of the new production – directed by Deborah Warner, one of the most gifted if unorthodox directors of the day – took place at a London rehearsal room called the Soho Laundry. Ralph, who had just bought his first car, a Peugeot, was wearing a multi-coloured Fair Isle sweater. He seemed nervous but gained in confidence with the passing days.

'Deborah sat us around a table,' recalls one of the cast, Susan Engel, and said, "I don't want you to read your parts. I want you to read other parts". So we all ended up reading each other's parts. It was part of her attempt to break down the barriers between the actors. She got us doing all sorts of improvisational exercises – be it rolling on the floor or having a tug of war with someone – for the same reason.'

This new version of *King John*, starring Nicholas Woodeson in the title role, began as a comedy about the arrogance and greed of Britain and France before shifting gear to become an archetypal Shakespearian study in evil. It opened at The Other Place, in Stratford, in May 1988.

The simple set, consisting of naked light bulbs and a network of ladders, was generally admired. But the cast's modern outfits were attacked for 'looking as if they had come from a jumble sale at an Army & Navy store'. The King himself was accused of 'looking like a visiting fireman or Dudley Moore unwontedly cast in an historical epic'.

By and large, the reviews were favourable – partly, one suspects, because there had been so few performances of *King John* in living memory by which to attempt to measure this latest production.

'It is a revelation to hear this play at close quarters,' said the *Financial Times*. Michael Billington, writing in the *Guardian*, confessed to being 'excited by the acting'. While the *Independent*, grudging in its praise at the best of times, called it 'a fascinating but flawed' production, adding: 'If one admits to being disappointed ...

it is only because one has come to expect nothing but excellence from Ms Warner'.

As before, however, Ralph's performance was virtually ignored by the critics. The fact is that neither role was likely to win wildly favourable press notices, as Susan Engel points out: 'Actors have never been able to shine in such unshowy parts. But if an actor has any sense he'll play the parts as Shakespeare intended and just bide his time.'

That was exactly what Ralph did. Besides, his moment was soon to come – in the RSC's most ambitious production of the 1988 season.

On arriving in Stratford, Ralph rented a pretty 150-year-old cottage with a small kitchen, a bathroom, lounge and two bedrooms, costing £70 a week, in the picturesque village of Ilmington, about eight miles from Stratford, on the edge of the Cotswolds.

'A lot of actors have stayed there over the years, including Helen Mirren, Jeremy Irons and his wife Sinead Cusack,' says owner Shirley Dingley, who lives in the adjoining house. 'The RSC would never tell us the name of the actor they were sending to have a look at the house. They would just tell you the part they were playing.'

The first time Fiennes turned up to look at the house, she says, 'he seemed quite shy and introverted and looked at the ground a lot when he talked'.

Ralph stayed at the cottage for the best part of a year and Shirley and her husband, Michael, got to know him and Alex, a frequent visitor, reasonably well. 'He was a quiet, homely chap,' she says. 'We talked about his cousin, Sir Ranulph, about Ireland, where we had also lived, and about whatever production he was appearing in at the time.

'He never struck me as a political sort of person but he was very supportive of the theatre's anti-apartheid stand refusing to invite the South African ambassador to the RSC's traditional Shakespearian birthday celebrations.'

If there is any one play that made Fienne's name as a great Shakespearian actor, it was his towering performance as Henry VI in

The Plantagenets – the nine-hour epic Adrian Noble adapted from Shakespeare's *Henry VI Parts I, II* and *III* and *Richard III*.

The idea to turn the four plays into a powerful new work came to Noble after he was invited by Terry Hands, the Artistic Director of the RSC, to take responsibility for the Stratford end of the company, with artistic control of all three auditoria: the main house, the Swan and The Other Place.

He had staged a highly praised production of Webster's *The Duchess of Malfi*, starring Helen Mirren, earlier in his career and, after joining the RSC as a director in 1980 had received acclaim for his strikingly imaginative productions of *King Lear* with Michael Gambon and Anthony Sher, and *Henry V* with Kenneth Branagh.

He says, 'The *Henry VI* plays seemed most appropriate for the 1988 Stratford season, with their vast gallery of characters, their high-octane theatricality and their simple but exhilarating metrical pulse – all ideal training for a new company.'

'The more I read them the more convinced I became our cycle should indeed take us through the pageant, through the heroics, through the whole convulsive world of Henry VI into the more closeted, dangerous, claustrophobic world of Richard III.'

Auditions for Henry VI – 'an almost uncastable role,' says Noble disingenuously – took place in the basement of London's Barbican Theatre. Dozens of young actors wanted the part but one, in particular, stood out. 'This man came along and he was quite electrifying,' says Noble. 'Henry VI is quite unworldly – a very fine creature in a hideous world – and Ralph inhabited that perfectly.' In the words of one admirer present at the audition, 'he possessed a natural aristocracy and nobility.'

The four original plays were reworked into a trilogy of three-hour segments: *Henry VI*, *The Rise of Edward VI*, and *Richard III, His Death*. Rehearsals – which turned out to be 'a genuine workshop', says Ralph – began in May 1988 in Stratford with a company of forty-two actors playing dozens of characters. Decisions were fought over but actors learned to balance the need to develop their own character with the needs of the company.

Ambition, destructive to both family loyalties and society, was the central theme of this sweeping saga of betrayal, violence and death – involving a bewildering web of tortuously entangled alliances – and spanning the period from the funeral of Henry V to the accession four reigns later of Henry Richmond, founder of the Tudor dynasty.

'The houses of Carrington and Ewing could take a few lessons from York and Lancaster's dynastic bully boys,' joked one pundit – but it was true. However, as the first night approached, there were those who wondered if the RSC had bitten off more than it could chew. Could modern audiences be expected to sit through a nine-hour play when they had trouble sitting through a 90-minute film?

Such fears proved groundless. Infallibly audible Ralph brought his trade marks of dignity and intelligence to the role. He proved himself worthy of the tag 'the new Gielgud' in Henry's great set speeches, including in the first segment, where having been 'chid from battle', he wonders if he would be happier if he were a simple peasant:

> *O God! methinks it were a happy life*
> *To be no better than a homely swain:*
> *To sit upon a hill, as I do now,*
> *to carve out dials quaintly, point by point,*
> *Thereby to see the minutes how they run –*
> *How many makes the hour full complete,*
> *How many hours bring about the day,*
> *How many days will finish up the year,*
> *How many years a mortal man my life.*
> *When this is known, then to divide the names –*
> *So many hours must I tend my flock:*
> *So many hours must I take my rest:*
> *So many hours must I contemplate;*
> *So many hours must I sport myself;*
> *So many days my ewes have been with young;*
> *So many weeks ere the poor fools will ean;*
> *So many years ere I shall shear the fleece;*
> *So minutes, hours, days, weeks, months and years,*
> *Pass'd over to the end they were created,*
> *Would bring white hairs unto a quiet grave.*

Ah, what a life were this! how sweet! how lovely!
Gives not the hawthorn bush a sweeter shade
To shepherds looking on their silly sheep,
Than doth a rich embroider'd canopy
To kings that fear their subjects' treachery?
O yes, it doth; a thousandfold it doth.

In the second segment, moments before being stabbed to death in the Tower by the treacherous Richard, Duke of Gloucester, he predicts the world:

Shall rue the hour that ever thou wast born.
The owl shriek'd at thy birth – an evil sign;
The night crow cried, aboding luckless time;
Dogs howl'd and hideous tempests shook down trees;
The raven rook'd her on the chimney's top,
And chattering pies in dismal discords sung;
Thy mother felt more than mother's pain,
And yet brought forth less than a mother's hope,
To wit, an indigest deformed lump,
Not like the fruit of such a goodly tree.
Teeth hadst thou in thy head when thou wast born,
To signify thou cam'st to bite the world ...

In the final segment, he makes a brief ghostly appearance the night before the Battle of Bosworth, tormenting King Richard III (formerly the Duke of Gloucester):

When I was mortal, my anointed body
By thee was punched full of deadly holes.
Think on the Tower and me; despair and die;
Harry the Sixth bids thee despair and die!

Bouquets showered down and the audience responded with a standing ovation at the end of the first night at Stratford's Royal Shakespeare Theatre in October 1988.

It was a triumph for all the cast. But a particular triumph for Fiennes's reinterpretation of Henry VI – a Henry whose fatal flaw as a ruler was not weakness, but goodness; a Henry more suited to the discussion of aesthetics than the exercise of power; a Henry hopelessly at sea in personal relationships, a man of peace overwhelmed by civil war. Subtle reinterpretation of this sort, which invariably saw him find the humanity until then absent in a character, would soon become a trademark of Ralph the actor.

The press was near-unanimous in its praise – both of the production and of the actor, whose white-robed, saintly portrayal of Henry had helped make *The Plantagenets* such a tour de force.

The *Guardian* hailed it as 'a triumphant production' asserting 'it was too short rather than too long', going on to praise Ralph's 'stained-glass profile and melodic voice'. While the *Financial Times* said, 'Ralph Fiennes is an outstanding Henry VI, less the saintly hermit of David Warner, more the wryly painted victim of circumstance.'

The *Daily Mail* went into rhapsodies: 'The heady scent of success and achievement – an all-too-rare aroma here in recent seasons – hangs once more around the RSC's Stratford stronghold. Ralph Fiennes's portrait of Henry VI as a raw, yet thoughtful and pious youth maturing into a remote but saintly martyr is one of the production's main glories.'

The magazine *Punch* lavished further praise, saying, 'It's good to find the RSC back on form', and categorizing Fiennes as an 'unusually powerful Henry VI'. The *Listener* called it 'a superb trilogy', and praised Ralph as 'well spoken and surprisingly gritty'. The *Jewish Chronicle* found the play 'an exhilarating journey through a key period of English history', adding, 'The triumph rests on performances of great strength and skill, notably from Ralph Fiennes.'

But the pleasure wasn't all the audience's. One of the highlights of being involved in *The Plantagenets* for Noble was getting the chance to work with an actor of Ralph's calibre.

'He's very unusual because he has a true vocation as an actor,' says Noble. 'He thinks there is more to acting than entertaining or telling a story. He is very aware that there is something privileged and responsible about an actor's job. He is a proper actor.'

*

The following year, 1989, Fiennes returned to Henry VI when *The Plantagenets* transferred to the RSC's London base, The Barbican. He also starred in two new RSC productions. They would be the first non-Shakespearian plays he had appeared in since his days at Oldham's Coliseum three years earlier.

The first play was *The Man Who Came To Dinner*, written by Moss Hart and George S. Kaufman, which ran for over two years when first staged in New York in 1939, fifty years earlier.

It tells what happens when the monstrous, egomaniacal critic Sheridan Whiteside (based on New York columnist Alexander Woolcott) breaks his hip during a lecture tour and is forced to spend several weeks around Christmas as the reluctant guest of even more dismayed hosts in a small Midwest town.

Within hours he wrecks the festivities with his unspeakable rudeness – he is inclined to pleasantries such as 'Hello, repulsive'. Before long, the family find themselves exiled from their living quarters and threatened with legal action. Meanwhile, his long-suffering secretary falls in love with a local newspaperman (Fiennes) and threatens to leave. True to form, though, the obnoxious Whiteside (played by John Wood) goes to absurd lengths to sabotage the romance.

Among those appearing alongside Ralph in the new production, which was directed by Broadway veteran Gene Saks, was Estelle Kohler – who has particularly fond memories of working with the actor. 'The two of us have always corpsed a lot on stage during rehearsals,' she says.

'One night we did just that during a performance when the bag next to John's wheelchair – where he kept his pipe – flamed up. Ralph grabbed a glass from the drinks tray and tipped out the coloured water. We did our best to cover up what had happened but when I reached for a drink the glass wouldn't move because all but the one Ralph had grabbed were glued down. We got an uncontrollable fit of the giggles. Thankfully we were appearing in a comedy so we got away with it. Offstage, Ralph was quite quiet but you often find that with exceptional actors everything happens on stage.' Again and again the observer of Ralph's career finds that his intensity, perception and presence are only really allowed to explode on stage.

The three-hour play opened at the Barbican in July 1989, but despite the good atmosphere among the cast and crew, it was, according to *The Times*, a dull evening for the audience. After his personal triumph as Henry VI, it was a shock to Fiennes to find himself in the critics' firing line, too.

'The pace seems laboured,' said the *Financial Times*, before turning its beady eye on Ralph. 'More Englishness from Mr Fiennes whose well-bred and melodious tenor bespeaks more English classical training than is good for a small town American newspaper man.'

The *Independent* took this one stage further saying that Ralph was 'hopelessly miscast' and that the play never stopped 'being a mechanically-antiquated, 1950s style Chevvy'. The *Daily Telegraph* echoed this view, saying: 'Ralph Fiennes, who plays the object of the secretary's affections, occasionally sounds as though he would prefer to be speaking the lines of Shakespeare.' His clear, melodious voice, with its reassuring timbre, refined diction and echoes of Gielgud in his prime – which had been so important in helping him become the leading romantic Shakespearian actor of the 1990s – clearly had its drawbacks.

'We were all desperately enthusiastic about the play and the audiences seemed to like it but it just didn't take off,' says Kohler philosophically. 'That's the way it goes sometimes.'

It looked as if Ralph Fiennes was in danger of becoming stuck in a Jacobean rut. His next play gave him the chance to climb out with Stephen Poliakoff's *Playing With Trains* – at the Barbican's smaller auditorium, The Pit. Dubbed 'the first Thatcherite play to be staged by the RSC', it told the story of a Clive Sinclair-like inventor-entrepreneur – Bill Galpin – whose success arouses the envy of an establishment which turns on him, sewing resentment in his soul and souring his relationship with his children.

Ralph's enthusiasm was still apparent years later. 'I loved acting in *Playing With Trains*,' he said, 'which was my first really new play.' Ralph's character, Gant, was a patent department employee who gave new meaning to the phrase 'unhelpful civil servant', and Ralph was flattered that civil servants who saw the play subsequently adopted some of his character's catch-phrases.

Despite the opportunity it presented to Fiennes, the play drew a mixed critical response. The *Financial Times* called it an 'efficient production', the *Listener* labelled it 'a worthy venture', and *City Limits* dubbed it 'a little gem'. But the *Daily Telegraph* felt that Poliakoff had been 'carried away by the unrestrained exuberance of his own inventiveness'. While *Punch* asked, 'Is it irony or poetic justice that Stephen Poliakoff's play about inventors is one of the least inventive plays of the year?'

By now, Ralph's parents were living in a smart, detached Victorian house in Therapia Road, on the right side of Peckham Rye Common in south-east London. He remained close to his family – in particular his mother – and would help to find his brother Joseph an evening job as a dresser at the National Theatre.

Even though, he kept his family at arm's length. A friend says: 'He loved them dearly and was undoubtedly proud to be a Fiennes. But he also relished his privacy and needed his own space more than his siblings. There was undoubtedly something different about him, and his family accepted this. They didn't try to change him but they knew he couldn't anyway. He was his own man.'

With growing fame, he grew more distant from his old Bishop Wordsworth friends. But he had never made any special contract to keep in touch with them anyway. He was moving in one direction, his old friends in another. 'As far as he was concerned, it was all in the past,' suggests one former classmate.

Having said that, Ralph was happy to return to Bishop Wordsworth's for a verse-reading evening – titled '*Is it Not Monstrous ...? (Hamlet, Act 2, Scene 3): An evening with Ralph Fiennes* – which saw him incorporate extracts from *Troilus and Cressida*, among other Shakespearian texts, before an invited audience of pupils, staff and parents. He would also happily invite old friends backstage if they had taken the trouble to see him perform – although sometimes these reunions could be 'laboured', according to one old schoolpal.

He and Alex appeared to be happy together – although one or two particularly perceptive friends feared that their differing fortunes were beginning to alter the balance of the relationship with potentially serious long-term implications.

But Ralph was happiest of all when acting, talking acting or socializing with actors. He became friendly with a number of his co-stars at the RSC, though relatively few – such as Simon Russell Beale who appeared alongside him in *Playing With Trains* – would become close friends. Increasingly, outside of his own family it was only in the company of those he knew well, invariably fellow actors, that he appeared to be able fully to relax.

At the start of his third year at the Royal Shakespeare Company, Ralph was the subject of his first media profile in an April 1990 story – headlined the 'Young Turks of the British Theatre' – appearing in *Time Out*, the London listings magazine.

'The actor's intimidating shyness and intensity of manner belie his growing status as a classical warrior,' stated the article, referring to his unforgettable performance in the title role of Henry VI in Adrian Noble's production of *The Plantagenets*. 'A performance that convinced the critics that here was a voice and presence for the great Shakespearian roles.'

By then Fiennes, deep into rehearsals for *Troilus and Cressida*, in which he played the male lead, was patently uncomfortable with being branded a young turk.

'You can't deny ambitious thoughts, or hunger, it's part of the motive of why one acts,' admitted Ralph, who from his RADA days had shown extraordinary pleasure and professionalism at working as an ensemble. 'But I can't see individual parts any more because everything is so integral to and dependent upon a whole group. Of course, it's exciting to play those big parts, but it's more exciting seeing eight or nine rich characters interacting.

'There's not much on nowadays which revolves around one role or one actor doing a star performance. It would be very worrying if companies put on plays simply because you have that actor.'

Noble ideals, for sure, but wouldn't plays such as *Hamlet* and *Ivanov* be staged in a few years time for no reason other than that the actor who wanted to play the parts, Ralph, was a star who could infallibly attract audiences?

The actor embarked on his usual painstaking preparatory research during the spring's rehearsals for *Troilus and Cressida*.

The play was first performed more than 300 years earlier not at London's Globe, but at the Inns of the Court, so it was somewhat fitting that the new production, directed by 24-year-old wunderkind Sam Mendes, who would go on to direct acclaimed productions of *Glengarry Glen Ross*, *The Birthday Party*, and the Palladium's hugely successful revival of Lionel Bart's *Oliver!*

Opening at Stratford's intimate Swan Theatre in April 1990, *Troilus and Cressida* tells the story of Troilus, son of Priam, the Trojan king. A young, naïve romantic, he is infatuated with Cressida, idealizing both her and the idea of love itself. And his feelings for her mean more to him than his battlefield duties. So when Cressida (played by Amanda Root) proves untrue, his disillusionment and hatred of her new suitor, Diomedes, drive him to reckless acts of valour.

'It sounds so stupid and glib to say it, but it is so modern, and awfully everyday,' said Fiennes, who played the part as a well-bred, mellifluous romantic. 'Just look at the stilted, rushed awkwardness about him when he leaves her after they've spent the night together and lost their virginity, and the way she asks, "Why are you going? Don't you like me anymore?" The embarrassment! It amazes me.

'One has so many preconceptions about the scenes one plays, but often a comic scene has romance in it, and a so-called romantic scene has a sinisterness and earthiness about it you hadn't anticipated at all. It's a constant process of learning – and of having to unlearn the lessons you think central to your acting and the role you are playing.'

The new production was certainly eye-catching. The props mixed ancient and modern – the soldiers wearing khaki tunics, medieval breast plates and Grecian helmets. For all the audience knew, they could have been fighting at the Somme, Agincourt or Marathon. Performed with a rare intensity, the play left one disillusioned about almost everything, as intended.

The *Financial Times* hailed it as 'a riveting new production, tipping the RSC's already goodish Stratford season into greatness.' It added: 'If Kenneth Branagh's chunky humanity marks him out as Ralph Richardson's heir, Fiennes is in the Gielgud succession, down to the quivering vocal throb.' Although the *Daily Express* claimed that pairing lofty Ralph Fiennes with petite Amanda Root made their *Troilus and Cressida* 'look like Little and Large'.

But most papers felt another actor stole the play. 'The chief glory of the evening is Simon Russell Beale's hilariously repulsive performance as Thersites, the vile chorus figure,' said the *Daily Telegraph*. 'Hunchbacked, rheumy-eyed and limping, he savours every syllable of his character's scabrous sneers and jibes.'

Happy though he was for his friend, Fiennes must have been disappointed that so few critics singled him out for praise after all the work he'd put into the part. If he felt a little crestfallen he kept his own counsel.

Like many actors, though, Ralph had always paid as much attention to the crowd's, as to the critics' reaction to a play. 'If the audience responded enthusiastically enough we knew we'd got it right,' says one member of the cast. 'And the applause was rapturous every night. That was good enough for Ralph and the rest of us.'

One afternoon the cast received as rapturous a reception from a matinée as an evening audience – a rare event in the theatre world. Part of the reason was that Ralph's younger brother, Joseph, was among the crowd. 'I was overwhelmed by the play and Ralph's central performance,' he says. 'It was so good I went back again in the evening.' What greater praise could there be?

One of the few people at the RSC who got to know the real Ralph – the man behind the actor's mask – was his dresser, John McCloud, a colourful, outspoken Geordie known throughout the company as 'Black Mac'.

'I dressed Ralph and the rest of the actors by the book, just like I dressed officers in the army,' says the ex-soldier who spent thirty years at Stratford but is now retired and not in the best of health. 'When he first arrived, he looked like he was just out of shorts. But he wasn't a bad lad – clean, neat and tidy.

'He reminded me of the great RSC actors of the past because, as far as he was concerned, acting was acting. He could soon do it standing on his cock. Some actors get into such a state before a performance but Ralph was always so professional. He was up there every night but never let the pressure get to him. He was a cool customer.'

Star turn or not, it didn't pay to get on the wrong side of Black

Mac, as Fiennes soon discovered. 'If an actor wasn't in the dressing room when they should be, I'd go and find 'em and give 'em a bollocking,' he says. 'I didn't stand for any nonsense. Mind you, Ralph was pretty punctual.'

'I used to have a bath ready for Ralph in the interval,' he says. 'Sometimes he'd say he didn't have time, so I'd tell him: "Listen, you're going to get your tackle and arse washed, boy!"'

And, old soldier that he was, Black Mac allowed no one – but *no one* into the dressing room – unless it was on the strict orders of young Mr Fiennes. Smitten female fans who sneaked backstage to see their idol were given short shrift. 'They didn't get near him,' says Black Mac proudly. 'Not with me around.'

Nor did Ralph's girlfriend fare much better. 'Once Alex asked if she could use his bath,' he says. "No you bloody can't – unless Ralph says so," I told her, shutting the door.'

The loyal Geordie dresser also got to see more of Ralph than just about anyone but his girlfriend – and takes responsibility for landing him with a nickname he'd presumably rather forget. 'He was always going around starkers, flashing his tackle – you know, in the nude – so I called him "Flasher",' says Black Mac. 'The name stuck.'

In his next play, *King Lear*, Ralph played Edmund, the bastard son of Gloucester, who is determined not to let his illegitimacy or his elder brother, Edgar, come between him and his father's fortune; he is a cruel, manipulative and ruthless individual who tricks his father into believing that his legitimate heir, Edgar, has been false to him and, furthermore, has his father's eyes put out.

It was a transparently obvious case of playing against type, but Ralph wanted to prove his versatility as an actor and show that he was just as able to play a Shakespeare villain as one of the Bard's heroes.

'You have to remind people that you're capable of other things,' he said. 'People are surprised when I tell them that I'm playing Edmund. A quizzical look appears on their face. "Why you?" I can hear them wondering. "Most Edmunds are quite coarse, or have a weight about them." I don't have those qualities really so I'll have to play them differently.' Yet a few years later he would cultivate both coarseness and weight for the finest performance of his career to date.

If anything, Ralph enjoyed the part even more than some of his other RSC roles, according to Adrian Noble who theorizes, 'Like many men who are good-looking, Ralph is usually happiest in disguise. Danny Day-Lewis is the same. He created a village idiot-type character and was absolutely mesmeric. But in another production, he played a good-looking young man and was absolutely dreadful. Ralph is much the same. He has these beautiful looks and a beautiful voice, but I think he is actually dying to play a character.'

Unfortunately, this new version of *King Lear* – Shakespeare's epic story of an ageing ruler's descent into madness following his cataclysmic decision to divide his kingdom between his three daughters – was not to be in the *Plantagenets* league. Nor was Ralph's performance.

Directed by Nicholas Hytner – who went on to direct big screen versions of *The Madness of King George* and *The Crucible* – this four-hour production, starring John Wood in the title role, opened at the Royal Shakespeare Theatre in Stratford-upon-Avon in July 1990. Interestingly, Ralph's long-time beau, Alex Kingston, played Lear's daughter, Cordelia. It was idiosyncratic and intelligent but also challenging – perhaps too challenging.

The bizarre, David Fielding-designed set, dominated by a large, swivelling cube, open on two sides, was criticized for everything from its 'symmetrical sterile design' to its 'diminishing the impact of the storm or any sense of the heath's hostile openness'.

The press was also quick to find fault with the players. The *Independent* criticized Wood for his 'mannered performance' and accused Fiennes of making Edmund 'sexless and unmachiavellian'. The *Daily Telegraph* called Wood's Lear 'a serious disappointment'. While the *Sunday Correspondent* thought the production 'vile jelly indeed' and felt that Fiennes 'lacked the devilish charisma of Edmund'.

Some newspapers did give it the thumbs up. The *Daily Mail* said, 'Such is the force of Mr Hytner's grasp on the play and its pace, it seems not a second of our time is squandered.' The *Observer* called it 'magnificent' and was impressed by Ralph's 'nasty Edmund who thrives on chaos'.

While the *Financial Times* thought Ralph's Edmund 'a very cold fish', but echoing Noble, predicted, 'One day this gifted young actor may be happier with the confiding leer and the humped back than the lyrical throb that currently falls to his lot.'

Whatever the critics thought, television director Peter Markham, who happened to be in the audience one night, was bowled over by the actor. 'I was astonished at his qualities,' he says. 'He had a very powerful and ambiguous presence – and it was that ambiguity between gentleness and pathology that I found fascinating. All eyes were on him when he was on the stage and other actors had to fall over themselves to get my attention.'

Later that year, Ralph appeared as Berowne in *Love's Labour's Lost*, a part he had played nearly a decade earlier at Bishop Wordsworth's School. This time, however, his performance would be slightly more polished.

The 'mirth-loving' Berowne is the sharpest and wittiest amongst the young men at the court of Navarre who agree to forgo women for academic study. And he takes great delight in mocking his peers when, one by one, they read out love poems dedicated to the objects of their desire. Of course, Berowne, too, falls in love – with Rosaline, the Princess of France's right-hand maid – and, to win her hand, must lay aside his 'taffeta phrases'.

While working with Ralph, the play's director, Terry Hands, observed, 'He carries a mystery with him. There is an enigma and it's very compelling. I remember rounds of applause at the end of his speeches. We were all very embarrassed by it, but it was the audience responding to the performer doing something superlatively well – they wanted to thank him for it. I have not heard that kind of reaction for decades.'

The upbeat production, which benefited from the autumnal splendour of Timothy O'Brien's sumptuous set, opened at Stratford's Royal Shakespeare Theatre in September 1990. It also starred Simon Russell Beale as the King of Navarre, Amanda Root as Rosaline and Alex Kingston as the country wench, Jaquenetta.

As one critic acknowledged, 'staging a play which Coleridge found of "little interest", Dr Johnson thought "childish and vulgar" and Charles Gildon called "one of Shakespeare's worst", can be a stiff task.' But the good reviews outnumbered the bad – and there was particular praise for Fiennes.

The *Daily Express* thought it 'a handsome production' and felt Fiennes and Root exhibited 'that vital spark as Berowne and Rosaline' – and there was particular praise for Fiennes. 'The languidly attractive Fiennes plays Berowne as an unconfirmed bachelor whose favoured position is obviously horizontal.' *Time Out* thought it an 'exuberant, many-layered comic feast', adding, 'The central performances of Beale and Fiennes are well-matched'.

The *Observer* said 'it could not be more beautiful' and continued, 'Ralph Fiennes's Berowne discharges his great speeches with admirable architectural control and once he deletes the dangerous Ian Richardson quiver from his voice and dispels his flopping quiff from his right eye, his will be the best Berowne imaginable.'

Three other newspapers gave the play largely favourable reviews but raved – there's no other word for it – about Ralph's performance.

The *Daily Telegraph* thought his ecstatic rendering of the great soliloquy at the close of Act 1 ('And I forsooth in love!') had 'all the bravura of a rousing operatic cabaletta', adding, 'Fiennes is a romantic Shakespeare actor of real stature for the 1990s.' The *Guardian* praised his 'Byronic Berowne' and the *Sunday Telegraph* said, 'When he gets to his feet and delivers his first great speech ("Why, all delights are vain ...") the production soars away.'

As usual, though, not everyone approved. The *Financial Times* claimed that Fiennes as Berowne 'contorts and belabours the verse, pausing oddly and not trusting the lines'. The *Independent on Sunday* labelled it 'a virtually throwaway production' that insulted one's intelligence while its sister paper, the *Independent*, thought Fiennes 'appropriately word drunk', but felt he wasn't 'in any way intoxicating'. But curiously, it had nothing but praise for his real-life other half. 'Behaving as though she has been hypnotized and ordered to strip any man in her path, Alex Kingston gives a delightful display of happy sexual instinct.'

While there were shades of Moll Flanders in her performance, one member of the cast reveals, 'It was tough on Alex seeing Ralph's character becoming so intimately acquainted with Amanda's Rosaline. Some of us wondered whether her suggestive performance was partly designed to remind Ralph that she was one very sexy lady.' It was an early indication of how the pressures of fame would affect Alex.

In the space of four seasons, Fiennes had gone from good, solid supporting roles to playing the leads in a trio of big plays – *The Plantagenets*, *Troilus and Cressida* and *Love's Labour's Lost* – impressing his peers, the public and the press.

'You could hardly hear Fiennes without connecting him with Gielgud,' reflected the *Financial Times* now in a more generous frame of mind. 'The surpassingly refined diction, the scholarly wit, the flair for romantic neurosis and the courtly smoothness – making music out of verse.'

Yet in 1991, the RSC in its wisdom let Fiennes go midway through its summer season because it had nothing 'suitable' to offer him. The decision angered many of Ralph's friends, including Estelle Kohler. 'It was extraordinary,' she says. 'I thought the way he was treated was appalling.' But if Ralph felt any anger, he typically didn't air it in public.

Among those who would be sorry to see him go was Simon Russell Beale, who says: 'He was a quiet man but had a delicacy and humour if you sought it out. He had a real artistic probity and a nice sense of self-irony. He was also an exceptional actor.' Sally Dexter, who appeared with Ralph in *King Lear*, would also miss him. 'I always found him very sweet and supportive,' she says.

However, Fiennes seemed anything but confident about his future prospects when, following his departure from the RSC, Robert Butler bumped into him at a café in Chelsea.

'After a couple of minutes' gossip there was the crunch question,' recalls Butler. 'What was he doing next? He didn't know. Come on, I joked. He must be doing something? "No," he said – he wasn't. His eyes darted uncomfortably. It was that familiar uncertainty. The look of anyone whose tax return is Schedule D. "Don't worry," I said, "something will turn up." He shrugged and ummed and erred. He didn't know about that. There was a moment of embarrassment. "'Course it will," I said. "You'll be all right."

'Walking down the King's Road, I thought, maybe he won't. Maybe he's just another good-looking actor with a nice voice. But too English, too pale, too posh. Maybe he'll be waiting at tables, seeing mates in other shows and writing "remember me?" letters to the Oldham and Clwyd.'

CHAPTER TEN

The Coming Man

It was asking a lot of a young actor, however talented, to reprise two roles immortalized by screen legends. But that was the fate – 'oh, what a fate,' you can hear a thousand actors cry – to befall Fiennes. For in 1992 he got to play not only Lawrence of Arabia – the part which shot Peter O'Toole to stardom thirty years earlier – but Heathcliff, so memorably played by Laurence Olivier more than fifty years earlier.

Ralph's screen career actually began with a sixty-second spot in a new television sensation called *Prime Suspect*. He played the bereaved boyfriend of a murdered girl in the first instalment of the acclaimed police drama series starring Helen Mirren. He got the part after television director Christopher Menaul saw Ralph in an RSC production. 'I threw him into a cell with Helen and he acquitted himself very well,' says Menaul.

But it was the two great romantic lead roles – one in a sequel to *Lawrence of Arabia*, the other in a new version of *Wuthering Heights* – that set him on the road to screen stardom.

Just how did he capture two such plum parts with his slender experience of on-screen acting? 'It was just a peculiar coincidence that these two roles came up at the same time,' was the typically self-effacing answer Fiennes gave at the time. 'Both roles were a gift,' he concluded.

In fact, Fiennes was already being tipped as the next big thing by – amongst others – David Puttnam, the man responsible for British

The magnificent sixteenth century Suffolk farmhouse where Ralph spent his early years. ©York Membery

The remote Irish bungalow - built by Ralph's father - where the Fiennes family briefly lived. © York Membery

In his blazer and tie, the young Ralph may not have looked like a future heartthrob - but even then he was proving popular with the girls.

The floppy-fringed actor during rehearsals for the National's 1987 production of *Fathers and Sons*. © Michael Mayhew

Making his Royal Shakespeare Company debut in *Much Ado About Nothing*. RST, Stratford-upon-Avon, 1988. © Joe Cocks Studio Collection / Shakespeare Centre library

A boyish-looking Ralph
appearing in Shakespeare's little-
performed play, *King John*, The
Other Place, 1988.
© Joe Cocks Studio Collection/
Shakespeare Centre Library

Ralph's towering performance as
Henry VI in 1988's acclaimed
production of *The Plantagenets*,
playing opposite Penny Downie,
made his name as a Shakespearean
actor.
© Richard Mildenhall

Bowing out of the RSC in style with his 'Byronic Berowne' in *Love's Labour's Lost*, Stratford-upon-Avon, 1990.
© Joe Cocks Studio Collection/Shakespeare Centre Library

Escaping the Jacobean rut: a new look for an up and coming star, 1991.
© Richard Mildenhall

Following in Laurence Olivier's footsteps in a disappointing re-make of *Wuthering Heights*, 1992. © Kobal

Evil incarnate: Ralph's chilling portrayal of a Nazi in *Schindler's List* shot him to stardom. © Kobal

screen triumphs like *Chariots of Fire* and *Memphis Belle* and the nearest thing Britain has had in recent years to its own Hollywood movie mogul.

'In the past ten years I have let Warners know about four people,' said Puttnam, in 1992, who occasionally tipped off studio bosses about emerging British acting talent. 'They were Jeremy Irons, Daniel Day-Lewis, Kenneth Branagh – and Ralph Fiennes. I felt an equal confidence every time that each would emerge as a major figure. I have no doubt that Ralph is the coming man.'

Until then, Ralph's reputation rested on the impressive body of work he had fashioned whilst at the Royal Shakespeare Company. But the irony is that he would not have even auditioned for the parts of Lawrence and Heathcliff had the RSC not 'let him go' – that all too common euphemism for showing an employee the door. As Estelle Kohler says, 'It's a perfect example of how good timing can make or break a career.'

Nevertheless, wasn't it tempting providence to try to follow in the footsteps of not just one, but two screen icons when he'd yet to prove himself outside the theatre?

'I was never exactly conscious of having to live up to two great men I could not hope to better,' says Fiennes. 'I suppose it was a hell of a responsibility in a way, and some might say arrogant of me to presume I might match two such formidable talents as Olivier and O'Toole. But the thing is, I never felt threatened by them.

'The greater challenge was the fact that the characters themselves – one real, the other fictional – were so huge. I simply felt that I had to rise to the occasion. That there was no choice but to raise my game.'

There can be few more fascinating figures in twentieth century British history than the soldier, scholar, and *Boy's Own*, and indeed Ralph's own, hero T.E. Lawrence.

Having learnt to live like an Arab during an archaeological expedition to the Middle East, he was recruited by British military intelligence following the outbreak of the First World War. His assignment was to help foment Arab revolt against the Ottoman Empire (which was allied to Germany and the Austro-Hungarian Empire).

Cloaked in flowing white robes and Bedouin head-dress, he

helped the Arab leader Prince Feisal secure a strategically-important port and then himself led the Arabs in a brutal guerrilla war. This struggle was as much about establishing Arab sovereignty as about defeating the Turks, and culminated in the capture of Damascus. Indeed, he established the principles of special warfare later developed so successfully by the SAS.

The erudite, Oxford-educated officer's thrilling exploits were glorified – first by the American journalist Jackson Bentley, and then in the sprawling, sun-drenched, David Lean-directed 1962 film, starring O'Toole, Alec Guinness, Jack Hawkins and Omar Sharif, which won a well-earned string of Academy Awards.

David Puttnam's Enigma Films had been struggling for the best part of a decade to find a new and revitalized angle on Lawrence. The core of the new story, written by Tim Rose Price, became Lawrence's relationship with Feisal, the thirty-three year-old Hashemite heir (presumptive) without a throne. It was set against the backdrop of the 1919 Paris Peace Conference.

In 1991, the £2 million television movie co-produced with Anglia Films – *A Dangerous Man: Lawrence After Arabia* – finally got the green light. 'We never considered anybody else but Ralph for the central role,' reveals Menaul, who directed the drama which also starred Siddig El Fadil as Feisal, Denis Quilley as Lord Curzon and Paul Freeman as a slippery French diplomat.

Most of the filming took place at a studio in London's East End, with a Royal Artillery indoor riding school in St John's Wood doubling up for a Paris stables. And a quarry near Sevenoaks, Kent, was turned into the Arabian desert with the help of a few sand dunes and camels. Lean's film, by contrast, had deployed hundreds of extras in a real-life desert setting prompting the *Daily Mirror* to run a story headlined 'Lawrence of Sevenoaks!'

With the neatly pressed khakis he wore for the part, Ralph looked every inch the military man – although in reality he was no more physically similar to the real Lawrence than Peter O'Toole – being at 5ft 11 ins, considerably taller for a start.

However, the depth of Fiennes' research would make up for any disparity in the two men's looks. He admits he had 'always had an interest in Lawrence', albeit 'in a schoolboy way', but he went on to visit the legend's Dorset home and even took lessons in Arabic and

French, for giving Lawrentian-style speeches. Furthermore, he galloped through every biography and known volume of recollections, even forcing his way through Lawrence's monumental *Seven Pillars Of Wisdom*.

'I'd only dipped into it before but I read the whole thing,' he said. 'It was pretty hard going in places. But if you make yourself concentrate, and really pay attention, you'll be moved to tears at the end. I feel a great affinity with Lawrence somehow. And yes, I like him enormously. I think lots of men feel it. He's a particular icon for many of us. There have been plenty of people all too ready to denounce him but they are probably jealous of his genius.

'A friend lent me a copy of a biography which slagged off Lawrence mercilessly. I couldn't read it. I was greatly comforted by another volume, *T.E. Lawrence By His Friends*, which has contributions from Churchill, Bernard Shaw and English officers he'd served with during the war. They all speak of his immense energy; of his being a "huge human being" – even though he was less than 5ft 6ins tall – who would walk into a room and light it up with his presence – or, conversely, enter a room and sit quietly in the corner with no one knowing he was there.'

The drama opened with Fiennes looking directly at the camera, saying:

> *All men dream but not equally*
> *Those who dream by night in the dusty recesses of their mind*
> *Wake in the day to find that it was vanity*
> *But the dreamers of the day are dangerous men*
> *For they may act their dream with open eyes to make it possible.*
> *This ... I did.*

This was just one of a number of Shakespearian-type speeches in the drama, for which Ralph's classical training had prepared him perfectly.

The story proper began with a show staged in London in 1920, celebrating the achievements of Lawrence – the 'Terror of the Turks', the 'Uncrowned King of Arabia' and the 'Twentieth Century Crusader'. The event's host regaled the audience with tales of his bravery, while a black and white film showing the desert-bound warrior in his flowing robes, flickered on a screen.

Suddenly, the camera cuts to the rear of the theatre. There, hidden in the shadows, is the object of the show's idolatry, T.E. Lawrence – looking like a frail shadow of the heroic screen figure. He has deep, dark rings under his eyes and the forlorn look of a beaten man. Who could have guessed they were one and the same person?

The story then goes back in time to Armistice Day, 1918. Victory has been won, albeit at a high price and the Great Powers – Britain, France and the USA – are preparing to meet in Paris to devise a peace treaty. A sunburnt Lawrence, fresh from his desert adventures, is determined to secure Syria for his friend, Prince Feisal. There's one small problem. France wants Syria, an aim Lawrence, a virulent Francophobe, abhors.

The film could never hope to reproduce the sheer spectacle of Lean's wide-screen action epic – with its great set pieces, cast of thousands and battles fought out in the shimmering desert sun. But the team behind the semi-sequel wisely never attempted to do so – it would have cost more than £40 million to emulate the original in the 1990s.

'Instead of sweeping desert vistas, this is a small, interior film about an idealist, a purist trying to manoeuvre in a pragmatic and cynical world,' observed Fiennes.

The film portrays Lawrence as 'a man apart' – not unlike Fiennes himself. He is highly intelligent, thoughtful and frequently self-effacing. There is something of the aesthete about Ralph's Lawrence. His Paris room is sparsely furnished, he doesn't drink and appears to have little time for life's frivolities. A Lawrence quite unlike the larger-than-life hero portrayed by Peter O'Toole in Lean's film.

It also shows that, in many ways, Lawrence was a man ahead of his time. His call for the establishment of an independent Arabia – 'the British Empire's first brown dominion', as he dubbed it – was about as radical as you could get at a time when most Englishmen still thought they had a God-given right to rule the world.

'He was truly a man with a vision, a genius, as Feisal describes him in the script, "not for this age, but for the future",' says Fiennes. His words and thoughts are as relevant today as they were then. He was fascinated by medieval literature and chivalry, and recognized in the Arabs the purest modern equivalent of the ethics and values of the crusading medieval knights. He understood that the problems of Christianity and Islam are fundamental and stem from the Middle Ages, if not even further back. It was these problems that he did his best to resolve.'

Before long, though, the British delegation begins to doubt Lawrence's loyalty to the Empire – a suspicion heightened by his fondness for Arab robes and Bedouin head-dress. He even stands up for Feisal in the face of the patronizing, near-racist behaviour adopted by most British – and European – diplomats to a man who in their eyes is a mere Arab, and as such, a subservient species.

At a dinner party, one guest condemns Lawrence for his 'disgraceful behaviour' in turning down a decorative medal from the king – even if it *was* designed to draw attention to the Arab plight. 'My action was prompted by a burning sense of shame at the likely betrayal of the Arabs by the country in which they had placed their trust,' says Lawrence calmly in his own defence.

The diner goes on to belittle the Arab revolt's importance, maliciously adding: 'I am even more dimly aware of the part played by Colonel Lawrence in the revolt.' But Lawrence remains a picture of calm. 'It was nothing,' murmurs Ralph's character self-effacingly. 'Nothing.'

Despite Lawrence's vehement defence of Feisal and the Arab cause, their relationship is not without tension, because, while Lawrence is being fêted as the great desert warrior, the prince he supposedly represents is all but ignored.

However, modern films about a great historical figure are rarely complete without some attempt at 'revisionism', which usually involves casting doubt on their heroism. In a similar way, this film highlighted the narcissistic streak in Lawrence's nature – his enjoyment at posing for portraits and his delight at seeing newsreels of himself in action.

'People say he was a show-off, that he liked the limelight and I think he did – but only in a little-boy way,' says Fiennes, forced to confront alleged character flaws in his childhood hero. 'He had an extrovert manner which actually stemmed from shyness, and he was intrigued by the attention he drew, but I don't believe he thirsted after it.'

Paradoxically, Lawrence was also publicity-shy. In one scene, he pretends to be someone else when a newsman asks him if he knows Lawrence's whereabouts. Later on, he comes to blows with the reporter when he turns up at the family home and asks if rumours about his alleged illegitimacy are true. 'For God's sake, get out!' yells Ralph's Lawrence, physically ejecting the man.

'Part of Lawrence was intrigued by the effect he had as a public figure, part was repelled,' says Fiennes, who even then was averse to sitting for photographs and being interviewed by the press. 'He felt the pleasure publicity can give you, but he was too intelligent to gloat.'

Much was also made of Lawrence's sexual ambiguity and alleged fondness for masochism.

When a beautiful French diplomat's wife tries to seduce him he giggles like a schoolboy, declining her offer before making a hasty exit. Shortly afterwards, he returns to his quarters to find the woman in his bed. But again he spurns her advances. 'I cannot respond to you as I fear you wish,' he says, intriguingly. 'It's simply not in my power to do so.'

Later on, Ralph's character reveals the terrible scars on his back – the result of a fearful lashing.

'What are those?' asks a shocked fellow officer.

'I was dragged through barbed wire,' replies Lawrence unconvincingly.

'Our treatment of the issue of Lawrence's sexuality was deliberately nebulous,' says Fiennes. 'My own feeling is that he was not inclined to sex, full stop. But Lawrence was forced to come to terms with his father's forbidden passion for their housekeeper, which perhaps inhibited his own sexual development.'

Most damaging of all, the movie casts doubt on the myth of the great desert warrior, suggesting that Lawrence was a self-publicist more interested in advancing his own career than in supporting Arab independence. 'That's precisely what I am, a fake,' says Ralph's character at one point. 'I'm imprisoned within a lie. My whole life is a lie. I was born to it, and I have sustained it throughout my life.'

The film even theorizes that Lawrence's mysterious withdrawal from public life, after his failure to secure Arab independence at the peace conference, may have been the result of an attempt to blackmail the government which backfired, leaving him no option but to disappear.

In many ways, Lawrence – who went on to join the RAF as an enlisted man, only to die in a motor-cycle crash in Dorset in 1936, aged 46 – was a tragic hero in the Shakespearian tradition: a man of intellect and drive, but a man whose integrity (or stubbornness) would prove his undoing.

'In co-ordinating the Arabs' aspirations, he took the first steps to greatness, but afterwards he denied himself the possibility of great achievement,' says Fiennes. 'He was devastated by a sense of having failed himself and the Arabs. I believe he found in the RAF the same astringency he had felt in the desert. Being yelled at by sergeants, cleaning latrines, denying himself any sexual life – this suited him, strangely. He went in for self-flagellation, like the saints he'd studied as a medieval scholar.'

When the man who conceived the project, Clive Irving, attended an advance screening, he was mesmerized by Fiennes's subtle, enigmatic performance, hinting at Lawrence's intellect and vision as well as his neuroticism, masochism and lack of self-esteem.

'Having worked on the project for eleven years, I knew that at last we had finally detached Lawrence from Peter O'Toole,' he says. 'Ralph managed to internalize the part, catching details like Lawrence's contorted body language and, particularly, his maladroit terror of sexual advances from women.'

After the long years on stage, Fiennes was relishing the chance to learn a new discipline. 'The thing I like about working in front of a camera is that so often it's as much about what isn't said as what is,' he explained. 'Shakespeare is so language-based, you have to keep going, you cannot allow pauses to sink in, or everything just falls apart.

'So it was a relief in a way to think, "I can just take my time here and not have to worry about being heard at the back of the theatre". But I think the kind of concentration and focus which I found I needed for the camera could be very effective on stage, while the discipline needed on stage could feed my film acting. The one complements the other.'

Unlike so many stage actors who think they have fathomed the art totally when they switch to television or film, he was aware that having mastered one discipline, he still had much to learn about the other; he was aware of the steepness of the learning curve and was determined to rise to the challenge. His sense of humility about the acting process, together with a constant striving to do better, would play as important a part as his photogenic looks in marking him out as a great screen actor.

The point is echoed by Clive Irving, who observes: 'One of the things about Ralph – and it's not often achieved by Royal Shakespeare actors – is that he made that transition from the sort of thespianism that works so powerfully when you're doing Shakespeare, to the entirely different kind of challenge that making a film like this demands.

'For all his brilliance, Kenneth Branagh is still the thespian on film, and Ralph isn't. Clearly the camera loves Ralph, but there's much more to it than that. It's the way in which he's able to internalize the lines. The lines go in and come out – they don't just come out.'

The two-hour television movie won acclaim both in Britain and abroad, and went on to win an Emmy Award in America. Fiennes was delighted. 'I am very proud of *A Dangerous Man*,' he said. 'I think it is the best thing I have ever done.'

Fortune appeared to be smiling on the actor and he wasn't yet 30. Within months of making his screen début he was becoming a name to drop, and the first gushing profiles penned by smitten female writers were appearing in the press. 'Is this the sexiest man in the world?' asked the *Daily Express*. The magazine *You* had no doubt about it, describing Ralph's lips as having 'the colour and sheen of rolled silk stockings'. Not even Peter O'Toole was praised for the lusciousness of his lips after starring in Lean's epic.

Fiennes was on his way – or so it seemed. But his next project would receive the sort of notices that could have sunk a lesser talent.

Ralph and Alex had meanwhile bought a flat in a large Victorian house in East Dulwich Road, London SE22, overlooking the curiously named Goose Green – about a mile from Ralph's parents' current home.

The property was approximately midway between Dulwich and Peckham. The former is known for its common, village and public school. While the latter – dubbed 'Del Boy territory' by one pundit – is a rougher, tougher, poorer inner-city area whose residents are more likely to live in a council flat than in their own home.

As *Secrets and Lies* star Marianne Jean-Baptiste says, 'When I tell people I live in Dulwich, they say "how posh" – then I say "East Dulwich".' Living in East Dulwich told people you were likely to have paid £100,000 less for a place to live than the £250,000-plus forked out by those in Dulwich Village.

Either way, it was a long way from neighbourhoods traditionally favoured by successful actors – such as Chelsea, Kensington and Hampstead. Indeed, many actors would never have considered even living south of the river, let alone in East Dulwich.

Alex says, 'We wanted as much space as we could afford. And we hated the idea of bumping into hundreds of people in the business. It was nice to feel at home yet anonymous.'

It wasn't such a bad place anyway. Until the 1850s, the area had been devoted to farming and market gardening. But the growth of the railways triggered extensive suburban development. And the leafy part of East Dulwich Road where Ralph and Alex set up home was one of the area's most desirable spots.

To outside eyes, they must have appeared much like any other young couple. They took pride in decorating the flat to reflect their exquisite taste, invited friends around for intimate dinner parties, popped around to Ralph's parents' Therapia Road home for lunch and took summer walks on Peckham Rye Common. They appeared to be very much in love.

Furthermore, their careers were both thriving – although Fiennes was obviously more of a high-flier. Reaching the top wasn't such an all-consuming passion for Alex as it was for her partner – and if Ralph had wanted her to stop working so they could start a family, she would have instantly agreed. 'Ever since I was 18 I'd wanted four children,' she says.

The one reality that all acting couples, Ralph and Alex included, had to face was the itinerant lifestyle inherent to their profession.

Fiennes had travelled to North Wales, Oldham and Stratford-upon-Avon in an effort to further his career. And Kingston had appeared at Birmingham's Repertory Theatre, Lancaster's Dukes Playhouse and Sheffield's Crucible. However, it was something they both, as members of a profession full of ups and downs, accepted.

By now, Fiennes was only too aware that he was being hailed as the next big thing – but it was something he preferred not to discuss, however flattered he might secretly be by the attention.

'It's dangerous,' he said at the time. 'It doesn't seem real to me. What does seem real is the work I'm doing in the studio or when I'm at home having a bath. If you start believing the hype and going around thinking "I'm promising", you're not going to do your job. It's satisfying to know people are interested but you've got to keep your balance.'

Living in East Dulwich at least helped him to keep his feet on the ground. He still lived modestly, and had little real idea of where his career was heading. He shopped at the local supermarket and made the weekly trip to the launderette.

However, that particular chore would soon be history – for a new role would enable him to acquire many more luxurious items than a washing machine.

The role in question was the central figure in a new big-screen version of *Wuthering Heights* – Emily Brontë's tragic 1847 story of the doomed love affair between the daughter of a wealthy family and the gypsy boy adopted by her father.

It would not be the first film based on the novel. As recently as 1970, Timothy Dalton had starred in a big screen version of *Wuthering Heights* alongside Amanda Calder-Marshall. This best-forgotten picture was nearly summed up by *Halliwell's Film Guide* which tagged it: 'A disappointing version that marks a Z-film company's first determined effort to enter the big-time.'

The best known – and best loved – version of *Wuthering Heights* was the 1939 black and white film starring Laurence Olivier, Merle Oberon and David Niven, directed by William Wyler.

At that time, Olivier was relatively unknown to American audiences. But he agreed to portray the moody Heathcliff only if his wife, Vivien Leigh, played Cathy. Oberon had already been given the role, though, and Goldwyn would not consider firing her. Eventually Olivier agreed to take the role and Leigh – in one of those twists of fate so common to the movie business – ended up shooting to stardom as Scarlett O'Hara in *Gone With The Wind*.

The Wyler film might have been shot in California – thousands of miles from the windswept Yorkshire moors where the story is set –

but studio bosses at Goldwyn spared no expense in creating the right atmosphere for the picture, which was altered from the Regency to Georgian period for no other reason than that it allowed them to dress its female stars in more lavish costumes.

A tract of 450 acres of land in the Conejo Hills was transformed into an authentic-looking setting with the help of 1,000 specially-imported heather plants, and a period manor was built on the site. When English weather was called for, Olivier and Oberon ran around in propeller-fanned winds with buckets of water being thrown at them.

It was a superb Hollywood production for that period of history and it caught the power of Brontë's classic. The *New York Times* hailed it as 'unquestionably one of the most distinguished pictures of the year', and it won a string of Oscar nominations.

The new version starring Fiennes was the first project to be green-lighted by the British arm of Paramount Pictures. The £5 million budget was small-scale by Hollywood standards, but the decision to film was nevertheless seen as an important boost for the British film industry, then in the doldrums.

'The studio sees Paramount UK as an opportunity to take chances at a relatively low price,' said Ileen Maisel, the British division's formidable head and the initiator of the *Wuthering Heights* remake. 'They're willing to take bets on movies with unknowns which they're not going to take on bigger-budget movies.'

Ironically, Fiennes originally auditioned for the role of Edgar Linton – the sensitive if bland gentleman (played by David Niven in the 1939 film) who is the obverse of the flamboyant, anarchic anti-hero Heathcliff, and eventually marries Cathy. 'People saw me as a lyrical actor and I, too, never saw myself as a Heathcliff,' said Ralph at the time. 'But when they offered me an audition for the lead part I wasn't going to say "no".' The difference between the two characters is elemental, and it's revealing that Fiennes initially assumed the foppish part over the fiery one. Brontë makes the difference between the two men quite clear as Cathy vocalises the different kinds of love she feels for Linton and Heathcliff. "My love for Linton is like the foliage in the woods. Time will change it, I am well aware, as winter changes the trees."

But of Heathcliff: "My love for Heathcliff resembles the eternal rocks beneath – a source of little visible delight but necessary."

The man who had come to believe nothing is forever needed a little persuasion to play that eternally rocky romantic hero – Heathcliff. The film's producer Mary Selway, who has cast more than ninety movies, sensed that here was an actor who could bring the character alive for a new generation. 'He had this extraordinary energy, power, romanticism and a surprisingly dark side, too,' she says. 'We needed someone as Heathcliff who could take on the film and have the power to dominate it. And I had no doubt that Ralph was that man.'

But the decision to cast the beautiful French actress Juliette Binoche as Brontë's quintessential English heroine, Cathy Earnshaw, sparked fury. 'It's absolutely disgraceful,' one leading screenwriter told the *Daily Mail*. 'So many English actresses would have killed for that part. The whole spirit of the story could be destroyed by someone with a lisping French accent.' The director of the Brontë Museum, Jane Sellars, echoed the criticism, saying, 'The idea of Cathy with a French accent is ludicrous.'

However, Maisel insists Binoche's screen test was 'head and shoulders' above the British competition. And director Peter Kosminsky – who had made the television thriller *Shoot to Kill* as well as documentaries on the Falklands War and the killing fields of Cambodia – hit back at critics, saying, 'People should stop banging on about the fact that she happens to have been born in Paris. It's so racist.'

Unlike the Olivier film which ended with the death of Cathy, the new adaptation – penned by Irish dramatist Anne Devlin – incorporated the second half of the book, which saw Heathcliff seek revenge on Catherine Linton, the daughter of Cathy Earnshaw and Edgar Linton. Devlin also supplied several additional sequences in which Emily Brontë (played by the Irish pop star Sinead O'Connor) herself appeared – the aim being 'to convey something of the creative process and the way in which Brontë's spirit infects the story'.

Despite *Wuthering Heights*' comparatively modest budget, there was a great deal at stake – not least the future of Paramount UK – and as far as finances allowed, everything was done to ensure that the film succeeded.

It was shot at Shepperton Studios, and in Yorkshire, where location scouts scoured the countryside looking for places that resembled the trysting points and lonely nooks described by Brontë. A vast Hammer Horror-style edifice was constructed at Grassington to double up as Wuthering Heights, along with a makeshift graveyard with fake tombstones wedged into the grassy earth.

James Acheson, the designer responsible for the lavish outfits in *The Last Emperor* and *Dangerous Liaisons*, was hired to ensure that the actors' costumes looked authentic. Expert advice was sought to advise on the appropriate musical arrangements for the time, and the acclaimed Japanese pop star Ryuichi Sakamoto was invited to compose the score. Meanwhile a specially employed 'distressing' assistant roughed up the clothes with paint and a stiff brush.

But Maisel was as keen to ensure the movie was accessible as to make it accurate. 'It's vital that the movie manages to express all the feelings and fears that young people have inside about their first love,' she said. 'It's got to be real as well as sexy. I'm looking to attract a *Pretty Woman* audience to the movie.'

One can visualize her pitching the idea for the remake to her Hollywood bosses as 'a *Pretty Woman* period drama'. But would Fiennes have wanted to star in such a film? Hardly.

Filming began in late September 1991. As the first day of the shoot approached, Fiennes spoke of his reverence for Olivier, the man in whose footsteps he was following. 'I think for every actor he represents something magical, a pitch of acting where you're taken into another realm and your senses are lifted,' said Ralph. 'I suppose he epitomizes the kind of instinct that people have when they want to act.'

But he expressed confidence that the remake would be every bit as good as the 1939 film, albeit different. 'This version of *Wuthering Heights* is truthful to the book, and follows it all the way through, whereas the Olivier film didn't,' he said. 'While Olivier cuts an amazingly passionate, romantic figure, the film suffers in comparison to the book. It's also dated badly.'

The new film opened with a storm raging. It's night and a lost horseman arrives at Wuthering Heights, seeking help. Enter Ralph's Heathcliff. Where Fiennes had appeared clean-shaven and austere in Lawrence, he had now donned designer stubble and a long, leather coat, his hair was dyed black and supplemented by a generous ponytail, and his eyes were wild like the moors.

It wasn't the easiest of film shoots with the scenes shot on the bleak, wintry Yorkshire moors proving a particular ordeal. The crew put on heavy, bulky clothes to shield them from the foul weather, while Ralph's attempts to deliver his great 'Haunt me' speech were repeatedly interrupted by squally 40m.p.h. gusts of wind. Some scenes required twelve takes – and tempers were quick to fray.

Fiennes sought to stay in character by remaining aloof from the cast and crew. 'I was moody and difficult to work with,' he admits. 'If you're playing a character suffering from pain, anger and aggression, it has to affect you. I tended to go very quiet and freeze people out.' So while everyone else stayed in a hotel, he rented a cottage alone on the moors. He claims his existence was anything other than glamorous, and he spent most evenings eating baked beans and watching television.

His co-star, Binoche, also hired a cottage. Ever since, there has been speculation about whether the couple's on-screen romance spilled over into their private lives. 'It crossed our minds, too,' admits one former crew member. 'But if anything did happen, they were very discreet. There was never any proof of a fling.'

As the film's October 1992 UK release date approached, Paramount's publicity machine went into overdrive.

A concerted, at times embarrassingly over the top, attempt was made to turn Ralph into an overnight sensation. 'I auditioned 100 actors for the part and I think he is the greatest British actor of his generation,' raved Kosminsky. 'He's one of the most extraordinary-looking men I've ever seen, the camera adores him and in his soul he's more Heathcliff than Ralph,' said Maisel, giving new meaning to the word hyperbole. While Selway spoke of the 'electrifying chemistry' between the leading couple.

'What chemistry?' scoffed Fiennes, refusing to play along with the publicity game. 'Juliette and I enjoyed working together, but when you're acting you don't think "Wow, there's a real fizz here", you're just pleased that a scene went well.'

He went on to say, 'There are plenty of people in the business who think I've been miscast. But people who really know me, especially my family, know how unpleasant, nasty, moody, selfish and monosyllabic I can be. I had been dying to play a brutal, unpleasant character for a long time because there's so much black in me.'

This was something of a revelation coming from a star who would become famous for being moody and monosyllabic in his dealings with the press. But how much was it simply an attempt to sell himself as something of 'a real life Heathcliff' to the public? And how much was it Ralph talking from the heart? Only Alex and his immediate family could, perhaps, give the answer to that question.

But despite the presence of a classical actor of Ralph's calibre, the reaction to the film at advance screenings was anything but positive.

One of the biggest problems was Binoche's accent. Maisel might boast, 'She's done a lot of work with the voice coach and her accent is pretty much eight-and-a-half out of ten, some days as much as a nine.' But was a nine enough? Clearly not, if audiences reacted the same way as the critics who fell about laughing when she came on and said 'Good moaning' – instead of 'Good morning' – at one screening.

It was no surprise when the film got a critical mauling. 'Pitiful,' was the *Independent*'s damning verdict. 'Sometimes the film is so thick with melodrama it's more like Withering Heights,' said the *Daily Mirror*. While a Sunday paper claimed, 'All the brooding, fiery passion of Emily Brontë's novel has been lost amid the soap opera slickness.'

However, there was praise for the leading man. 'Fiennes's flowing black locks and piercing blue eyes make Heathcliff, striding the moors swathed in skins, a powerful, darkly attractive figure,' conceded *Time Out*, but added: 'Binoche's Cathy lacks the wild sensuality that should underpin her wilfulness. There are problems, too, with her wavering accent.'

Even Fiennes couldn't escape being caught up in the critical back-lash and was attacked by one critic for portraying Heathcliff's agonies 'as though he had permanent indigestion'.

The film scraped into London's Top Ten but failed to chart nationally following a limited release at just thirty-six UK cinemas. It performed so poorly that it consequently got a video release in the USA. Who was to blame for the débâcle? Some criticised Kosminsky's lack of feature film experience. And Binoche, fine actress though she might be, was clearly miscast. It is a difficult book to film, its story in some ways more suited to the melodramatic style of the pre-war cinema. But giving it a glossy, soap opera-style look in the hope of appealing to a *Pretty Woman* audience ensured it would become just another forgettable remake.

Luckily for Fiennes, he emerged relatively unscathed from this mess. Indeed, he was probably the only member of the cast and crew to benefit from being involved in the picture. For a certain Hollywood movie mogul was so impressed by Ralph's dark, brooding performance that he would offer him a leading role in a film that would make his name worldwide.

CHAPTER ELEVEN

A Watershed Year

Before taking the fateful call from Steven Spielberg that would change his life forever, Fiennes worked on a couple of projects in 1993 which, in view of his subsequent career, can only be described as oddities. The year would also see momentous changes in his personal life.

The first project was a thoughtful television drama, with echoes of Hitchcock's *The Birds*, about a family who escape from the rat race to a house they have inherited in Wales. The second was a typically controversial film from the arthouse director Peter Greenaway.

Based on the novel by Stephen Gregory, the Screen Two film *The Cormorant* (a Holmes Associates/BBC Wales co-production) provided a marked contrast to much of the formulaic fodder which passes for entertainment on television – and, as such, the project had obvious appeal for Fiennes.

The £1 million drama follows the trials and tribulations of writer John Talbot (Fiennes), his wife Mary (Helen Schlesinger) and their young son Tom when they move to the remote Snowdonia house he has inherited from his Uncle Ian. The raw butt of the deal is that his late uncle's beloved pet cormorant, Archie, is part of the inheritance.

Despite its cage, Archie is a wild creature. But where John is fascinated by the strange-looking seabird, with its long neck and glossy black plumage, the superstitious Mary is terrified, fearing its cruel beak and sharp claws could harm their young son. It relieves itself over the carpet when Talbot takes it indoors. 'Get that thing out of here!' screams his angry wife. But, when he tries, it flaps its wings, sending ornaments flying and furniture crashing to the floor.

Although bitten by Archie, Ralph's character forms a bizarre bond with the bird, even taking it for walks along the beach on a makeshift lead. But it gradually drives a bigger and bigger wedge between husband and wife. If they get rid of Archie, they risk losing the house, a risk Mary is prepared to take but John is unwilling to countenance.

Mother and child flee the house when the cormorant kills their pet cat. But Ralph's character still can't bear to do away with Archie, so he resorts to driving it from the house. Within hours, it's back. His wife returns but the final straw, as far as she is concerned, is discovering their son, Tom, alone with the creature in its cage.

As the film draws to a close, we discover that Uncle Ian died in mysterious circumstances in a rowing boat, alone with the cormorant. Despite the mauling his body received, Talbot insists he died of natural causes. 'But the bird picked out his eyes,' the pub barmaid says accusingly in one scene. 'It was kissing him,' replies Talbot defensively, his obsession with the bird now in full flood.

Eventually he kills off Archie in a fit of rage, yet still the family can't seem to escape the bird's malign influence. For when Mary tries to burn the bird on a bonfire, young Tom makes a beeline for Archie. Luckily Ralph's character sweeps him up in the nick of time. Only then, with the cormorant reduced to ashes, are the family freed from its evil curse.

The original story called for a horrific ending and Ralph was 'disappointed' when the filmmakers decided against having his character burned alive in the fire. 'I felt something horrendous needed to happen,' he says, his dark side once again in evidence.

The two-hour film, directed by Peter Markham, took five weeks to shoot, in Snowdonia and south Wales. It is notable both for the beautiful shots of the cormorant fishing under water, and for the fact that it is the only film Fiennes has made to date in which he wears glasses!

Four different birds – which were taken from the wild as chicks and specially reared and trained by experts – played Archie. But even though 'filming went very smoothly considering there was a lot of bird footage', things didn't always go according to plan, according to Fiennes. 'Three of the cormorants were fine but one was totally unpredictable,' he says. 'It had a tendency to go for me and once pecked me on the face. After a while I developed a fondness for the other birds, though; one in particular was very tame and liked to rub his beak against my face and nose.'

Most critics admired the film's underwater film footage of the birds – which were subsequently released back into the wild – yet they couldn't hide their ultimate disappointment in the slender tale.

'By the weak ending, it's difficult to see what it all amounts to,' said *Time Out*. 'A dull, unedifying TV drama' was *Sight and Sound*'s damning verdict. As for the *Independent*, it commented: 'It was beautiful to look at, nicely-written and well-acted.' But, putting its finger on the drama's central weakness, it added: 'Somehow, though, wildfowl don't quite cut it as predators.'

Even Ralph's performance drew mixed reviews, one critic observing that with 'his hawk-like beak, Fiennes is perfectly-cast as the bird-obsessed protagonist' while another memorably claimed: 'If anything, Fiennes is upstaged by the bird.' This conveniently ignored the fact that John Talbot, with his taste for corduroy trousers and woolly cardigans, was 'a bookish, academic person' – in Ralph's words – without the charisma of a Lawrence or a Heathcliff.

In the final analysis, it's inconceivable that Spielberg would have offered Fiennes the part as an SS commandant in *Schindler's List* simply as a result of viewing *The Cormorant*.

In contrast, *The Baby of Macon*, starring Julia Ormond as well as Fiennes, was a very different proposition. Made on a shoestring budget in Germany for £1.6 million, this Peter Greenaway film was a sumptuous, gorgeously photographed work that looked as if cost ten times as much to make. However, it was even more controversial than previous films of his, such as *The Cook, The Thief, His Wife and Her Lover*.

It was reportedly inspired by two photographs – the one in the Benetton advert featuring a blood-smeared baby, and another showing a model dressed as the Virgin Mary on the cover of *Elle* magazine. Although quite how they evolved into *The Baby of Macon* is anyone's guess.

A play within a play about miracles set in a seventeenth-century

Macon theatre, it opened with a naked, skeletal man caked in mud, suspended in a go-go dancer's cage, jabbering like an idiot. It is chiefly memorable for its full frontal assault on the senses, featuring corpses, brutal sex, an on-screen birth, the suffocation and dismemberment of a baby and a ten-minute rape by 200 men of one woman.

Dressed in white and wearing a saintly countenance, Ralph plays a bishop's son who is lured to a stables and seduced by a self-proclaimed virgin mother – played by the striking Ormond.

In a blasphemous scene parodying the birth of Jesus in the manger, she invites him to suck at her breast. 'Taste my milk,' she says teasingly, before begging him: 'Now take me with your prick.' However, Ormond's 'baby boy' puts a curse on the by now naked Fiennes who is attacked by a bull and gored. Little is left to the imagination in what critics branded 'one of the most explicit sex scenes ever committed to film' with the camera homing in on Ralph's blood-splattered genitalia as he falls to the floor, writhing in agony and choking on his own blood.

'That was a funny scene to shoot,' admits Fiennes. 'We didn't have much in the way of special effects. We used a cow's head and a pair of polystyrene horns covered in wax, and it was shot with such rapidity that the viewer wouldn't notice that there wasn't any real goring going on. I spent the whole day covered in blood, naked, on straw which irritated my skin, in this sort of nativity set-up with real pigs, sheep, hens and cows around. It was rather wonderful.'

While Fiennes was unperturbed by the need for nudity, his then girlfriend Alex admits: 'I really didn't like it. I was quite happy seeing other actors naked, not bothering to wonder what their wives were thinking, but when it came to my own situation, I got a little bit panicky.'

The trouble with a Greenaway film was that while the costumes might be colour-coded and the scenes exquisitely set up, it was likely to be virtually incomprehensible to the average cinema-goer. The director himself argued that he was breaking taboos and blurring the boundaries between art and actuality. But while a minority acclaimed his brilliance, the majority of critics felt his work was self-indulgent and pretentious, more spectacle than substance.

True to form, *The Baby of Macon* sparked mass walk-outs and critical indignation when it was released in September 1993, and the critics gave it a justified pasting.

One said it was no more than 'a posh, glossy excuse to milk every sickening perversion in the book'. Another dubbed it 'the most outlandish erotic film ever made'. The *Daily Mail* called it 'the most shocking film of the year.' While the BBC's veteran film critic Barry Norman commented: 'Peter is a spectacular, painterly film-maker whose images are always unforgettable. It's just a pity you don't want to remember them.'

Even though *The Baby of Macon* was never distributed in America, the *New York Times* perhaps summed up the film best, dubbing it a 'stew of grotesque religiosity, slavering voyeurism and sexual violence'.

Unperturbed, Greenaway hit back: 'We think a film ought to be a cathartic, masturbatory act where we let down our emotional hair. But we live in a violent world. My film reflects the feeling that, if we're not careful, we'll be having a visit from the Four Horsemen of the Apocalypse.' His views were echoed by Fiennes who said: 'It's difficult to watch but I liked it, and I loved working with Peter. It was wonderful to see his vision become a reality – like a live painting, really.'

However, the public appeared to share the critics' views, for the film performed poorly even in London – the one place where Greenaway films, such as *The Cook, The Thief, His Wife and Her Lover* were usually guaranteed an audience. Not that Fiennes was worried. By then he had made a film that would be viewed by more people than would ever hear about, let alone have to sit through a Greenaway picture.

Interestingly, he's not the only Fiennes to have worked with Greenaway. Ralph's sister Sophie worked for several years as his personal assistant.

Less than two weeks before *The Baby of Macon* opened, Ralph finally made an honest woman of Alex Kingston, his girlfriend of nearly ten years.

The wedding took place on 5 September 1993, at Holy Trinity Church in Blythburgh, once a thriving port on the River Blyth but now a small village on the A12 just a few miles from Ralph's old childhood home in Wangford, Suffolk. It was also close to where his by now sickly mother was staying. 'It was a familiar sight to him as a boy and he always dreamt of marrying at the church,' says a friend.

The fifteenth-century worship place, famous for its magnificent Angel ceiling, is often described as the 'Cathedral of the Marshes'. And with its 83 ft-high tower, lit up at night, it could be seen for miles around.

It was a joyous day, according to vicar Harry Edwards who conducted the service. Family and friends lined the pews of the airy church. Ralph's former RSC co-star, Simon Russel Beale, sang his favourite song, 'Over the Hills and Far Away'.

The couple appeared happy enough, but the more observant members of the congregation would have noticed Ralph's frequent, anxious glances at his mother, Jini. For, despite joining her family on the dance floor at the after-wedding reception, she was dying.

In 1990, with the cancer in remission, she had set out on a pilgrimage to the holy sites of France and Spain, recounting her experiences in her book, *On Pilgrimage*. But within eighteen months the illness had returned with a vengeance, moving from her breasts to her lungs.

Like most people who look back on their life as the end draws near, she had regrets. But she could at least be proud that her children – her special project – had all grown up so strong and determined to achieve their dreams. She was particularly proud of her eldest son, who had made his mark, first on stage and now on screen. However, she had one remaining wish – to see Ralph walk down the aisle with the other woman in his life, Alex.

As the couple emerged from the church into the bright Suffolk sunshine, Jini – frail though she was – could breathe a sigh of relief that he had found someone who could love him and care for him now that her time was nearly up.

However, for all the smiles and laughter that day, the newly-weds themselves harboured a secret: their relationship was in trouble. The years of touring, the time spent apart, and more recently the divergence in their careers, had all taken their toll. The cracks in their relationship might not be obvious to the outside world, but they were deep – and getting deeper. 'Ralph had been away filming for most of the year and came back only three days before the wedding,' says Alex. 'We were like strangers but somehow we thought the wedding was going to heal everything.'

One charge no one could level at Ralph and Alex was the old one about 'marrying in haste'. They had been stepping out together for so long that some friends were shocked when the wedding invitations dropped on to the door mat.

Why suddenly tie the knot now? Was turning 30 the catalyst that had triggered Ralph into finally proposing? Were he and Alex planning to start a family? Or was there another less obvious reason? Such as a desire on the part of a loving son to fulfil one of his dying mother's last wishes?

That year Jini had retreated to the isolation of a Suffolk cottage where a friend had said she could stay. Like Ralph, she did not fear being alone; she wanted to be alone with her thoughts. But when the illness became too much she was admitted to hospital at Odstock, Wiltshire, and then to a nearby hospice.

It was hard not to admire her courage as the end drew near. 'She could hardly speak,' says Ralph. 'Two words and she had to take a breath. But there was an amazing sense of acceptance about it. I could imagine her seeing all these faces of concern and encouragement crowding around, and I could see her acknowledging us and smiling, but at the same time distancing us.'

On 28 December 1993, Jini died. She was 55. Ever since, the Fiennes family has shown a tendency to mythologize Jini as an artistically inclined Earth Mother – which is understandable given her premature death. But as Kim Kent has hinted, Jini had troubled elements in her character as well.

'There were enormous problems,' concedes Martha. 'My mother often went through a great deal of distress. As a young woman, she was diagnosed an "incurable hysteric" and there was a side to her that was very, very unpredictable. She was close to the edge at times and as children we all witnessed it. It was frightening. She would scream, break crockery and threaten to kill us all.'

After Jini died, the conventional pieties were kept to a minimum. In accordance with Buddhist teachings her body lay for twelve hours on her death-bed, on a linen cloth stitched with a map of Ireland, her prayer-beads twisted in her hands, while candles were lit and her family and friends sang religious chants at her bedside. 'She looked wonderful,' says husband Mark. 'She had a Victorian nightdress on and all her lines had disappeared.'

Dispensing with the distrusting conventions, Mark, Ralph and the rest of the children made the funeral arrangements, and even buried Jini themselves. 'I did not want black suits and black cars and funeral directors with their professional piety,' says Mark.

Her coffin was painted electric blue in tribute to 'Silencia', the blue-coloured symbol of strength in *Tristram and the Power of the Light*, a book Jini had written for the children. As the coffin was too big for the family car, it was transported in a friend's VW camper van to the cemetery outside Tisbury, near Salisbury.

Finally, her four strapping sons, Ralph, Magnus, Jacob and Joseph – carried the coffin up the slippery path, eased it over the webbing straps, lowered it into the grave and covered it with earth, while an Irish piper played a final lament. 'Ralph thought he might not be able to do it at first, but he did,' says Mark. 'He ended up brushing her hair.' It was a fitting Celtic send-off for the matriarchal Jini.

The year 1993 was a watershed year for Fiennes – in more ways than simply losing his beloved mother and gaining a wife.

The days when he could appear in an offbeat little television drama that caught his fancy or work with a director he admired, yet still wander the streets of London unrecognized, were about to end. His career was moving up a notch. Yes, he would finally achieve the stardom he'd always secretly cherished. But there would be repercussions, not least in his private life.

CHAPTER TWELVE

Evil Incarnate

It was a balmy Californian evening. The boyish-looking movie mogul pressed a button on the remote control unit and the massive television screen in the lounge of his LA home lit up.

He had just finished shooting *Jurassic Park* and would soon start work on a project that meant more to him personally than anything he had ever worked on before. Its name? *Schindler's List*. There was only one problem. He had yet to find someone to play the Nazi commandant, Amon Goeth, and time was running out. There were plenty of bad-to-the-bone-looking heavies he could cast but he didn't want Goeth to come across as a comic-strip Nazi. He was looking for something different. But what?

Meanwhile he stroked his famous grey-flecked beard and adjusted his wire-rimmed glasses before settling down to watching a satellite television movie about Lawrence of Arabia, a man who had always fascinated him.

Two hours later, Spielberg picked up the phone and in a state of high excitement, called an aide. 'Find out all you can about an actor called Ralph Fiennes,' he said. 'I think we've found our Nazi.' Seeing *Wuthering Heights* only served to confirm his initial reaction. The film was no masterpiece, but Spielberg instinctively felt that in Fiennes he'd found someone who could bring his vision of a more ambivalent movie villain to life.

'I liked him as Lawrence,' he affirms. 'He took a lot of chances, especially with Peter O'Toole looming above the part like a guillotine. And I thought he pulled off a difficult part well in *Wuthering Heights*. His Heathcliff was a feral man, a kind of grown-up Wild Child.'

He met Fiennes and tested him for Goeth. 'Ralph did three takes,' reveals Spielberg. 'I still, to this day, haven't seen Take Two or Three. He was absolutely brilliant. After seeing Take One, I knew he *was* Amon. His eyes had a sexual evil. It's all about subtlety: there were moments of kindness that would move across his eyes and then instantly run cold.'

Within days, Fiennes was on board. Few actors, whether denizens of LA, let alone East Dulwich, would have hesitated about signing on the dotted line after being offered a role in a Spielberg movie, and Ralph was no exception. He would earn more from this one picture – $250,000 – than for all his previous roles combined.

The film, based on Thomas Keneally's Booker prize-winning 1982 novel, *Schindler's Ark*, was the extraordinary tale of an opportunist, Sudeten entrepreneur called Oskar Schindler, a gambler, a womanizer and a man of doubtful scruples, played in the film by Liam Neeson. For all his frailties, though, Schindler proved to be a saint in disguise.

With the help of his chief accountant (played by Ben Kingsley) he employed more than 1,300 Jews at his enamelware factory, providing humane conditions and bribing Nazi officials with his workers' money, to save them from the gas chamber.

As the course of the war turned against Germany, Hitler's henchmen became ever more zealous in their pursuit of the Final Solution. But Schindler miraculously marched his charges away from the threat of Auschwitz to his home town of Brinnlitz, Czechoslovakia, where they remained in safety until the war had ended.

In hindsight, this audacious behaviour was all the more remarkable for being pulled off under the nose of one of the Final Solution's most enthusiastic advocates, Hans Frank, the Nazi governor-general of Poland, who resided in Wawel Castle, Krakow.

Shot in southern Poland, *Schindler's List* was the biggest movie ever to be made in the country – even though its £15m ($23m) budget was modest by Hollywood standards. In addition, it was unique amongst Spielberg-directed films in that all three lead parts were played by British actors – Neeson, Kingsley and Fiennes.

The four-month shoot was preceded by controversy over Spielberg's plans to film within the precincts of the death camp at Auschwitz. But in the face of condemnation from organizations such as the World Jewish Congress, Spielberg (who is himself Jewish and lost seventeen relatives to the Nazis) erected five mocked-up barrack huts just outside the camp.

Most of the filming took place in a disused lime-quarry 35 miles to the east where a replica concentration camp was constructed. It was modelled on the Plaszow site where many of 'Schindler's Jews' were rounded up and held. With its newly-built, grey-painted huts encircled by barbed wire, it looked chillingly realistic.

It was a massive project, involving a 200-strong film crew, more than 1,000 extras and scores of location shoots. Indeed, so vast was the web it weaved, so ramificatory were its tentacles that one Warsaw director complained that he could not even get a television commercial made – because so many Polish actors had bit parts in the movie.

It was also shrouded in a secrecy, bordering on paranoia, that was customary in the world of big budget Hollywood movies, particularly those directed by Spielberg. Photographers were warned by burly security men not to snatch sneak pictures of the set or the props – if they transgressed this demand, their film would be 'gently' removed. While queries about the film's plot were met with the blunt reply: 'Read the book. It's called *Lista Schindlera* in Polish.'

Before joining the cast and crew in Poland, Fiennes prepared for the role by reading Keneally's novel, steeping himself in Nazi literature and history and watching films ranging from Leni Riefenstah's *Triumph of the Will* to SS recruitment movies showing combat training and what he calls 'finely muscled Aryan young men doing gymnastics'.

He says he came to understand the appeal – 'the sense of power, the order and hierarchy, and the patriotism' – of the SS and how it touched 'that sense being part of a clan gives one'. Fiennes also discovered, from reading transcripts at London's Imperial War

Museum of interviews with Plaszow labour camp survivors, how the syndrome which led to grossness overcame Goeth's originally fine features.

So Fiennes started to eat large quantities of pasta washed down with pints of Guinness in a bid to put on the necessary weight. He accelerated the process by consuming a weight-enhancing substance made of vegetable fat which eventually helped him gain nearly two stone, most noticeably around his stomach and jowls. 'I just had to force-feed myself,' says Ralph, who had noted as far back as his RSC days how often villains were characterized by excessive body weight. 'But I remember sometimes seeing myself in the mirror and hating myself.' One also wonders how his wife Alex viewed his newly-acquired fatty flesh, but a family friend insists, 'She was very supportive.'

Spielberg allowed Fiennes a great deal of leeway in choosing how to play Goeth, who came from a middle-class Roman Catholic family in Vienna. 'Steven wasn't dictatorial or autocratic,' says Fiennes. 'He trusted me, and never got involved in the motivation of the character. But he underlined the fact that he did not want me to play a cliché; he wanted him to be human.

'He was also very relaxed about not being word perfect about the script. It was a very good script, but above all he was concerned with keeping the freshness of the performances. And sometimes, if things are getting a little bit tired, it can help if you change the phrases a bit.'

The three-hour-long movie was filmed in black and white, which served to highlight the struggle between light and dark, good and evil, and made the story that much starker while also evoking a newsreel-style period atmosphere. Cinema-goers had to wait fifty minutes for Fiennes to make his first appearance and when he did there was no forgetting him – his chilling portrayal of Goeth lingering in the mind long after *Schindler's List* has ended.

In Fiennes' first scene, Goeth is receiving a guided tour of the Krakow ghetto, in a German staff car. A junior officer sits in the front pointing out Ghetto A (the industrial workers) and Ghetto B ('surplus labour' – that is, the elderly and infirm). 'Any questions?' asks the officer when the tour is complete. The camera cuts to Fiennes. He's wearing a long army overcoat and a peaked cap, with the distinctive death's head crest of the SS. His face is puffy but is semi-obscured by the handkerchief he holds to his running nose. But it's the words he utters that make the scene so terrifying. 'Yes, wind this top down,' he replies coldly. 'It's fucking freezing.'

As the *New Yorker* observed, 'If he had merely complained about the Jews around him, we might have grasped the nature of the man, but he doesn't even notice them. In his mind they are already cancelled out.'

He's then given his first glimpse of the newly-established labour camp that he will commandeer, at Plaszow. Snow lies on the ground and inmates are erecting makeshift barrack blocks that will offer pitifully little protection against the bitter Polish winter. Looming above the camp is the opulent château that will be Goeth's home.

Striding down a line of young Jewish women wrapped up in coats and headscarfs against the cold, Goeth says: 'One of you is a very lucky girl. There is an opening for a job away from all this back-breaking work.'

One of the girls, Helen (played by Embeth Davidtz), is prettier than the rest. 'Which of you has domestic experience?' he asks, looking at her out of the corner of his eye. Everyone else puts up their hands. Looking her way, he puffs on his cigarette before adding, 'On second thoughts, I don't really want someone else's maid.' Of course, Helen's duties will include considerably more than keeping Goeth's house clean.

Minutes later a female inmate, an engineering graduate who is overseeing the construction of a barrack block, runs up complaining that it's structurally unsound and must be demolished. 'Ah, an educated Jew,' says Ralph's character scornfully. 'Like Karl Marx himself.' He then casually orders for her to be shot and she's gunned down in full view of her fellow inmates.

Cut to Goeth, in a long leather coat – not unlike the one he wore as Heathcliff – giving a speech to German troops in the parade ground outside the camp's military barracks. 'Today is history and you are part of it,' he proclaims. 'For six centuries there has been a Jewish Krakow. By this evening those six centuries will be a rumour.' The rounding up of thousands of innocent men, women and children then begins. Goeth leads from the front, a snarling

Alsatian straining at its leash. Anyone who dares resist – or makes any attempts to reason with the German troopers – is shot and left to die in the snow.

(The real-life rounding-up of the city's Jews was carried out with typical German efficiency in 1943. In pre-Nazi days Krakow had a thriving Jewish community of 70,000 people. Now just 150 ageing Holocaust survivors remain.)

But worse is to follow the next morning when Goeth strolls bare-chested on to his bedroom balcony carrying a rifle, his unsightly paunch hanging over his trousers. 'Everyone comments about my putting on weight,' says Fiennes. 'But Goeth was a man with a sense of his own incredible power, a power to let people live or die. Powerful men often carry around a paunch with them in a way that demonstrates that power. It makes them more expansive, it creates extra space around them. There's something almost phallic about it.'

As a roll-call of inmates is taking place in the camp below, he raises the weapon to his eye and starts picking off victims with abandon, 'using his rifle as if it were God's lightning', to quote one film writer. A man drops here, a woman there – while, a few feet away, his 'domestic help' lies naked in his bed, covering her ears with her hands to block out the sounds of the senseless slaughter.

To prepare himself for such a harrowing scene, Ralph 'tried to understand what it was like to be a brainwashed SS officer who thought that Jews were vermin who had to be got rid of like rabbits', says his father Mark. He also dredged up the memory of primitive – but comparatively innocent – long ago sensations he had experienced as a child.

'I think Goeth experienced an extension of that boyish thrill with an air rifle when you aim at cans in front of a wall,' said Fiennes at the time. 'He got the same sense of satisfaction you get when you hit a target. It gave him a kick. It's as basic as smashing a fly with your hand as a kid and standing in front of a window and seeing how many flies you can kill.'

Furthermore, he theorized: 'I'm not a psychologist but I'm convinced the brutality Goeth became addicted to was related to his obesity. He also became an alcoholic and an insomniac. I think he was so steeped in this kind of brutality that unconsciously, as a kind of remedy or palliative, he had to stuff himself with food and drink to numb his sensibilities.'

His character commits numerous other wanton acts of unbelievable cruelty – for example, shooting dead an inmate at random when a chicken is stolen, and beating his domestic help, Helen, for throwing away bones he was storing up for his dogs.

In one scene, a drunken Goeth finds the girl cowering in the basement of his house. 'I realize you are not a person in the strict sense of the word but I feel for you, Helen,' he says, touching her breast. 'For a crucial moment,' as one critic put it, 'evil paused to consider itself.' Then his mood changes, he looks at her coldly and says: 'No, I don't think so – you are a Jewish bitch.' With that he flings her to the floor and his fists flail out as her cries echo around the room's four walls.

In another scene, Goeth kills 25 men after a member of a work party escapes – and it is impossible to forget Fiennes's blood-splattered, furious face as he walks through its thinning ranks, randomly shooting every other man. There is chilling cruelty in those laser-like eyes. As Spielberg says: 'When Ralph, as Goeth, looks you in the eye, it makes your blood run cold.'

Yet the reason Fiennes was so terrifying in the role was that he made Goeth so terrifyingly believable. 'He became Goeth', in the words of a fellow actor.

'The thing is to connect with the part of you which can relate to the character you're playing,' said Ralph, explaining how he had got under Goeth's cruel skin. 'I had to say, "What's the part of me that can get really angry with a person?" and use that as a spring-board for playing Amon.'

So chillingly lifelike was his performance that when Fiennes, in full Hauptsturmführer regalia, was introduced by Spielberg to Mila Pfefferberg, a Schindler survivor depicted in the film, the old lady trembled. 'Her knees began to give out from under her,' recalls Spielberg. 'I held her while Ralph enthused about how important it was for him to meet her – and she shook with terror. She didn't see the actor. She saw Amon Goeth.'

The actor made enormous efforts to understand Goeth's psychology, commenting, 'I feel that inside this man there must have been some deep void. He found in Nazi ideals a wonderful release for himself, a channel for his anger and frustration. If anything, I felt a kind of sympathy for him. Portraying Goeth as a simple monster is too easy. Whether you're dealing with a Nazi commandant, someone who orchestrated a Stalinist purge, or whoever, they came out of their mother's womb, wore nappies and grew up. To make any sense of it all you have to open these people up as human beings.'

It is quite something to express sympathy for a man such as Goeth. Especially if you have seen an old woman quake at fifty-year-old memories of him. But it is a mark of the extent to which Fiennes will identify with, climb inside, his characters.

'What surprised me, was the way survivors of the camp talked about Amon Goeth' said Fiennes. 'Although they say he was the devil – if they lost count of the number of strokes when he whipped them he would start again from the beginning – there was a part of them that found something compelling about his awfulness. Like Hitler. And though Oskar Schindler was benevolent where Amon was destructive, the two men shared a fondness for hard drinking and raucous parties.'

The film was a long, hard and exhausting shoot, as Fiennes indicated: 'Everyone felt depressed to some extent because these awful things appeared to have happened only yesterday.'

Playing someone as relentlessly evil as Goeth involved paying a price. 'If you are instrumental in dehumanizing other people, you yourself become dehumanized,' says Fiennes. 'Everything that is unique about a human being's capacity to create and love and construct is destroyed and negated. Playing Goeth raised all sorts of question marks – about acting, about human behaviour, about the fact that our capacity for evil is probably closer to the surface than we like to think.'

Nevertheless he sought to shake off the part at the end of each day's filming – at least for a few hours. 'I would have found it hard to come back to the hotel still speaking in an Austrian accent and giving everyone a steely glare,' he admitted. 'It would have made life hell for other people as well as myself.' Allowing himself a rare smile, he added: 'Though I think I would have got served a lot faster at the bar.'

To his horror, he discovered that even in the hotel where he was staying there were people prepared to give voice to the anti-semitic

With actress wife Alex Kingston - at the *Schindler's List* premiere, 1994.
© Alan Davidson

A night of triumph: Fiennes with Steven Spielberg at the Bafta Awards, 1994. © Alan Davidson

Playing fall guy Charles Van Doren in Robert Redford's powerful moral fable, *Quiz Show*, 1994. © Kobal

From Hollywood to Hackney - the cast of the 1995 Almeida production of *Hamlet* at the Hackney Empire; (left to right) Ralph Fiennes, Francesca Annis, Tara Fitzgerald, James Laurenson. © Alan Davidson

The Grunge Prince: exhibiting what one critic called his 'goatish sex appeal'.
© London Features

The Action Hero: Ralph playing against type in 1995's futuristic flop *Strange Days*. © Kobal

The English Patient, 1996: The Count reads Herodotus. © Kobal

Washing away the desert sand with the help of Kristin Scott-Thomas.
© Kobal

Francesca Annis, by his side at
the opening night of *Ivanov*.
© Alan Davidson

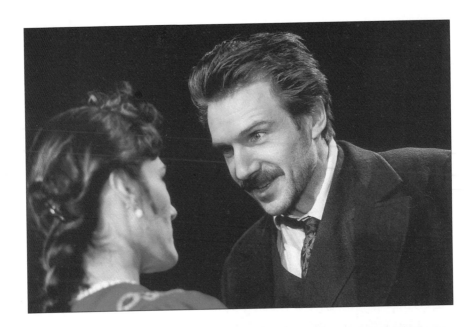

Playing another introverted hero
in 1997's triumphant revival of
Chekhov's *Ivanov* at the Almeida.
© Geraint Lewis

Filming Peter Carey's *Oscar & Lucinda*.
© London Features

A film star's residence, West
London, 1997.© York Membery

Today's intense, brooding matinée idol. © Kurt Krieger/Famous

sentiment that made the Holocaust possible more than fifty years earlier.

One night, Ralph was having a drink at the hotel bar with Ben Kingsley and a Jewish co-star, Michael Schneider, when a German tourist strolled across the bar and said to Schneider, 'Goodnight, Jew. You are a Jew, aren't you?' The three actors tried not to let their tempers get the better of them but, as Ralph says, 'The incident shook us all and gave our work an added sense of immediacy.'

Before the film's release, many people thought Fiennes, with his angular, classical good looks, was a left-field choice to play Goeth. But despite his real-life diffidence, and what one pundit called 'the slightly distracted, angst-ridden air of an existentialist poet', his performance was set to mesmerize cinema audiences.

The film opened in America in December 1993. President Clinton led the accolades and virtually every critic followed suit. The *New York Times* declared, 'Spielberg has made sure the Holocaust will never be thought of in the same way again.' The *Los Angeles Times* said, 'Never before has Spielberg come close to this kind of film-making.' And *Newsday* hailed it 'as a masterpiece by any standard'. While 'the extraordinary Fiennes', as *Variety* labelled him, was praised for creating 'an indelible character in Goeth, like a minor-league Roman emperor gone sour with excess.'

One of the creepiest aspects of the film was that despite the intense and extreme brutality inherent in his character, many women found Fiennes strangely sexy in the part. 'It was his eyes that did it,' said one lovestruck woman after a screening of the film, in a not untypical female response. 'They just bore right into me. I can't quite explain it but I thought there was something frighteningly sexy about Ralph Fiennes's Goeth.'

Women were also attracted by his character's unpredictability, power and, unbelievably, in some cases they were hugely impressed by the sheer volume of his girth. It was a strange phenomenon that revealed more about the human psyche than was perhaps desirable. But didn't Sylvia Plath (whether or not, at the time, overwhelmed by an emotional breakdown) write that every woman loves a fascist?

There were those who voiced their unhappiness with the film. The

Village Voice claimed *Schindler's List* presented the transportation of the Jews as 'a transport of under-privileged waifs on a special trip to Disneyland'. And the *New York Post* accused Spielberg of making the Jews 'bit players in their own tragedy'. While Oskar Schindler's widow, Emilie, insisted the real Goeth was an Ivan the Terrible-type figure, rather than the complex, recognizably human fiend – who, in true Devil-like fashion, got to say many of the film's best lines – of Ralph's characterization.

The following February, the film was released in Britain. Spielberg, Neesom and Fiennes, accompanied by Alex, all attended the opening night première at the Empire in Leicester Square, London. Among the celebrities present was the writer Salman Rushdie. As in America, the film was greeted by near-universal acclaim with *The Times* – among other papers – hailing *Schindler's List* as 'truly one of the greats in cinema history'.

The media also singled out Fiennes for extensive praise. One broadsheet spoke of the 'revoltingly mesmeric charisma' with which Ralph played the part of Goeth, thus making the German 'the film's most indelible presence'. While *GQ* described his character portrayal as one which 'moved Fiennes into the edge of a realm where sagacious complexity meets instinct and becomes known as genius'.

The film was nominated for a string of Oscars and, as expected, Fiennes was nominated for the Best Supporting Actor award. Among those who thought the nomination well deserved was Spielberg, who predicted: 'If he picks the right roles and doesn't forget the theatre, I think he can eventually be another Alec Guinness or Laurence Olivier.'

As the day of the Academy Awards ceremony dawned, the smart money was on *Schindler's List*. 'After all, how could Hollywood ignore such an important film?' asked one movie industry insider.

Despite his best efforts, Ralph – whom Barbara Streisand asked to be seated next to at the pre-Oscars dinner – discovered that it was impossible not to be swept up by 'award fever'. 'I found myself getting expectant amidst the whirlwind of chatter,' he admits. 'All the papers run articles, people were telling me they had put money on me – and you catch yourself taking it quite seriously.'

The movie duly swept the Oscars in March 1994. As well as

winning the Best Picture and Best Director awards, it won gongs for its screenplay, cinematography, art direction, editing and score. After years of being snubbed by the Academy Award judges, Spielberg finally achieved the recognition he deserved. And, on the crest of the wave engendered by its Oscar success, *Schindler's List* went on to gross more than $90 million in America and nearly £15 million in the United Kingdom. Its worldwide gross would eventually exceed $300 million.

Despite sharing in Spielberg's triumph, Fiennes must have felt a tinge of disappointment for, on the big night, his own potential 'greatest moment' was instead awarded to Tommy Lee Jones for his role as a tough police chief in *The Fugitive*. Now Jones is a fine actor, and *The Fugitive* was among the best big-budget thrillers to come out of Hollywood for a long time. But most critics felt his performance paled besides Ralph's Amon Goeth.

However, Fiennes was philosophical about the result, only too aware of the behind-the-scenes wheeling and dealing that played so big a part in deciding the eventual winners.

He was also comforted by Liam Neeson, who in some ways looked upon Ralph, ten years his junior, as a younger brother. Says the Irishman: 'I told him, "I'm thrilled you got nominated, and I think it's wonderful you didn't win – because if you did, you'd end up wearing Goeth around your neck like an albatross. Tommy Lee Jones won and rightly so, because it wasn't just for *The Fugitive*. It was for years of hacking away at his craft. You've arrived, you've been acknowledged, you don't need a statuette." '

But Ralph did win the New York Critics' Circle and National Society of Film Critics' Best Supporting Actor awards as well as a Golden Globe nomination. He also picked up the Best Supporting Actor prize at the BAFTA (British Oscar) Awards in April 1994 – tearfully dedicating it to his late mother, Jini, who, while not living to see the world acclaim her son, was taken in a wheelchair to see a private screening of the film two weeks before her death, the cancer by now in her lungs.

'I'd like to remember my mother for this role because of her compassion,' said Ralph emotionally, after hugging Spielberg who was also at the star-studded London ceremony. 'She was more a friend than a mother. No one could have had a better mother.'

Even though Jini was no longer with Ralph and the rest of the family in body, they were convinced she was close to them in spirit. 'She is still around,' said Mark Fiennes. 'I've felt her sitting next to me on a flight to Los Angeles.' They were convinced Jini was there listening to Ralph on the night of the BAFTA Awards too.

CHAPTER THIRTEEN
A Different Kind of Villain

Within weeks of finishing work on *Schindler's List*, Fiennes was off to America to start work on the Robert Redford-directed *Quiz Show*. He would again play a villain, but a very different one, in this film about a real-life scandal that erupted when a former contestant claimed that one of America's most popular quiz shows was rigged.

The year was 1958, and the US was in the grip of a television quiz show phenomenon – with more than three dozen airings every week – holding out the promise of vast wealth for the winning contestants. 'To a post-war generation mesmerized by the promise of upward mobility and endless riches, quiz shows were an extension of the American dream,' says Redford.

Rivalling *I Love Lucy* at its peak, *Twenty-One* was a prime-time general knowledge show, watched by millions. Every Wednesday night the streets would empty as people gathered around their black and white television sets as two contestants attempted to answer questions of escalating difficulty. The first to reach '21' won.

The loser was never seen again but the masterminds who won week in, week out, became national celebrities. The greatest mastermind of them all was academic Charles Van Doren who kept his title for a record-breaking fifteen weeks.

The Columbia University lecturer, with 'a Greek God aristocratic brain', was a product of one of the country's most renowned literary families and became an American folk hero. In the words of

121

Redford, Van Doren became 'the academic world's answer to Elvis Presley' and with each victory became more celebrated until he eventually graced the covers of *Time* and *Life* magazines.

His $130,000 prize money acquired during his 'winning' streak was powerfully attractive to a lecturer earning just $86 a week. Week after week, he seemingly drew from his vast knowledge to give the correct answer to obscure questions. Little did his viewers realize they were being duped.

When disgruntled contestant Herbie Stempel claimed the game was a fraud, Congressional investigator Richard Goodwin winkled out the true, scurrilous facts, sending shockwaves through Eisenhower's America.

In reality, quiz show cheating has a long history. The very first of the big-time quiz shows, *The $64,000 Question*, which became an instant hit when first aired in 1955, supplied the required answers to selected contestants. The success of the show prompted a flood of imitators, including the popular *Twenty-One*, which first aired in September 1956. But it was not an overnight success. 'The show's première was a dismal failure,' admits co-creator Dan Enright. 'It was just plain dull.'

Worried sponsors told Enright to do 'whatever was necessary to turn it into a success'. Contestants were (accordingly) fed the questions and answers beforehand and coached to sweat and stammer for the camera as they 'searched' for the answers. Having pumped up the drama, *Twenty-One* went on to become a huge ratings success.

Rigging a television game show would cause few ripples in today's America after the exigencies of Vietnam and Watergate. But the story held a particular attraction for Redford, the golden-boy of American cinema and the star of films like *Butch Cassidy and the Sundance Kid* and *All the President's Men*, and director of the Oscar-winning *Ordinary People*. For not only did he grow up at a time when quiz shows were king but was himself a contestant – on a show called *Play Your Hunch*.

'It really marked the end of a period of innocence in our social history,' says Redford who, like Fiennes, studied art before becoming an actor. 'No longer did people believe that what you saw on television was the truth.'

✻

The casting presented Redford with a unique challenge – for all three leading actors in the drama would be portraying individuals who were still living.

The talented John Turturro was cast as Herbie 'The Unstumpable' Stempel – 'the abrasive, annoying, Jewish guy with the bad teeth and sidewall haircut' – whose six-week reign as quiz show king was brought to an abrupt end when the producers dumped him in favour of the telegenic Van Doren. And *Northern Exposure* star Rob Morrow was cast as Richard Goodwin, the ambitious Harvard Law School graduate and Washington DC attorney, a man eager to make a name for himself as a champion of truth and justice.

Redford was less successful in his search for his Van Doren. After auditioning thirty actors he had almost given up. 'I had a picture in my head of the character – he had to have a natural grace and charm – to the manor born,' says Redford. 'The shell had to be almost perfect but, at the core, something was not right. I was looking for the character weakness in Charles, to be found somewhere in the eyes, the face. A confident, smiling, articulate fellow, but with something haunted underneath, something in trouble. I couldn't find all those elements together.'

He didn't want to go abroad to cast this American hero-turned-villain, but *Quiz Show* was already in pre-production and he still hadn't cast the film's pivotal character. He began to panic.

Like Spielberg, he had seen Fiennes in *Lawrence After Arabia: A Dangerous Man* and been impressed by his performance. Despite the scepticism of some of the film's money-men, Redford began to wonder if the little-known English actor could be the man to play Van Doren. He certainly had the requisite aristocratic looks – not surprisingly given his patrician ancestry.

Fiennes was then shooting *Schindler's List* in Poland but after taking a call from Redford, agreed to fly to New York one weekend to meet the director. It was the first time he had set foot in the States. He arrived considerably plumper than usual, having gained nearly two stone to play Amon Goeth, and says, 'I didn't feel remotely like a clean-cut American intellectual. I was carrying an extra twenty-five pounds and had a very aggressive, short hair cut.'

Redford comments that 'everything was going against him', except the thing that mattered most – possessing the charismatic qualities integral to the part of Van Doren. 'I just felt Ralph had this wonderfully interesting interior – this dark, haunted quality beneath a perfect shell – and that is exactly what I wanted for Van Doren,' he says. 'Ralph's eyes were what interested me most. I felt they would carry the message I was looking for, for the whole character.'

The actor himself has a different recollection of the events which led him to the coveted role. 'I read for the part before *Schindler's List* opened in New York, then I heard it was being offered to someone else,' he says. 'The moment word on *Schindler's List* came out, over three weeks later, I get this fulsome letter from the director offering me the role. It made me feel slightly cynical. Usually, if you read for something and the director is interested in you, you hear in a few days.'

That was how the show business world operated, as he was fast discovering. 'Hollywood is a tough town where success is all that counts,' observes one industry veteran. 'There is no time for professional modesty or outdated civilities.'

But Fiennes had already shown he was learning to play the game – and was ruthless enough to succeed – by firing his original US agent, Clifford Stevens, and signing up with the all-powerful Creative Artists Agency. His former agent, Stevens, saw the move as a betrayal and said, 'I hope he gets everything he deserves.'

Sources close to the actor, though, insist he landed the plum roles of Goeth and Van Doren without Stevens's help. And Ralph says, 'Clifford began to represent me through a connection with my British agent. I never actively sought his representation. I accept that the way I handled leaving him was inept and hurtful – due to my being anxious, inexperienced and nervous – and I regret the way I left him. But I don't regret the decision.'

Whatever the behind the scenes chicanery, Fiennes eagerly accepted Redford's invitation to play Van Doren – a role that could potentially establish him as a romantic Hollywood leading man.

His wife Alex – who was still soft-pedalling in her career, though she had played a lawyer in the hit television drama *Crocodile Shoes* – was delighted at her husband's good fortune. And she was convinced that their relationship was strong enough to survive another enforced separation so soon after *Schindler's List*.

'We've had a fantastic grounding,' she said. 'For our first five years together after RADA, we were both jobbing actors, and it's that which enables us to keep going even though we're separated by the Atlantic.'

Those of a superstitious cast of mind would have winced to hear her apparently tempting fate in this way – did Alex, in her heart, have an inkling of the problems to come?

It was a humid afternoon. Charles Van Doren was reading a book on the verandah of his home in the charming village of Cornwall, Connecticut. A car pulled to a stop outside, and a young man got out and walked over.

'I seem to be lost,' he said in a refined English accent. 'I was wondering if you could kindly point me in the direction of New York.'

With great courtesy, Van Doren re-directed him. The stranger thanked him, and the two men went their separate ways.

The encounter lasted less than five minutes but the Englishman had noted his Ivy League accent, his body language, the graceful way he moved – and his air of sadness.

Unlike Turturro and Morrow, who got to have lengthy meetings with the characters they were playing, Fiennes was denied such an opportunity – in fact the reclusive Van Doren had declined every interview request since the quiz show scandal of 1959.

So he studied kinescopes of Van Doren's numerous appearances on *Twenty One*. 'What I observed from watching the old shows,' says Fiennes, 'was that Charlie was a very gifted actor. He had a quality of being slightly different yet charming, and adapted to the pretence of not knowing the answers, and then finding them by thinking aloud.'

He also met friends of the élite family, noting how they dressed, spoke and behaved. 'Initially, they just seemed very American to me, but the more Americans I met the more I realized the peculiar cultural and class differences of these WASPy people,' he says. 'I liked their old-world East Coast courtesy. They behaved in a gentlemanly, unaffacted way and there was no self-conscious image projection going on with them. They may have been conservative in their dress and attitude to life, but they seemed trusting and open.'

But perfectionist that Ralph was, he was desperate to meet Van Doren himself. Hence the trip to Connecticut. 'I just wanted to hear what he sounded like,' says Fiennes who, while not regretting the deception, adds: 'I felt guilty for disturbing his solitude. I know what it's like to have people interfering and coming up to talk to you when you just want to be left alone.'

Few actors apart from Fiennes can have faced the challenge of achieving such a startling transition in character in so short a space of time.

Firstly, he had to spend three weeks shedding the two stone he had gained for *Schindler's List*. 'I was frantic,' admits Ralph. 'The studio hired a personal trainer who helped me lost twenty pounds and I was put on a strict diet. The trouble was, that took a toll of my stamina and made it all the harder to get into Van Doren's head.'

Secondly, he had to perfect an Ivy League accent having spent a mere weekend in the States and played an American just once before – in the RSC production of *The Man Who Came To Dinner*. 'The danger was in trying to do a contemporary twangy American,' he says. 'It takes time for an English person to learn the subtleties and nuances of American dialects.'

His co-star, Turturro, admits: 'It was hard for him. He hadn't really had enough time to prepare the accent – and he was quite nervous when he arrived. He gained confidence as he went along, but he was in a very vulnerable situation, in part because of the newness of New York. He was in a daze, basically.'

Redford wasn't troubled by Ralph's jitters. If anything, it pleased him. 'I guess I thought we could use some of that in the character,' he says. 'Because Charles had a slight ungainliness about him, which had to be mixed with a shrewd, smart, slippery quality that I knew would come in time. I knew Ralph's seriousness would lead him to the right place.'

But in a few weeks Fiennes gained confidence – so much so that screenwriter Paul Attanasio was too intimidated about making suggestions under the actor's intimidating gaze. 'When Ralph fixes you with those eyes,' says Attanasio with a chuckle, 'he's so intense you just don't feel up to it.'

Shooting on *Quiz Show* began in Manhattan in late May 1993. A former discotheque was turned into a 1950s-style NBC studio; scenes were shot in the lobby of the Roosevelt Hotel; streets were blocked off to recreate the simpler New York of the past; and a beautiful country home in Ossining, in upstate New York, doubled up as the Van Doren family home.

Despite his relatively low American profile, whenever Fiennes appeared on the street to film a scene, female admirers would appear, according to his co-stars. 'Women went for him in droves,' says Christopher McDonald, who played *Twenty-One* host Jack Barry. 'He was a chick magnet. I've never seen anything quite like it. He has an aura. Women are just drawn to him.'

The film opened with people rushing home to catch the show, which was being broadcast 'from New York to Los Angeles and Seattle to St Petersburg'. Among those watching was Ralph – looking every inch the blue-blooded, Ivy League academic Van Doren.

'Ever watched one of these quiz shows, like the *$64,000 Question* or *Twenty-One*?' he asks his father Mark, played by British actor Paul Scofield – a 1966 Oscar-winner for his performance as Sir Thomas More in the screen version of Robert Bolt's *A Man For All Seasons*, and a long-time hero of Ralph's.

Soon afterwards, Van Doren tries out for another NBC quiz show. As soon as *Twenty-One*'s producers realise he is a Van Doren, they anoint him successor in waiting to Stempel – flattering him into believing that he is the 'intellectual Joe di Maggio' they are looking for. There's one catch – the pair want to give him the questions to the answers.

'I don't follow,' says Ralph's character, puzzled.

'You wanna win, don't you?' asks the first producer.

'I'd really rather win honestly,' says Van Doren.

'What's dishonesty?' asks the second. 'When Gregory Peck parachutes behind enemy lines, do you think it's really him?'

The first director pipes up, disingenuously arguing: 'It's like we would be giving you the answers just because we know you know.'

While his partner in persuasion tries the high-minded approach, asking, 'Just think what you being on the show could do for the cause of education.'

Van Doren naïvely thinks their inducements are part of the 'examination test' for scanning new contestants – an impression the producers encourage – and the following week he turns up at the studio to challenge Stempel. Little does he know that Stempel – superbly played by Turturro – has been told to answer a question wrongly. Von Doren goes on to win the contest and the $20,000 prize money. Only later is it revealed that Ralph's character has been secretly fed the winning answer.

Within weeks, Van Doren is a hero to his students and to all America. During a television interview he reveals, with his apparent New England modesty, that when his stint on *Twenty-One* ends he plans to finish the book he's writing on President Lincoln.

'How do you think Honest Abe would do on a quiz show?' the interviewer asks, innocently enough.

'Why,' stammers Ralph's character, momentarily shamed, 'I think he would do very well.'

But the storm clouds are gathering. Investigator Richard Goodwin has launched a probe into scandalous allegations of quiz show rigging and wants to question Van Doren. The two have similar Ivy League backgrounds and, in a bid to win him over, the academic invites him to meet his parents at their beautiful country home with its enormous garden that is reminiscent of the Suffolk garden of Ralph's childhood.

A battle of wits ensues in which Goodwin puts ever-mounting pressure on Van Doren. And during the recording of the next quiz show, the worried academic gives a wrong answer in a forlorn attempt to escape the net closing in around him. But it's too late.

He is duly called to give evidence at the Congressional hearing into quiz show rigging. In a touching scene beforehand he tells his father of his nervousness at appearing before such an august body.

'Just tell the truth,' says Mark Van Doren reassuringly. 'You'll do fine.'

'Dad,' says Ralph's character slowly. 'I can't simply tell the truth.'

'They gave you all that money to answer questions you already knew?' asks Van Doren Sr incredulously, as the horror of the situation slowly dawns upon him. 'Oh my God, Charlie …'

The film culminates in Van Doren's riveting speech to the Congressional committee, resonating with the anguish Ralph's character so clearly feels at his public fall from grace:

'I would give almost anything I have to reverse the course of my life in the last year. The past doesn't change for anyone. But at least I can learn from the past. I've learned a lot about life. I've learned a lot about myself, and about the responsibilities any man has to his fellow men. I've learned a lot about good and evil – they're not always what they appear to be. I was involved, deeply involved, in a deception. I have deceived my friends, and I had millions of them. In a sense, I was like the child who refuses to admit a fact in the hope that it will go away. Of course, it did not go away. I was scared, scared to death. I had no solid position, no basis to stand on for myself. There was one way out, and that was simply to tell the truth. It may sound trite to you, but I found myself again after a number of years. I've been acting a role for years, maybe all my life, of thinking I've done more, accomplished more, produced more than I have. I've had all the breaks. I've stood on the shoulders of life, and I've never gotten down in the dirt to build, to erect a foundation of my own. I've flown too high on borrowed wings. Everything came too easily. That is why I am here today.'

"I can't decide if you think too much of me, or too little."

Fiennes gave a sympathetic, keenly observed portrayal of a diffident but charismatic man, who took a surprisingly childlike pleasure in his new-found fame and whose anguish at his disgrace was ultimately rooted in a terror of finding himself mediocre.

'In preparing for the part I understood the ease with which one can go down a path of behaviour that is morally wrong,' says Fiennes. 'He's seduced by the attention, the celebrity and by the producers themselves. I thought he was a rather tragic figure and suffered more than necessary. Whatever his intellectual gifts, he shared a perfectly normal desire for recognition, achievement and, to some degree, money – and in this lay the seeds of his downfall.'

What a downfall it was. Following the scandal, the illustrious Van Doren family was frozen out of polite society. Charles lost his teaching job at Columbia, narrowly escaped going to prison and spent the rest of his working life writing for the *Encyclopaedia Britannica*. And what was all this in aid of? Fifteen weeks of fame.

Promotion of the film focused on its fledgling English star; massive billboards sprang up along Sunset Boulevard showing Fiennes in a quiz show isolation booth, head tilted forward in concentration, listening to a question. For even though both Turturro and Morrow were better known in America at the time, Ralph's character was the linchpin of the story. For all intents and purposes, it was his first lead role in a Hollywood film.

To publicize its US release, Fiennes embarked on the lengthy round of newspaper, magazine and television interviews that is the lot of today's movie star.

By now, Hollywood's publicity machine was creating 'a palpable whirr around him', as one writer observed, and he was about as hot as it was possible to get in Tinseltown – but was also having to learn to live with the hype that comes with being the Next Big Thing.

Fawning profiles appeared in glossy American magazines such as *GQ* and *Vanity Fair* which proclaimed in a story headlined 'King Ralph' that 'Ralph Fiennes is the biggest movie star you've never heard of.' He was acclaimed as one of the year's 'Fifty Most Beautiful People' by *People* magazine, enthusiastic female journalists sang paeans of praise to his 'fine bones, tapered nose, delicate, almost perfectly-shaped nostrils, long curly eyelashes and piercing eyes' and he was tipped as 'the new Daniel Day-Lewis'.

However, the comparison with Day-Lewis clearly rankled. 'Comparisons are odious,' snapped Fiennes. 'Each actor is what he is. I'm not the next anyone. I'm just myself.'

His unusual name also occasioned some confusion – as had Sean Connery's in the old days. Interviewers found it hard enough to grapple with Ralph's Christian name, let alone his surname – the result being that he was called everything from Fiends to Feenies while *Time* magazine mistakenly informed its readers that the name was Welsh. (The US media also showed a poor grasp of British geography – with one newspaper claiming that he 'hailed from Sussex, a county north of London'.)

'People think you're being wilfully perverse or affected if you point out that it's a perfectly legitimate Old English pronunciation,' said an irritated Fiennes. 'As I'm learning, we are two countries divided by a common language. But I'm so sick of the fucking pronunciation thing. I hate it being made an issue of.'

In a bid to set the record straight once and for all, the promotional pack accompanying the release of *Quiz Show* went to the unusual length of stating that his name was 'pronounced Rafe Fiennes'. Such episodes only served to fuel claims that the actor took himself a mite too seriously. Did he even need to stress that Rafe was the 'Old English pronunciation'?

Ralph's portrayal of a character who had been seduced by the glamour of fame guaranteed that journalists would seek to find out what Ralph's motivation was in becoming an actor. Was he, like Van Doren, driven by a desire for fame and fortune?

'I hope I'm the kind of actor who wants to be – and will be – a good actor,' he said, shuddering at the comparison and attempting to explain that he was not interested in the rest of the package. 'If any sort of so-called celebrity is starting to attach itself to me, it's not something I'm really interested in or want to be concerned with. I recognize that it's something that goes with the job and I try to do it as efficiently as I can; then I want to get on with doing my work.'

But he was already, at this early stage in his screen career, tired of journalists asking him the same repetitive questions, be it on the West Coast, East Coast, Midwest or Deep South. 'His posture, along with his bored demeanour, sums up his attitude to the media: "Let's get it over with",' observed a *San Francisco Chronicle* interviewer. 'But he'd better get used to it. This is just the beginning.'

The film was acclaimed by *Première* for its 'superior intelligence, surgical precision and witty elegance', the magazine praising Fiennes for creating 'startlingly effective moments'. The *Los Angeles Times* wrote: 'It's Ralph Fiennes's poignant, ravaged portrait that provides *Quiz Show* with its centre of gravity. His ability to project pain behind a well-mannered façade is devastating.' And the *New Yorker* commented: 'No wonder Redford scrutinizes Van Doren from the side in half-face shots – for Fiennes is like a silent-movie star in his ability to carry a close-up, to let his eyes and composure do the work for him.'

The US reviewers were critical only about his accent – with *Première* noting that 'his American accent wavers throughout' and *GQ* concluding, 'he delivers on all counts – except, possibly, the accent.' (To cruder British ears, it sounded more convincing, faltering only occasionally.)

The movie performed respectably, if not spectacularly, in America – grossing a rather disappointing $25 million following its September 1994 release. In Britain, it garnered equally glowing reviews, with newspapers praising Fiennes for 'catching perfectly the slippery glamour of Van Doren'. It opened in London's West End in February 1995, before being released nationally – but grossed a meagre £1.5 million despite favourable write-ups and word of mouth recommendations.

Sadly, intelligent films such as *Quiz Show* were facing an increasingly rough ride in a market dominated by big-budget – and essentially mindless – Hollywood event movies. But the cast and crew could take pride in the fact that it bagged a cluster of honours – an Oscar nomination for Best Film, an Oscar for Best Supporting Actor for Paul Scofield, four Golden Globe nominations, and the New York film critics' Best Picture award. It also consolidated Ralph's reputation in Hollywood. As Turturro says: 'It was real confirmation that what he did in *Schindler's List* was no fluke.'

CHAPTER FOURTEEN

From Hollywood To Hackney

Once Ralph had become a movie star, the Royal Shakespeare Company's Adrian Noble predicted that he was unlikely to return to the stage, saying: 'As soon as you become what he's become, it's difficult to do the long theatre stint.'

It was fair comment – but, as it happened, miles wide of the mark. The last thing Fiennes was planning to do was turn his back on the theatre. And having achieved honour playing a string of tormented souls on the big screen, he returned to the London stage to play that most tormented of souls, *Hamlet*.

With two big budget Hollywood films under his belt, he could have easily taken *Hamlet* to the West End. Finding a venue would not have been difficult. Instead, he opted for the riskier, more adventurous option of staging the play at the 'off-off West End' Hackney Empire in London's East End, about as far as it was possible to get from the bright lights and glamour of the capital's theatreland.

Some people found mirth in the very idea of staging *Hamlet* in Hackney, the third poorest borough in London, with one of the highest unemployment rates in the capital and an unpleasant reputation as a run-down, no-go area. Abandoned rubbish swirled underfoot and some shop fronts looked as if they hadn't seen a lick of paint, let alone a customer, in years.

'Talk about staging high art in a lowly area!' scoffed one critic. 'Will the Prince of Denmark get touched for a few spare kroner by a spiky-haired youth with a dog on a string? Will he dare park his car around the back of the theatre? If he does, the chances are he'll never see it again!'

The Hackney Empire itself stands on the site of the first theatre in London, long since torn down. (It was built in Hackney, then a village, because the sixteenth century Tudor monarchy had prohibited theatres in the city proper for fear of corrupting public morals.)

The beautiful Frank Matcham-designed building – seating 1,000 people – now occupying the site dates back to 1901. Soon becoming the East End's premier music hall, it played host to Flamenco dancing, fire-eating and opera during the first decades of the century and later witnessed performances by legendary comedians such as Charlie Chaplin, W.C. Fields and Dan Leno.

But with the advent of cinema, and then television, the Empire went into a long decline – eventually suffering the ultimate indignity of being turned into a bingo hall. In 1985 the domed building's very existence looked threatened until an unlikely alliance of artists, actors and local residents launched a campaign to save it from destruction.

The sumptuous red and gold interior, with its gothic-style wall masks, and cherubs smiling mischievously down on the audience, has since been restored to its former glory, though in recent years it has been more likely to echo to the *risqué* gags of 'in-yer-face' alternative comedians than to Shakespeare's poetic verse.

The £250,000 *Hamlet* production was the brainchild of the Almeida Theatre's Jonathan Kent who first discussed the project with Ralph's agent eighteen months earlier, and the actor was quick to accept the challenge. There were those who wondered why a British actor, on the verge of becoming a major movie star, would jeopardize it all to return to the stage. But they conveniently ignored the fact that, in addition to all his screen successes, Fiennes remained a card-carrying member of the RADA-Royal Shakespeare Company alumni.

His mother, Jini, had first introduced him to *Hamlet* when he was 8 years old and, finding him enthralled, presented him with a long-playing record of Olivier's version of the play. 'I remember being fascinated by it,' says Ralph, 'my mind even then trying to embrace the idea of parental betrayal. As in any story you're told, there's a point at which you identify with one of the protagonists. One tries to imagine: what would it be like if I were that person?' The part subsequently 'became encoded in his relationship with his mother,' adds Kent.

Furthermore, at 32, Fiennes felt the time had come to play Hamlet, saying, 'If I'd played it when I was, say, 23 or 24, I don't think I would have played it the same way.' But as one observer pointed out, 'Playing Hamlet for a worthy but impoverished theatre lent a certain *gravitas* to an actor without undermining his earning power in the movies.'

It was felt the Hackney Empire – where the shades of the past always seemed to be present – would be a more suitable venue for such a big budget version of the play than the cramped, stucco-peeling Almeida Theatre in Islington. However, all the profits would go to the Almeida. The Empire also enjoyed the advantage of being far away from the West End sharkpit.

Preparations for the production began in earnest in October 1993, and by the end of the year the exquisite Francesca Annis had been cast as Hamlet's mother Gertrude – 'something guaranteed to make the play even more Freudian than usual,' noted one critic. Tara Fitzgerald would be the tragic Ophelia and Peter Eyre Polonius.

The classic revenge tragedy, probably the best-known play in the English language, was first performed in 1600 – with Shakespeare himself playing the ghost of Hamlet's father, according to tradition.

Playing the Danish prince, Max Beerbohm once said, was 'the hoop through which every eminent actor must jump'. It was 'the big one' as Olivier said when he undertook it in 1937 – a sort of graduation role for the cream of promising English actors.

Clocking in at 1,530 lines, Hamlet was the most vocally and physically demanding of Shakespearian roles – one that had proved too much for many a fine actor – including Nicol Williamson who threw down his sword and walked off the Round House stage in 1969, and Day-Lewis, who fled the stage midway through a performance at the National twenty years later, suffering from nervous exhaustion and, some said, having seen his own father in the ghost of the old king.

Having lived with Hamlet in his head for so long, Fiennes had no doubt how he would approach the part. 'I've always been drawn to the distress of Hamlet,' said Ralph, during a break in rehearsals which took place at St George's Church Theatre in London. 'I'm much clearer now about the struggle he has with himself about not being able to kill Claudius. I'm much clearer about his rage and his frustration with himself.

'The conflict in Hamlet is between what's expected of him as a prince, a man of action – a leader who should take good, pure, strong action for the good of the state – and the most simple human confusions, pieties, frustrations and angers, which are rooted in the child in him. His path to action begins to take shape when the travelling players arrive at Elsinore. They come on, he listens to them, addresses the audience and admits that he's been unable to take action. But he takes a step forward; he will use the players; they become, in effect, a foothold for him in trying to clarify the situation.'

Fiennes knew he would be compared with stage greats like Olivier and Gielgud who had long ago stepped into the troubled prince's shoes, but he deflected questions about them by declaring that he wanted to clear away the mythology about the play 'and do it as if it were a new play that had never been performed before'. When asked if the reason charismatic actors like himself and Olivier had been attracted to the part was Hamlet's movie-star charisma, he scoffed, 'Hamlet doesn't think he's a star.'

He also knew he would be competing with other recent Hamlets by Mark Rylance, Daniel Day-Lewis, Alan Cumming, Jonathan Pryce, Kenneth Branagh and Stephen Dillane. Peter Hall's well-received Dillane *Hamlet* finished its successful West End run just ten days before Fiennes's opened.

But Ralph argued: 'Hamlet is who he is, and whoever the actor is who's playing him. The extraordinary genius of the role is that it can mutate in so many different directions. Daniel Day-Lewis's Hamlet was charismatic and striking-looking, while Alan Cumming's was awkward, adolescent and funny. The Hamlets I've liked have been played by the actors who are true to themselves.'

The pressure on the cast mounted as the production's very own D-Day approached but Kent was confident everything was falling into place. He also found working with Fiennes a revelation, saying, 'The great thing about Ralph is that he's got phenomenal classical technique. He can speak in heightened verse as if that were the only way he *could* express himself. He also has astonishing breath control.'

Unusually for a show of this scale, its star decreed that he would give no interviews beforehand. This wasn't a total surprise to journalists. As one said: 'This is a man who would rather go to the dentist than be locked in a room with a journalist.' However, publicizing the starry Almeida production was the least of the Hackney Empire's problems. Such was the hype that one wit joked: 'Anyone would think it was a new Andrew Lloyd Webber musical.'

Tickets, which cost up to £17.50, were expensive by Hackney Empire standards but the five-week run still sold out within days. Women rang the box office in despair, declaring, 'I don't care where I sit as long as I can see Mr Fiennes.' Teenage girls usually more interested in the latest pop pin-ups than in the works of the Bard snapped up tickets and 250 tickets given away by *Time Out* in a special offer went in just forty-five minutes. 'We've never known anything like it,' said one ticket-agency booker. Fiennes also offered a couple of free tickets to Charles Van Doren, perhaps out of a sense of guilt over his little deception. But the offer was declined.

The production certainly put humble Hackney on the map, and the Automobile Association even took the precaution of erecting signposts to help Shakespeare fans venturing into the urban jungle of the East End for the first time. 'It's the new centre of the theatrical universe,' joked Fiennes. And as the first night – March 1 – approached, the press was full of talk of 'Hollywood coming to Hackney'.

'How was Ralph going to arrive,' speculated one newspaper. 'Wearing shades, perhaps? Weaving his way through Hackney's narrow streets in a stretch limousine past the municipal toilets to the stage door?'

It was a strange opening night. The weather was wild and stormy to a Gothic degree. Limousines queued up to file into what the AA signs referred to as the 'Hamlet Car Park'. And a crowd of – largely female – fans stood expectantly outside the theatre. 'God, he's so handsome,' cooed one slip of a girl, as Fiennes jumped out of a limousine and made a bee-line for the stage door.

The great and the good duly descended on the Empire – the Hollywood contingent, led by Demi Moore, arrived late in a chauffeur-driven Daimler but still ended up with a seat in the front row of the theatre's ornate dress circle.

Big-time Tinseltown agents were also much in evidence. One was heard asking at his plush West End hotel whether he could land a helicopter on the theatre's roof. It was politely explained that this wasn't a wise idea unless he planned on crashing through the roof and joining Mr Fiennes on stage. 'You gotta point,' the American replied, chomping on his cigar.

The *crème de la crème* of the British showbusiness establishment also turned out for the occasion. Those present included Emma Thompson, who sneaked in through a side entrance, Ralph's *Schindler's List* co-star Ben Kingsley, former *Avengers* star Diana Rigg, Zoe Wanamaker, David Hare and the National Theatre's Richard Eyre. 'It was wonderful to see so many stars in Hackney,' said Ralph's wife, Alex. 'I never expected to see police controlling the crowds. I couldn't believe all the fuss.'

A palpable air of anticipation filled the auditorium as people took their seats. Meanwhile, in his dressing room, Ralph took a last look at his mother's photograph, which he had pinned to the wall. The final bell rang, then the curtain went up on the starkly designed set.

Ralph's Hamlet took to the stage – his lank hair hanging down to his shoulders and his eyes blazing with even more intensity than usual – and there was a collective quickening of the crowd's pulse. He launched into his first great set speech ('O, that this too too solid flesh would melt ...') with dizzying speed.

This set the tone for the tremendous pace of the production as a whole, with one soliloquy after another delivered as if in a race against time. 'At times it seems like turning into a "highlights from Hamlet",' sniped one critic. There was speculation as to whether Ralph's 'To be or not to be' speech was the fastest on record.

His passionate bedroom scene with Gertrude raged with Oedipal intensity. Fiennes violently shoving Annis's face into the mattress and miming sex with her. 'She seems unnaturally fond of her son, caressing and kissing him with a warmth that would make Freud straighten up and polish his glasses,' said one critic.

Ophelia, the one person who needed to be kissed, got short shrift. Ralph's prince casually flipping up her skirt and grabbing her by the crotch before directing her to a nunnery.

Only the previous year, the actor Jeremy Brett had acknowledged in a BBC documentary, *Playing The Dane*, that the 'incestuous bed' was at the heart of his Hamlet because his mother had only recently been killed in a car crash. 'That is true for me, too,' Fiennes later revealed. 'It is about those primal blood relationships. They are the one thing Hamlet's reasoning cannot handle. Not only is his father dead but his mother has been fucking Claudius and that infuriates him beyond reason.

'It is, in that sense, personal to me. I was very influenced by my mother, especially in the area of art and literature and I know she would have loved to see me play Hamlet. I sort of feel she will in a way. Losing a parent has a big effect on your life. Your sense of self is completely redefined and you re-evaluate your own mortality and the child in you. All those things come into relief.'

Elsinore was represented by an eerie series of dark, drafty chambers, sparingly illuminated by shafts of piercing, chilly light – made even more sinister by the mysterious rumblings heard from behind the set caused by the Empire's tin roof flapping in the gale force winds.

The production sought not to update, reinterpret or discover explosive new contemporary meanings in the text but simply to deliver a hard-hitting, tighten-the-nuts, get-its-hands-dirty *Hamlet*. A Hamlet who smote his own forehead with his fist during his great rant against Claudius – 'Remorseless, treacherous, lecherous, kindless villain!' – and who smeared dirt from Yorick's grave on his cheek during the last act. A grunge Hamlet for the grunge generation.

As the play hurtled onwards and the prince degenerated into madness, Ralph grew shabbier, his unbuttoned shirt exposed more of his chest and his swirling mane sprayed rock-star sweat over his front-row female admirers, who appeared impervious.

Three hours after the curtain had risen, Demi Moore led the standing ovation, the crowd cheering as Fiennes and his fellow actors took their bows. 'It was spectacular, it was breathtaking and very moving,' said the *Indecent Proposal* star, who had never seen *Hamlet* before, and was reportedly only in London to see her 'friend' Ralph's performance. Other celebrities in the audience were equally enthusiastic. 'It was fantastic,' said Ben Elton. 'If it doesn't get the rave reviews it deserves, there's no justice.' While Antonia

Fraser declared that he was 'the very embodiment' of 'her *Hamlet*'.

Afterwards Moore fought her way through the crowds to Ralph's dressing room and as Fiennes emerged from the theatre, his wife on one arm and Moore on the other, he was mobbed by photographers. He said he was 'pleased' with his performance but 'irritated' by the gale which kept rattling the theatre's glass dome, adding, 'It would have to happen on the first night.' All three then crossed the road to the first night party at Hackney's Central Hall where hundreds of revellers partied until the early hours.

The following morning's newspapers gave Jonathan Kent's production, and its prince, decidedly mixed notices.

'High Voltage Hamlet' proclaimed the headline over the *Evening Standard* review which said: 'Fiennes's performance, in a production by Jonathan Kent which has the right, hurtling speed and revenge drama's sense of danger, turns out to be brilliantly original and power-packed.' The *Observer* shared the enthusiasm, applauding it as 'an exciting, intelligent and absorbing production' and commenting that its Hamlet 'exudes the appeal of a true star.' It also made the point that 'Fiennes succeeds on the patch left disappointingly vacant by Daniel Day-Lewis: that of the well-bred, well-educated and confused aristocrat'.

But the *Times* dubbed the play 'excessively Oedipal' and accused Ralph of transforming Hamlet's 'To be or not to be' speech into 'the kind of jumble of obsessive anxiety you might hear from a tramp in a park.' It acknowledged, however, that Ralph's prince had 'an intensity and unpredictability of his own'. While its sister paper, the *Sunday Times*, warned, 'This is certainly not a sweet prince. This is a harsh, lyrical reading, savage and ruthless, giving no hostages to affection or romantic admiration.'

In a review headlined, 'This worthy Hamlet fails to rise above the rest', the *Daily Mail* admired Ralph's bravery in 'playing the part as if he were in the politest, poshest part of the West End', but added, 'it is not that Fiennes is not adequate to the demands of the Prince of Denmark. It is simply that he does not rise above anything one has seen before in this curiously old-fashioned production.'

Echoing the criticism, the *Independent* branded the play 'a desperately disappointing Victorian period production', adding: 'The eyes have it with this actor. But in the well-nigh permanent longshot of a theatre, this actor's eyes look so hooded that you can't get into his face, let alone his soul, while his "To be or not to be" soliloquy is rattled out with all the rhythmic modulation of a rap record'.

The *Daily Telegraph* commented: 'Despite his undeniable stage presence, Fiennes is a big disappointment. He too often seems weary, stale, flat and unprofitable.' While the *Guardian* complained that Fiennes 'rattled through the soliloquies as if he has a train to catch,' adding: 'Although he is clearly one of nature's Hamlets, the speed of the productions prevents him from reaching the heights.'

It was left to the *New York Times* to articulate the feelings of the actor's many fans who were firmly convinced that his Hamlet had been given an unjustifiably rough ride by the critics.

'Movie success doesn't come cheap,' observed the newspaper astutely. 'In the case of Ralph Fiennes, the cost has been a certain credibility, at least in the eyes of the local press. Many of the reviews were condescending in ways that said more about the press than the production. In this newspaper's view, Mr Fiennes could be on his way to creating a singularly romantic, obsessed Hamlet, less cerebral and pretty than Laurence Olivier's platinum-haired prince, but tougher, grittier and more dangerous.'

On May 2, Ralph's *Hamlet* transferred to New York's historic Belasco Theatre on West 44th Street and Broadway which was every bit as grand as London's theatreland palaces.

His wife Alex had originally planned to join him in New York for his three-month Hamlet stint. But she noticed a new coolness about him. 'It was as if he didn't want her there with him,' says a friend. So when she was offered a part in the British television series, *The Knock*, she jumped at the opportunity to fly home, only accepting the part on the condition that she could have long enough breaks in her working schedule to join Ralph wherever he was performing.

Ralph's interpretation of Hamlet – unlike other recent London incarnations of the prince – made the journey across the Atlantic purely because of the man in the lead role. A man who was seen even more in America than in Britain as the heir to Olivier, Gielgud and Guinness.

A full-page advertisement, a painting of Ralph's prince holding a skull in his hands, appeared in the *New York Times* several weeks before the play transferred to Broadway. All 100 performances would soon sell out, a sizeable slice of the audience being made up of movie-goers tempted away from the multiplex by the prospect of seeing a screen idol in the flesh.

Unlike London, which was spoilt for choice when it came to Shakespeare, the critics reacted extremely favourably to Ralph's prince. 'He is the best Hamlet I've ever seen,' said *WCBS Television*'s drama critic. 'I felt his every agony.' While the *New York Post* raved: 'This is an extraordinary fine Hamlet. Fiennes is a dark genius as an actor. He broods with true melancholy, moves with a princely grace and manipulates the verse with conversational passion.'

Despite the absence of Alex, Fiennes had a fast and glamorous time in New York. Champagne flowed like wine at show business parties and his *Hamlet* became the toast of Broadway, attracting luminaries such as Meryl Streep, Barbra Streisand, Tom Hanks, Bruce Willis, Steven Spielberg, Paul Newman and Joanne Woodward, Cher, Lauren Bacall, Keanu Reeves, Bette Midler and Courtney Love.

'I rather wish I'd kept a book so everyone who came backstage could have signed it,' said Ralph later, revealing something of the star-struck little boy who had once hero-worshipped Lawrence of Arabia and 007. 'I was thrilled to meet people like Kirk Douglas and Liza Minnelli. It was very exciting.'

One of the highlights of his New York stay was attending a lavish party on a private cruise ship, with Francesca Annis and the other members of the cast. 'We went around Manhattan, past the Statue of Liberty at night and saw all the sights,' says Annis. 'It was absolutely fabulous.'

To cap it all, Ralph was nominated for a Tony Award. Established in 1947, they have since been offered every year for 'distinguished achievement' in the American theatre. One of the most prestigious awards in the States, a Tony could dictate the box office triumph or demise of a show.

That year's prize-giving extravaganza, with its usual complement of glamour and slickness, was held at New York's Minskoff Theatre where actors Alec Baldwin, Kathleen Turner and Lauren

Bacall were among those handing out the gongs.

The night was dominated by Andrew Lloyd Webber's *Sunset Boulevard*, which scooped seven awards, including best musical. But, despite numerous other British nominations, the nation's hopes were repeatedly dashed, and Ralph must have wondered whether he too was going to be disappointed.

Then, Kathleen Turner announced that Fiennes had won the 1995 Tony Award for Best Performance by a Leading Actor in a Play, and the theatre erupted in applause. He bounded on to the stage to accept his gong and paid tribute to the rest of the play's cast and crew, but especially to the Almeida's Jonathan Kent. 'You are my heart's friend, Jonathan,' he said emotionally, clutching the Tony in his hand.

It was a fitting reward for Ralph's intellectually and physically agile Hamlet – a Hamlet that was, despite the reservations of some, a Hamlet for the 1990s. It was also a fitting rebuff to Ralph's British critics.

With success, though, Fiennes was noticing a change in people's attitude towards him – both in Britain and America. 'They say to me, "Oh, God, are you OK? It must be weird for you at the moment",' he said, showing what some felt were early signs of paranoia. 'And *that's* what's weird. People assume certain things are happening to you. They're waiting for you to suddenly be different and starry and aloof. They're waiting to see you being corrupted or destroyed.'

Ironically, Fiennes was about to show that he was indeed different and do something that a couple of years earlier would have seemed totally out of character.

CHAPTER FIFTEEN

Black Friday

'Friday the 13th' is widely regarded as an unlucky day. And Friday 13 October 1995 would go down as an especially black day in Ralph's life, not to mention Alex Kingston's. For that was the day the world discovered the couple had separated – just days after their second wedding anniversary.

The *Daily Mail* broke the story in a front-page exclusive which asserted that a spokesman for the star had confirmed that 'Alex and Ralph are leading separate lives.' The 'scoop' came hot on the heels of news that another of Britain's best-known show business couples, Kenneth Branagh and Emma Thompson, had announced they were going their separate ways.

Within hours the rest of Fleet Street was chasing up the story. There was much speculation about a possible romantic link between Fiennes and Demi Moore, who had crossed the Atlantic earlier that year to see Ralph's prince at the Hackney Empire. But Moore, who was married to actor Bruce Willis, insisted she and Fiennes were just good friends.

It emerged that Fiennes had arrived in London earlier that week but – instead of going home to the couple's East Dulwich flat – had gone into hiding at a West End hotel, only to surface again a few days later in New York.

The press, at a loss to explain the separation, fell back on the old journalistic cliché that 'it was believed that, as with the recent break between Thompson and Branagh, pressure of work had taken its toll'. Few people entirely believed this story but friends were fiercely protective of the intensely private actor and his wife.

The fact was Fiennes was so private – indeed secretive – that even his family knew very little about the events leading up to the shock split. So just what had gone wrong?

A year earlier, they had seemed an entirely steadfast couple and the *Daily Express* had dubbed their relationship 'a Fiennes romance'. Kingston had even spoken of her wish to start a family with Ralph in 1995. With their specially installed Mercury 'phone line they attempted to bridge the gap between Britain and America.

The actor had echoed his wife's attempts to show the strength of their relationship. 'Alex and I have made our adjustments,' he said. 'Every actor-actress couple has to go through enforced separation. Hollywood is a necessary exile, but it's not a permanent one.' He claimed to be happy living in East Dulwich. 'I'm not going to move anywhere in a hurry – we're making our home really like a home, like a pair of shoes that become part of you'.

They had been pictured strolling happily arm in arm through Dulwich Park, 'looking like any other couple who are in love and have only been married eighteen months,' said an eye witness. 'They were oblivious to the crowds, kissed and cuddled, and appeared to only have eyes for each other.' Just three months before the split, Alex appeared to be deeply in love with the man in her life, describing him as 'intelligent and sensitive' and talking about his 'amazing looks'.

But, if you probed a little deeper, the cracks in the relationship became apparent. Success appeared to be changing Ralph – at least in Alex's eyes and she later lamented that they hadn't had enough time together.

There were other causes of conflict. As happy as Alex might have looked standing beside her man at star-studded events like the 1994 Academy Awards – when Ralph was nominated for an Oscar – she actually felt very insecure. 'I hated schmoozing in Hollywood,' she says. 'I felt like an appendage. People would be introduced, I'd say "hello" and you'd just see their eyes glaze or flick over my shoulder so they could see if there was anyone famous around. It's very strange when all the attention is focused on the person next to you.'

It was *Schindler's List*, which had made Fiennes a star, which also signalled the beginning of the end of their marriage, then just a few months old. 'He never wanted to marry me,' Alex now says. 'I don't know why in the end he decided he would. His mother was dying and when that happens it can bring people closer together. It was a decision he made after almost nine years and then instantly regretted.'

The actor spent much of 1994 and 1995 away from home, in Poland, New York or Los Angeles, but for all the couple's brave talk of not letting the distance interfere with their relationship, it inevitably did.

'I supported Ralph's career wholeheartedly,' says Alex. 'Not because I felt his was the greater talent but because I felt our relationship was the most important thing. And I gave him the space to go and do whatever job or amazing opportunity came along. But I could see him becoming more distant, and the more distant he became the more insecure I became.'

In an attempt to put things back on track, she started seeing a marriage guidance counsellor to 'work out how to say everything that needed to be said'. However, Fiennes never accompanied her.

'He said he would come but he was always busy or had meetings,' she says. 'I was doing a play in Hampstead, rehearsing all day and getting home late but I still found time in the mornings to see the counsellor. "Why are you doing this?" Ralph asked me. "Just lie in." But I thought "No, I have made a commitment".'

His heart was no longer in the marriage. He'd given up on it in all but name. His view seemed to be that what was going to be was going to be. If it was doomed, it was doomed. The catalyst that would drive them apart was not long in coming.

Six months after Ralph's split from Alex became public, a curious item appeared in the *Daily Mail* – the paper which broke the original story – claiming Fiennes had 'developed an intense bond' with his former *Hamlet* co-star Annis.

The pair had recently appeared at a gala night of poetry and prose at New York's Laura Pels Theatre, celebrating romance in Britain and called *Love In A Cold Climate*. The actors Natasha Richardson and Alan Rickman also performed at the benefit show for London's

Almeida Theatre. In one scene, Francesca sat in Ralph's lap to illustrate a poem and, according to an onlooker, 'for a brief, shimmering moment, she caught his eye and they shared what seemed to be a glance of romantic significance'.

The previous evening they had been guests at a starry dinner party hosted by Tina Brown, the British-born editor of the *New Yorker*. Again, fellow diners spoke of the 'couple's closeness' and the fact that they appeared to be 'more than just good friends'.

The *Daily Mail* story was carefully worded and the newspaper further covered itself by reflecting: 'We could have simply misjudged the signals and the two actors may merely be platonic buddies who have kept up a close relationship after working together so closely for six months.' Nevertheless, to assume that Francesca Annis was his inamorata – the woman who, in Kingston's words, 'he fell in love with' – was an inspired guess.

When the news of their relationship came out, it made the headlines. Celebrity break-ups happened all the time, providing endless fodder for the Sunday tabloids which made it their business to lift the lid on the stars' often tawdry love lives. But the Fiennes-Annis romance was an altogether different spin on an old story – because she was eighteen years his senior.

The daughter of a wealthy French-Brazilian shipping heiress, Marquita, and actor-director Anthony Annis (who played Laurence Olivier's double in several films and worked for British Intelligence during the war), Francesca was born in Brazil on 14 May 1945. She spent the first six years of her life in Brazil before her parents moved to a huge house in Kensington. Here, she had an upper-middle-class, Catholic upbringing, and as a child wanted to become a Carmelite nun.

She went on to study ballet at the élite Corona Stage School, and with her delicate bone structure and supple body looked set to become a professional ballet dancer. Then, at 16, she was spotted by a film producer in a studio corridor and cast as a handmaiden to Elizabeth Taylor in the epic movie *Cleopatra*.

Fortune smiled on the 'impossibly beautiful' Annis who, despite her petite figure, possessed an inner steel and, it was said, 'the arrogance that goes with good looks'. By the time she was 18, she was financially independent and when she left home at 21 she rebelled against her conventional upbringing, embracing first hippiedom and then feminism.

She chalked up successes as Ophelia to Nicol Williamson's Hamlet, and Juliet to Ian McKellen's Romeo, during her years with the Royal Shakespeare Company, and afterwards played Lady Macbeth in Roman Polanski's 1971 nude film version of *Macbeth*.

Annis went on to star in the hit television series *Madam Bovary* and *Parnell*. She also appeared in David Lynch's disappointing sci-fi movie, *Dune*, and played Jackie Kennedy in the American mini-series *Onassis* – but is probably best-known for portraying Lillie Langtry in the television drama *Lillie*, which won her a Best Actress award.

Emotional and highly-strung, she enjoyed a string of romances with – among others – Jon Finch, her co-star in Roman Polanski's *Macbeth*. There were also rumours that she had been involved with the afore-mentioned controversial Polish director himself.

When news of her romantic attachment to Fiennes became public knowledge, the press was quick to highlight the Oedipal overtones in their relationship. Recalling their sexually passionate encounter in *Hamlet*, it leapt to an almost foregone conclusion – that he was looking for a mother figure to fill the emptiness left by his mother's premature death.

Anyone who saw Annis in the flesh would have questioned such a simplistic hypothesis. For she was the sort of classic beauty age could not wither. If you compare photographs of the actress in her twenties with photographs of her in her forties, it's hard to escape the feeling, like a fine wine, she had matured with age. Then there were her eyes. If Ralph's sea-blue eyes could set a woman's heart aflutter, Francesca's chocolate-brown eyes could make a man go weak at the knees. 'She had the most beautiful eyes I've ever seen,' says Ralph's old RSC dresser, John McCloud, who worked with her in Stratford.

The future lovers first met when Annis was cast as Gertrude in Jonathan Kent's production of *Hamlet* in late 1994. But Ralph had long admired her from afar. 'She was the archetypal older, experienced woman of our dreams,' says a classmate at Bishop Wordsworth's. 'She had a regal, untouchable quality but oozed sex appeal.'

There were tantalizing glimpses of Ralph's burgeoning passion for his stage mother during *Hamlet*'s run. It had once been remarked that Fiennes 'smelt like fresh soap' and a woman writer who interviewed him jokily told him that she could smell his soapiness from the Empire's front row. Laughing, he replied, 'It may have been Francesca Annis. She smells rather wonderful.'

The exact date when their relationship began remains a mystery but Kingston has since said, 'People in the theatre company knew about the affair but Francesca kept well away from me and I was the last to know.' Not surprisingly, the lovers sought to keep the lid on the relationship for as long as possible.

For if anything, the affair forced Annis to make an even greater sacrifice than Fiennes – in effect, walking out on Patrick Wiseman, the man who had been her live-in lover for twenty-three years, and who was the father of her three children – Andreas, 12, Taran, 15, and Charlotte, 17. (A product of her time, she described marriage as 'a ludicrous concept' and refused to give up her name.)

The bearded Wiseman – who described himself as a photographer-turned-writer but was more of a 'long-suffering house-husband', according to friends – was devastated by Annis's decision, and moved the children out of the family home in Kensington, west London, into his own small flat.

By March 1996, Annis admitted for the first time that she and Wiseman were living apart. She went on to say – as Fiennes might have done: 'If a relationship breaks down, it breaks down, and that's an end to it.' But she was still maintaining the pretence that there was no third party. 'I'm not involved with anybody else,' she said before adding, intriguingly, 'but I don't think of myself as a single woman.'

If Annis had counted on the support of her octogenarian parents when, a week later, the world finally learnt of her relationship with Ralph, she was in for a shock. Her mother, Marquita, was outraged at her daughter's behaviour, saying, 'I am very sorry, especially for Patrick and the children. I suppose this is how people behave these days.'

It was the third time in ten years Annis had left him for a younger man, leaving him to care for their children, her heartbroken ex-partner revealed.

'The first time we managed to keep it from the children,' said

Wiseman, who at 56 preferred tweed jackets and jumpers to the fashionable clothes favoured by Fiennes. 'But Francesca's quest for younger and younger men has taken over her life. She is adamant that age is not relevant, yet the men in question have been ten years, fourteen years and now nearly twenty-five years younger than me.'

Hitting 40 'did something to her', he claimed. She started going out clubbing until the early hours and their domestic situation suffered as a result. Wiseman says that it became almost an inevitability that she would have an affair.

Her first affair was with Ian Ogilvy, her handsome co-star in Elijah Moshinsky's West End production of Chekhov's *The Three Sisters* but an actor best known to the public for appearing in the short-lived 1970s series *The Son of the Saint*. 'I don't think Francesca saw it as a particularly big deal,' said Wiseman. 'But for me it destroyed the whole fabric of our relationship.'

A few years later Annis was unfaithful again with another co-star whom Wiseman declined to name because the man had a family, too. However, newspapers at the time carried reports of an alleged relationship with former *Shoestring* idol Trevor Eve, her co-star in the BBC production *Parnell*. Annis and Eve, who is married to the actress Sharon Maughan, protested against the rumours – but Annis moved out of the home she shared with Wiseman for the best part of a year. She returned in 1992, but only after she had been dumped, according to Wiseman, adding: 'That was a first.'

Three years later, Annis was cast as Gertrude in Jonathan Kent's *Hamlet* – opposite Fiennes.

'At first, I thought she was having an affair with Kent,' says Wiseman, who guessed it might be Fiennes when, at *Hamlet*'s first night party, the actor kept giving his wife what he felt were 'peculiarly proprietorial' looks. 'Every time I looked across the room I caught this man's eye, watching Francesca, upon which he would hastily look away. This went on until it got annoying, at which point Francesca said, "That's Ralph. He's terribly shy – he probably just wanted to come and join me".'

Six weeks later, Annis flew off to America with Fiennes and the rest of the *Hamlet* cast. But when she eventually returned, to be met at the airport by Wiseman and her children, he noticed a change in her manner. Shortly afterwards, she told him she was leaving – again.

'The fault, of course, was entirely mine,' says Wiseman sarcastically. 'She was not guilty of anything. The children were informed that she had not left them, only me, and that I'd not been left for anybody else. And finally, and most importantly, that Ralph was in no way responsible for breaking up the family home.'

The day after she moved out, Francesca told Wiseman that she was seeing Fiennes.

The day the story of her marriage split broke, Alex was driving to her parents' house in Epsom, Surrey. She stopped at a garage *en route*, and, to her horror happened to see her and Ralph's faces adorning the front page of the newspaper.

'I just shook,' says Alex, who had separated from Fiennes just days earlier. 'I was in such a state I don't know how I managed to get to my mother's. When I got back to Dulwich I found reporters camped outside the flat. It was a horrible time. I didn't know it at the time but Ralph was actually in London, secretly staying at a hotel. The papers didn't know so he had no problems at all while I was hounded. Initially, he didn't even call but when he heard what was happening he rang to apologize. By then it was too late.'

The weeks and months ahead would be the most difficult of Alex's life. So low did she get that she twice ran a bath at her East Dulwich home, took a Stanley knife from the toolbox, and prepared to slit her wrists. 'I just thought "That's it, it's over",' she says. Only the thought of the blood and the mess she would leave behind for someone else to clear up made her put the knife down.

An actress friend with a young daughter moved into her flat to keep her company and Alex joked that having the little girl around helped to fulfil her maternal instincts.

'Looking back, we were both very young when we got together and maybe it wasn't healthy because neither of us had the chance to be single adults,' she reasoned, trying to be philosophical. 'I was so bound up to him that I thought he was the love of my life, and would be the love of my life forever.'

However much Kingston sought to view things objectively, the truth was devastating – the man she had loved like no other had walked out on her, leaving a gaping void in her life. When she leant across the bed to feel the warmth of his body, he was not there – and, what was worse, she knew he was never coming back. At times like these it was hard to hold back the tears.

His possessions – a shirt here, a suit there – still littered the house, constantly reminding her of their life together. But he didn't respond to her requests to move them out. 'I wanted him to pick up his things because I didn't feel I should have to do it,' says Alex. 'But he was busy, and I couldn't bear to see his things around, so in the end I realized I was going to have to box them up myself and put them in another room just to get him out of my mind.'

Even then, Alex admitted she was unlikely to stay put in East Dulwich. 'At one time I was very rooted to the place but they are roots I don't want to have any more because the flat has too many painful associations,' she said. 'I've tried to rid it of all the memories and make it my place but when you've been through what I've been through it's as though the very walls have absorbed the pain and anguish.'

In the months ahead, Kingston threw herself into her work – appearing in *Crocodile Shoes*, landing the female lead in the second series of *The Knock* and enjoying a cameo role in the Emma Thompson film *Carrington*. In her spare time she went salsa-dancing with girlfriends and sang backing vocals in a rock band called Henry Kissing Her.

But in those dangerous moments of solitude she still couldn't help wondering why things had gone so terribly wrong and even turned to therapy to soothe the wounds and reach that elusive stage counsellors refer to as 'acceptance'. The therapy involved re-examining her youth and, says Alex, helped her to find herself. But still she pointed out, 'If you've spent eleven years of your life with someone, you never stop loving them completely.'

Why did Annis and Fiennes embark on what some people saw as an extraordinarily reckless affair?

In Francesca's case, there were obvious grounds for an initial attraction. Wiseman said, 'Look at me and look at Fiennes. One's a battered, middle-aged man, the other the trendiest thing since Daniel Day-Lewis.'

But here, also, was a woman who was inherently unconventional – be it in her attitude to marriage or in the way she refused to be a prisoner to the passing years – even at 50 wearing impossibly short red skirts with the confidence of someone half her age. 'Getting old is a fact,' observed Annis, even though it was hard to imagine her ever being cast as a dowdy, middle-aged housewife. However, she saw nothing out of the ordinary in an older woman going out with a man young enough to be her son.

In Ralph's case, things were more complicated. The sexual passion had obviously gone out of Ralph and Alex's relationship. But after ten years what relationship does not become a little stale in that department?

Then there was Ralph's apparent attitude towards Alex. She admits she wanted to marry him as soon as they met. He was the man of her dreams. But one never gets the impression that she was the woman of Ralph's dreams.

Perhaps Alex's mistake was to love too quickly, and then too forgivingly. Never short of female admirers, as his Bishop Wordsworth's classmates reveal, one gets the feeling that part of Fiennes wanted a woman who would be more of a challenge. A woman whose unpredictable moods would reflect his own restless temperament. A woman whose emotions were as extreme as his mother's had been. If anything, Alex's fatal flaw was to love her husband too much.

At first, Ralph's family were every bit as upset about the turn of events as Francesca's, with his father, Mark, saying: 'I'd much prefer my son was known for his career than for his affair with Francesca Annis. I want nothing to do with it.'

For all the alleged Oedipal overtones in Ralph's relationship with Annis, she was first and foremost an intelligent, sexually desirable woman. Kingston might have an earthy, voluptuous sexuality, but Francesca possessed a delicate, swan-like beauty. And it was their mutual sexual attraction which first drew them close, not Ralph's search for a substitute mother-figure. And Annis did not, after all, have a very maternal image, or a particularly conventional attitude towards motherhood.

The fact was any man could have fallen under her spell even at her comparatively mature age. Besides, age is less of a factor in an era when Farrah Fawcett can pose for *Playboy* at 50 and still look fabulous.

Human nature has always been a battle between the animal passions that lurk deep within us and the desire to do the right thing or at least to appear to do the right thing. In this instance primeval desires carried all before them. By the time the dust had settled, two hearts may have beaten as one but two hearts also lay battered and broken.

CHAPTER SIXTEEN

Lenny

His private life might be unnervingly complicated, but Fiennes had not put a foot wrong career-wise since 'side-stepping from kill-guy to fall guy' as one critic put it. His next film, though – which, by coincidence, opened in America on Friday 13 October 1995, the day his split from Kingston became public – would be the most controversial of his career.

The futuristic action-thriller *Strange Days* began life as an ambitious story conceived by James Cameron – director of the hugely successful *Terminator* movies – in the mid-1980s. 'I wanted to do a David Mamet science fiction film,' he says, referring to the Pulitzer Price-winning playwright and screenwriter famous for his dense, gritty dialogue. But, he never found the time or inclination to develop it into a full-blown script.

So, in 1993, Cameron, at that time committed to the new Arnold Schwarzenegger movie, *True Lies*, gave his ex-wife Kathryn Bigelow the green light to develop the project and bring in Jay Cocks to write the final screenplay. Bigelow was the gutsy and glamorous director who had made a name for herself directing dynamic action films like *Blue Steel* and *Point Break*.

Set in an apocalyptic, riot-infested Los Angeles of the future, *Strange Days* brought us a warped world where SQUID clips – bought-and-sold memories pirated from human brains – are the newest form of illicit entertainment in the digital underground.

Seedy cop-turned-street-hustler Lenny Nero is a small-time dealer in these stolen dreams. He sells 'clips' – bits and pieces of people's lives, consisting of what they have seen, heard, and felt on a 30-minute digital recording. His virtual reality discs capture the intensity of the raw human experience. Sight, sound, taste, smell and touch. Sex, thrills and violence. And maybe a little vicarious love. If it can be recorded, it can be experienced – and Lenny is the man who can make it happen. The only thing he won't deal in is 'blackjacks' – death clips.

But somebody is setting Lenny up for a fall, and he suddenly finds himself enmeshed in a maze of paranoia, deception and murder that could lead to his own death.

Impressed by Fiennes's ability 'to connect to his characters' in *Schindler's List* and other films, Bigelow offered him the part of Lenny. 'His performances are so seamless and complete, and his transformation so genuine in every character he's played,' she said. 'The role of Lenny Nero required somebody who had tremendous intelligence, complexity, depth and a wide range of emotion – qualities I really felt only Ralph could supply.'

By now, though, everyone wanted to know and work with Fiennes. 'He's a terrific actor, handsome, personable and eager to please,' said a leading Hollywood producer. 'His name comes up right after Daniel Day-Lewis for every leading man role going. And in some cases it comes up before because Dan's gotten a bit of a reputation for being difficult.'

The days of waiting for a script to land on his doorstep were long gone. Twentieth Century Fox wanted him for *Anna Karenina*. His friend Demi Moore had already failed to talk him into starring opposite her in the ill-fated screen version of Nathaniel Hawthorne's *The Scarlet Letter*, which subsequently bombed at the box office.

Fiennes also declined a leading role in Barbra Streisand's long-planned screen version of Larry Kramer's play about Aids, *The Normal Heart*. Streisand was one of his biggest fans, emotively describing him as 'the best young actor of our time – one with the charisma of Brando or Dean'.

In addition, he had turned down a reported $4 million to star in a big screen version of *The Saint*, the classic 1960s television series which made Roger Moore famous. 'It had an appeal to the little boy in me who wants to drive fast cars,' admitted Fiennes. 'But I'm more interested in the Sam Spades and Philip Marlowes, who have a rough edge.' It was a wise decision, as it turned out, for the 1997 movie, starring Val Kilmer, proved to be a travesty of the original, damned by the critics and largely ignored by the public.

Perhaps the most enticing prospect for an actor who had once penned the numbers '007' on his school shoes was the chance to play Bond. For in April 1994, Timothy Dalton had announced he would not be stepping into the secret agent's shoes again, and the race began to find his successor.

Fiennes, along with Mel Gibson and Liam Neeson, were among those approached by the producers. Asked at the time if he was interested in donning 007's tuxedo, he replied, 'Only if the film is set in the 1950s.' The part went to Pierce Brosnan who saw his career prospects transformed when *GoldenEye* grossed $350 million around the world.

The question, now, was not so much whether the producers of *Strange Days* wanted Fiennes as whether he wanted to be in the film. Fiennes was drawn to its dark, unconventional hero and attracted by the prospect of working with the controversial Bigelow, who seemed to relish making more violent movies than her male peers.

'I was thrilled to be offered the part because it's not a part some-one would necessarily think of me for,' he said. 'Having just played two psychologically intriguing roles, I'd like to follow them up with something that offers the same kind of challenge. Lenny's weak, emotionally screwed-up and a bit of a jerk – but likeable. Knowing Kathryn's work, I knew I would be a part of something special.'

Ralph duly signed on for a reported $1 million – even though Fox were initially unenthusiastic about him playing Lenny, and Cameron himself admits that he originally visualized the character 'as being a little glibber and slicker'. He was later won round, though, conceding that the British actor would 'make Lenny a much sexier character'.

Shooting on *Strange Days* got under way in the summer of 1994. It was the third Hollywood movie Fiennes had made on the trot, and the first which found him as a contemporary action hero.

He rented a warehouse near that well-known hot spot Venice Beach, on Los Angeles's Westside. With its weight-lifters, hippies, roller-bladers and drunks, it was worlds apart from anywhere he had ever lived before and one female journalist who observed him walking along the boardwalk thought that 'he looked a little like Christ among lepers'.

It was 'stranger in a strange land' time but Fiennes found much to admire about America. 'It has an energy and an attitude to life that is reflected in the grid system you find in its cities,' he said, looking at the country through his artist's eyes. 'It has a clearly thought-out approach to things, which makes life easier.'

Though his view of Los Angeles was more ambivalent. 'I don't particularly like LA,' he said. 'It's not somewhere I'd like to live but its architecture, diverse lifestyles, different ethnic groups and the way it's so messily put together make it an endlessly fascinating place.'

As always, work-related matters were Ralph's overriding consideration. To research his role as a former police officer, Fiennes rode with Los Angeles Police Department (LAPD) vice and narcotics detectives in the city's drug-infested south central district where gangland murders are a nightly occurrence and human life is shockingly cheap.

'It gave me a real insight,' he says. 'There's a way of life out there that's sad, dirty and lonely, with people selling themselves just to get a few minutes' kick from ecstasy or crack. It's like the Wild West. But I also discovered that there was a weird sort of rapport between people on the street – such as prostitutes and drug dealers – and the police.'

The experience also gave Fiennes an insight into how his character might have fallen foul of the LAPD. 'I suspect Lenny wasn't a good cop,' he admits. 'Working vice you tread a thin line. You go into gambling houses and brothels. You do drug deals. You have to seem genuine so you start to play a role. One minute you're a policeman on the right side of the law, the next you've slipped over to the other side. It happens all the time. And if a guy working vice is found to be having a relationship with a prostitute, he will be kicked off the force.'

This, he presumed, was Lenny's fate when he fell for a spirited young runaway called Faith, (played by Juliette Lewis). 'She inspired him, and he wanted to rescue her from the dark pit that she was in,' he says. 'Unfortunately, his LAPD bosses didn't see it the same way.'

In addition, Ralph worked with a dialect coach and read Raymond Chandler out loud to familiarize himself with the Angeleno patois; spent time acquainting himself with the multi-national, culturally polyglot metropolis that is modern Los Angeles; and explored the nightlife, even visiting a 'girlie bar' – apparently 'out of curiosity'.

The movie was set in the year 1999 – just five years into the future – and giving it the right look would be integral to the success of *Strange Days*, explains production designer Lilly Kilvert.

'Highways, buildings and even car design are not going to change that radically in the space of a few years,' she says. 'What are likely to change are the small things like telephones and computers. Our focus was therefore on the details like universal phone numbers, widescreen TV sets and multi-media communications consoles that can transcribe spoken language in real time.'

Technology was only one of the influences at work on the future. 'The emphasis was just as much on creating the social fabric of the film,' says Fiennes. 'We anticipated a future based on the tensions witnessed during the 1992 riots. The film depicts a society that's falling apart, with racial tension and violence on the streets.'

To create this tense urban environment, Kilvert made use of city life to portray an LA where doomsday is just around the corner, where bonfires rage on the streets that are the uneasy province of pimps, hustlers, hookers and punks; teenagers dart furtively between troop-carriers; and shop owners protect their premises with flak jackets and Uzis.

Weeks were spent exploring the relationship between glitz and grunge, night-time shoots took place in deserted factories and warehouses in desolate areas of LA such as San Pedro, and several scenes took place in a night-club where Lenny's ex-girlfriend-turned-pop-singer Faith performs. By the time Kilvert had worked her magic, 'it featured all kinds of extraordinary visual dioramas,' says Ralph. 'There were old women ironing, Nazis burning books, blindfolded men and women chained to a wall, and patrons queuing up to take shots at them with guns.'

It was going to be a strange kind of film. In fact, the strangest film Fiennes had made since *The Baby of Macon*. Some movie business insiders thought it was a strange sort of film to make if you wanted to be a major league star.

The film opens with four masked gunmen committing a burglary. They burst into a building, lashing out at anyone who gets in their way and mouthing a string of obscenities. Suddenly, the police arrive, the gang run up to the rooftop and a raider flings himself off the edge of the building and plummets towards earth.

It then cuts to Ralph's character pulling off a virtual reality headset in disgust and angrily telling a fellow clip dealer: 'You know I don't do blackjacks. I hate that zap when they die. It brings down your whole day. I've got ethics.' Nevertheless, he still offers him $5,000 for the clip.

Back in his dark, depressing apartment, Lenny escapes reality himself by pouring a whisky, popping a virtual reality disc into a player and remembering the good times he once shared with his ex-girlfriend Faith. 'He's totally obsessed with her,' admits Fiennes. 'He's recorded some of his happier experiences with her and likes to relive them by himself. He's living in a sad world of nostalgia.'

Hopeless wirehead that he is, when he's not buying bits and pieces of other people's lives or viewing them for his own pleasure, he's selling them. 'You're there, you're doing it, you're seeing it, you're feeling it,' he tells a would-be customer in a seedy bar in his slick salesman's patter. 'It's about what you can't have; it's about the forbidden fruit. It's about running into a liquor store with a 357 Magnum in your hands feeling the adrenalin pump through your veins.

'This is like TV – only better. This is life – a piece of somebody's life, straight from the cerebral cortex. You wanna girl? You want two girls? You wanna guy? Maybe you wanna *be* a girl? Hey, think of it! Maybe you want a nun to tie you up? It's all do-able. Because I'm your priest. I'm your shrink. I'm your main connection to the switchboard of your soul. I'm the magic man. I'm the Santa Claus of the subconscious.'

The scene makes clear why his fellow ex-cop and lowlife buddy

Max (played by *Heat* star Tom Sizemore) crudely but not inaccurately describes Lenny as 'a fucking pimp who'd sell a goddam rat's asshole for a wedding ring'. While his dreadlocked female friend Mace (played by Angela Bassett) goes even further, accusing him of living a life consistent with 'backstroking in a toilet bowl'.

Ironically, given the ambivalence of their feelings towards him, they are 'the only two people he can really trust in these strangest of days', according to Bigelow. But despite Lenny being 'a hustler and loser', in Bigelow's eyes he 'possessed an undiscovered conscience'.

Furthermore the character – as played by Ralph – oozed sex appeal. And with his long, lanky hair, sideburns tapering to a point, designer stubble, black leather trousers and slinky 1970s-style shirts unbuttoned nearly to the navel he looked 'woundingly handsome', according to one insider, and 'more like Hamlet than Hamlet'.

Fiennes didn't accept the analogy, pointing out, 'Hamlet is alert and articulate, and so much more intelligent than Lenny. Hamlet is able to rationalize the complexities of the moral situation he finds himself in, whereas Lenny doesn't see a problem in his life because he has very little objectivity. I don't know if there is much of a parallel.'

Lenny's life is turned upside down when a prostitute called Iris who used to do 'wire work' for him is brutally murdered. When someone slips him the killer's playback recording of her rape and murder, Lenny can't help but become an emotional accomplice to the crime. The clip opens a door into a mirror-maze of intrigue, betrayal, pursuit and chilling violence involving Faith, his ex-girl-friend.

Horrific SQUID discs start appearing all over the place. On viewing one, he discovers that an intruder has been into his apartment while he's sleeping, and run the blade of a knife along his neck. He teams up with Mace and together they try to solve Iris's death – though in a neat role-reversal, Bassett plays the gutsy, capable, karate-kicking partner to Fiennes' crumpled failure.

Then Lenny discovers a disc showing rogue LAPD cops indulging in a Rodney King-style racial execution of a controversial rap star – 'a lit match that could bring the entire city down in flames' in the words of the film-makers.

Despite the movie's brutal, indiscriminate violence, it had a sprin-
kling of entertaining one-liners. Furthermore, for the first time
Ralph played a big screen character who possessed a sort of ready,
self-deprecating wit – badly-needed by the look of LA's futuristic
mean streets.

The five-week, night-time film shoot put a lot of pressure on the
movie's key players, particularly Ralph. 'Lenny is constantly on the
move, thinking about the next deal he can cut, and I became very
restless,' he reveals. 'I wasn't sleeping and I had a lot of energy. Then
when I'd hit the bed, I'd crash and get up at midnight.'

But his co-star, Juliette Lewis was among those impressed by his
concentration and professionalism. 'It would be four in the morning, it would be ninety degrees, there would be a million extras talking, and he'd be so focused it blew me away,' she says. 'He would do
take after take with the same precision as the first time.'

The visually dazzling film, part *Blade Runner* and part film noir,
eventually premièred at the Venice Film Festival in 1995 amid much
controversy which centred on a rape scene sadistically viewed
through the eyes of the attacker's video camera which gave viewers
the sensation of participating in the act. 'Ironically for a film directed
by a woman, more than a few women will have problems with these
scenes,' said *Variety*'s Todd McCarthy.

But Bigelow – an admirer of Oliver Stone whose *Natural Born
Killers* was among the most gratuitously violent films of the 1990s –
argued: 'There is violence in society. Art imitates life and you have
to be unflinching to be faithful to the truth.'

And Fiennes himself, while admitting he had initially been
concerned at the film's handling of such sexual violence, echoed her
views. 'Either you never portray any violence against women or you
find a way of doing it,' he said. 'The thing is: it's real the way war is
real. It's the job of a drama to reveal how humanity behaves though
it would be foolish to deny that some people may be titillated by
such scenes.'

The movie's October 1995 US release was accompanied by the
usual hype accompanying a Hollywood movie release, and publi-
cists put the word out that it was set to make Fiennes 'the British

Elvis'. However, despite the pedigree of those involved, its violence provoked a critical backlash and at two hours twenty-five minutes it was almost certainly too long.

It duly slunk into the Top Ten on its first week on release but grossed a disappointing $5 million. In week two it grossed a further £2 million but by week three was fading fast. In all, *Strange Days* grossed less than $10 million in America.

The film received an equally hostile reception when it finally hit British screens in March 1996, the lengthy delay in its release an indication that it was regarded as a problem movie.

The *Sunday Times* acidly commented, 'Sitting in high court listening to two shrieking divorcees battling it out over their record collection would be more fun than watching this film.' The *Guardian* branded it 'amoral and brutal'. The *Evening Standard* said: 'Not just women, but men too, will be deeply disturbed by *Strange Days*.' While *Empire* observed that the film was 'no easy business' and its 'freefall through voyeurism and violence' offered a depressing vision of the future.

Even the *News of the World*, which usually has a soft spot for action movies such as *Strange Days*, gave it the thumbs down. 'It fails miserably,' wrote the paper's film critic, Jonathan Ross. 'And the ending is as unbelievable and as pointlessly unexciting as the rest of the film.' One of the few upbeat reviews was by the *Sun*'s Steve Wright, who wrote, 'It's a fascinating film but the sound effects and grungy music left me feeling as if I'd been watching MTV at full volume.'

However, Ralph largely escaped the critics' wrath. The movie magazine, *Première*, declared, 'Fiennes, as always, manages an extraordinary luminescence'. And the *News of the World* thought he was 'great, almost managing to save this dodgy, badly-scripted turkey from certain death'.

Certain death being the operative words, for after scraping into the UK Top Ten in its opening week, *Strange Days* sunk without trace, grossing little more than £500,000.

Far from making Fiennes 'the British Elvis' – a somewhat dubious honour in the first place – the failure of *Strange Days* put a dampener on the way he was perceived in Hollywood. Controversy is all very well if it turns a film into a hit. But *Strange Days* would be his least successful film since the low-budget *Wuthering Heights*. Nervous studio bosses, newly doubtful of his box office appeal, would subsequently come close to scuppering his next project – a project especially close to his heart.

CHAPTER SEVENTEEN

The Mysterious Count

A balding, cuddly-looking man looked out of the window of his hotel room on the corner of 77th and Columbus. The streets below were swarming with yellow cabs, coaches and cars. Tiny figures dotted the sidewalks. It was a sweltering New York summer morning but the hotel's air-conditioning cocooned him from the intense heat and the sounds of the city far below.

Despite his exotic-sounding surname, Anthony Minghella grew up in the seaside town of Ryde on the Isle of Wight where his Italian-born parents ran an ice-cream factory. To the initial disappointment of his mother and father, Gloria and Eddie, he had forsaken the family business for a career in academia. In 1981 he had left his job as a lecturer at Hull University to become a playwright and gone on to become an editor of the children's television show, *Grange Hill*, before making his directorial feature film debut in 1991 with *Truly, Madly, Deeply*.

He poured himself a cup of strong coffee and sat down with a novel he'd long been meaning to read – *The English Patient*, written by the Canadian Michael Ondaatje. The 1992 Booker prize-winner, a shimmering, impressionistic, 300-page book with rich, poetic prose, inspired strong reactions and was not an easy read. What the hell, thought Minghella. He'd give it a couple of hours. By then he'd know whether it was his kind of book.

Morning turned into afternoon and afternoon into evening. But Minghella read on. He ignored the telephone, too engrossed in the story to contemplate distraction. When he eventually finished the book twelve hours later it was dark, and he initially wondered where he was: Cairo? Italy? The Sahara? He got up and looked out of the window but the streets below were still filled with yellow cabs, coaches and cars.

He was convinced that this story, centring on an overwhelming, and finally destructive, love affair, was something he had to film, however complex it might be. He admits, however, that 'A lot of friends thought I'd gone mad because it defied conventional adaptation.' The very next day Minghella contacted Saul Zaentz, the only Hollywood-based producer he thought 'crazy enough to countenance such a project' and suggested he read the book.

Described as 'perhaps the last of the great independent producers' by *Variety*, Zaentz had been responsible for helping to adapt acclaimed literary properties like *One Flew Over The Cuckoo's Nest* for the cinema, had produced respected films such as *The Mosquito Coast* and *The Unbearable Lightness of Being*, and 'was one of the few movie-makers who loves to read', according to Minghella. 'I've never seen him without a book within reach'.

A few days later Zaentz, born in New Jersey of Russian-Polish parents, called Minghella back to say the he loved *The English Patient* and thought it worth exploring but, astute businessman that he was, added that he could not immediately see how the story could be adapted for the big screen.

The novel was set in two distinct time periods – in the immediate pre-war era of the late 1930s, spilling over into the outbreak of World War Two; and in the spring and summer of 1945, as war finally gives way to peace – the two time-frames linked by the unidentified 'English' patient of the title who is later unmasked as a Hungarian, Count Laszlo de Almasy.

The pre-war section was set in the Sahara and the Egyptian capital, Cairo, focusing on two of the archaeological expeditions that criss-crossed the desert in search of traces of lost civilizations. But at its core lay the giddily passionate love affair between the mysterious Count Almasy and Katharine Clifton, the beautiful, headstrong, upper-class wife of a fellow member of the expedition. The end-of-war section focused on the love affair between a young Canadian nurse called Hana and Kip, a Sikh sapper working his way up Italy defusing unexploded bombs and clearing the area of mines.

Within weeks of Minghella's call to Zaentz, the two men had arranged to meet with Ondaatje in Los Angeles, where he was giving a book reading.

Born in Ceylon at a time when the country lived in fear of Japanese attack, Ondaatje was the son of an alcoholic tea plantation manager. When his parents' marriage broke down, he was shipped to England and educated at prestigious Dulwich College. At 18, he emigrated to Canada, started writing poetry while at Quebec University and published his first novel when he was 33. By the 1980s, he was an established author in his adopted homeland but it was *The English Patient*, which took six years to write and required six drafts, that shot him to international prominence.

Novelist Edmund White described it as 'the best piece of fiction in English I've read in years' and *Time* magazine called it 'a magic carpet of a novel that soars across worlds and times'. But the very complexity of the lyrical, dreamlike tale, drifting between time zones, and circling a story rather than telling it, made people question how such a literary *tour de force* could possibly be turned into a film.

'We told Michael that if he wanted to make the book word for word then Anthony and I weren't the people to do it,' says Zaentz bluntly. 'It would be a boring eight-hour movie.' The literary world had become accustomed to Hollywood turning great novels – such as Tom Wolfe's *Bonfire of the Vanities* – into cinematic howlers, but Ondaatje showed a flexibility of outlook and trust rare in an author.

'The novel was my version of the story,' he said. 'The script has to be something new. Film isn't a reflective medium. You can't throw in someone dreaming in his bed about a love affair he had in Cairo five years earlier. Something like that obviously has to be recreated. The information has to be simpler.'

Following the meeting, Minghella returned to England and was granted access to photographs and papers at the Royal Geographical Society and the British Library. He gathered up a large collection of books on Egypt, compass reading, Second World War military campaigns and the geography of the Sahara, and then headed for a remote cottage deep in the Dorset countryside to write a film script.

Given the book's non-linear plot, Minghella realised he could never write a traditional, three-act film. 'The prose is oblique, mosaic-like and doesn't automatically offer a narrative route,' he said.

So instead the director took the novel's basic premise of four strangers converging on a Tuscan village in the dying days of the Second World War and played up the story's love interest. Several months later he emerged from his self-imposed isolation with a first draft of over 200 pages – about twice the length of the usual screenplay. 'It had too many characters, not to mention too many countries,' says Zaentz, who was unimpressed.

But as successive drafts materialized – each subject to the ruthless, rigorous scrutiny of Ondaatje and Zaentz at meetings in Toronto, London and Tuscany – a blueprint for a wide-screen version of *The English Patient* slowly began to emerge.

Key decisions included playing up the love affair between Almasy and Katharine Clifton at the expense of the book's secondary love affair between Hana and Kip, and narrowing the age gap between Almasy – who was considerably older in the novel – and Clifton. Once Minghella had completed the final screenplay, Zaentz began assembling the financing for the film. He put up $6 million but Twentieth Century Fox agreed to provide the bulk of the $33 million budget. The all-important task of the casting then got under way.

In early 1994, the script was sent to Fiennes, whom Minghella admired for his 'intelligence and great emotional complexity'. As soon as the actor read it, he committed himself to playing the part of Almasy, the taciturn explorer who, with his love for the solitude of the desert, resembled Ralph's boyhood hero, Lawrence of Arabia.

'The screenplay spoke to something inside me,' says Fiennes. 'It's a love story, a tragic, multilayered love story about several protagonists. But I was also attracted by the way the dialogue lived on the page.' Minghella was delighted to have him on board, saying, 'He can play a chord which, however sweet, contains the threat of discord.'

From the outset, both Zaentz and Minghella had the beautiful French actress Juliette Binoche (who starred opposite Fiennes in *Wuthering Heights*) in mind for the part of French-Canadian nurse Hana – though initially she wanted to play Katharine Clifton. That part eventually went to the elegant English actress Kristin Scott

Thomas, (until then best known for appearing in *Four Weddings and a Funeral*) who beat off stiff competition from Demi Moore and Andie McDowell. The fourth key role of Caravaggio (a character created by Minghella), went to *Platoon* star Willem Dafoe.

Bringing *The English Patient* to the screen was always considered a high-risk project in Hollywood's eyes. Movie moguls at Fox were concerned that none of the actors in the key roles were sufficiently 'bankable'. And *Strange Days'* dismal reception at the US box office further dampened their confidence. At the eleventh hour, Fox backed out because Minghella and Zaentz refused to replace Thomas with Moore or Michelle Pfeiffer, or even consider replacing Fiennes with a big-name Hollywood star who could be relied upon to enhance the image of a picture. Pre-production work in Italy ground to a halt.

It was a body blow to everyone involved in the venture, including Ralph. 'All the studios found it hard to commit to this film,' admits Minghella. 'They thought it was too European and too ambitious, and thought I should have been casting US actresses. They were looking for an "insurance policy" before committing money to the film. We could not come up with a portfolio that interested them.'

A desperate search for alternative sources of financing began. At one point it looked as if Minghella and Zaentz might have to call it a day but then Miramax's Harvey Weinstein came to the rescue, offering a $27 million lifeline. 'It was a close call,' says one insider. 'But for Harvey, the movie version of *The English Patient* would have died a death.'

Principal photography began in the autumn of 1995 at Cinecetta where sets had been constructed on two of the Roman studio's main sound stages. After three weeks, cast and crew travelled to the town of Pienza in Tuscany, thirty miles south of Siena, and then to Viareggio, a coastal resort town near Pisa, to create the emergency field hospital tent and to film scenes which took place in and around the monastery in the story's end-of-war section. The beautiful Hotel des Bains in Venice doubled up as the famed 'Shepheard's Hotel', a popular watering hole for upper-crust explorers, diplomats and military officers in pre-war Cairo which had been destroyed in the 1950s.

In mid-November, cast and crew flew out to Tunisia for nine weeks where the remaining North African scenes were filmed. Initially, the film-makers hoped to film in Cairo itself but it was felt the Tunisian city of Sfax better conjured up the Egyptian capital of the 1930s while the nearby town of Mahdia doubled up for Tobruk. The inaccessible area around Tozeur, a six-hour drive from Mahdia close to the Algerian border, provided the 'kind of Lawrence of Arabia desert' so crucial to the film's narrative. But filming in the desert posed unique problems. 'Mistakes could not be made shooting scenes in sand dunes as the footprints took days to disappear,' reveals one crewman.

No expense was spared in the search for authenticity when it came to recreating the period outfits – items such as tan leather jackets or silk scarves – that helped give the film its distinctive look, and Ralph was fitted for his clothes by the Savile Row tailor who had worked for the Duke of Windsor, Gary Cooper and Fred Astaire. And after all the off-set money worries, everyone had a burning desire to do the book justice. Leading by example, Fiennes carried out meticulous research into the real Count Almasy – the inspiration for Ondaatje's novel.

The film opens with the camera focusing on a brush coaxing to life a primitive painting of a body that seems to swim or fly. The painter was actually Fiennes, though he's never identified. 'I immediately recognized the stroke of the brush as being Ralph's,' says his old art teacher Duncan Davies. 'It possessed the same lightness of touch.'

The story then cuts to a bi-plane flying over the desert where the planes of sand look like smooth ripples of flesh. Hit by a shell, the plane plunges to earth and bursts into flames. The pilot is rescued from the wreckage by Bedouin tribesmen, but he's been burned to a crisp and his face transformed into a grotesque mask of twisted flesh. Fast forward to a beach in Italy in October 1944. The patient (Fiennes) lies on a sun lounger. His face is hideously scarred, he is blind in one eye and is bald but for the odd tuft of hair peeping through the blotchy-skinned scalp – leaving Fiennes looking more like a ghastly Hammer horror-style film freak than a movie heart-throb.

Typically, Ralph – whose third-degree burns make-up took six hours a day to apply – consulted a top plastic surgeon for advice on how to play a burns victim, and to discover the degree of pain that would have been felt. 'When your skin heals after you've been badly burnt it loses its elasticity,' he says. 'It can't breathe like skin. Before they really understood the way burns heal, scar tissue would just tighten up leaving people crippled. Victims lost huge amounts of fluid, their internal organs were badly damaged, and try as they might to sweat they couldn't, so they suffered all sorts of shooting pains and irritations beneath the surface of the skin.'

Despite his laudable quest for authenticity, Zaentz took the decision to go gently on the scar make-up because he felt if the burns were too realistic it might prove more than the audience could bear. Even so, Binoche confesses: 'I was shocked the first time I saw Ralph in make-up because his injuries looked so real.'

An officious British soldier asks the patient for his name, rank and serial number.

'I think I was a pilot,' he murmurs with difficulty, his lips having been burnt away.

'You were married?'

'I think so, but I believe that is true of some Germans too,' replies Ralph's character sarcastically. 'My organs are packing up. I'm a bit of toast.'

The next scene finds the morphine-pumped Ralph in an Allied hospital convoy in Italy. A truck in front is blown up by a mine – bringing the rest of the vehicles to a halt. Every time he is moved he is suffering intense pain so his nurse, Hana, insists on removing him to a crumbling monastery high in the Tuscany hills where she can let him die with dignity.

Once installed, his mind wanders and he experiences the first of many flashbacks ...

Cut to the Royal Geological Survey expedition in the Sahara in the late 1930s and a closely-cropped Fiennes as his fans know and love him. The camera lingered lovingly over his fine features, razor-sharp cheekbones and chic desert apparel. As Almasy he spoke in an even more refined English accent than usual. Yet there was an unmistakable air of melancholy about his character, as there sometimes seems to be about Fiennes himself.

The caring, free-spirited Hana with her wild, untamed hair forms a special bond with her mysterious patient. To play the nurse, Binoche learnt how to administer morphine and bathe a burns victim – but she and Fiennes disagreed over just how their characters should behave towards each other. 'Ralph was angry with me at times,' she says. 'He would tell me "Hana wouldn't do that because the patient is anonymous" but it wasn't just about a nurse and a patient, there was a platonic love between the two of them.'

She finds a fragment of his writing in which he states that 'the heart is an organ of fire' – hinting at the passions of a past life . . .

Cut to a desert camp-fire scene at night-time. The other members of the British geographical party, which includes Geoffrey Clifton (Colin Firth) and his wife Katharine, are singing songs and telling jokes.

The action shifts to a Cairo market and a seemingly chance encounter between Almasy and the newly-married Katharine. He offers to haggle with the traders for her. Later, Clifton asks him why he has followed her.

'I was concerned for you,' lies Almasy.

'Why follow me?' she asks. 'Escort me, by all means. Following is predatory, isn't it?'

He doesn't reply – just fixes her with that famous Fiennes stare.

The arrival of Caravaggio, a mysterious Canadian thief turned intelligence operative, adds a new dimension to life at the monastery.

'You think he's a saint because of the way he looks but what if I told you he did this to me?' he says, holding up his thumbless hands. 'Ask your saint who he is. Ask him who he's killed.'

With Europe on the brink of war, the British government had been keen for expeditions, such as that organized by the Royal Geographical survey of which Almasy was a member, to complete map-making duties in North Africa as soon as possible.

But when the decent if dull Geoffrey Clifton flies off on a secret mission, he leaves his pliable wife ripe for seduction. As a sandstorm rages, Almasy tells her stories about the desert and strokes her hair. While pasting some sketches into his journal, Katharine finds scribbled, loving observations about a certain 'K' – and clearly these are referring to her.

And, when she appears uninvited at his Cairo hotel, they begin a passionate affair. He drops to his knees, wraps his arms around her

172

and rips off her dress, and they make love in a torrid scene that didn't actually exist in the book.

Afterwards as they're relaxing in a warm bath, he dreamily asks, 'When were you most happy?'

'Now,' she replies.

'When were you most sad?'

'Now,' she replies.

'What do you love?'

'Water,' she replies, stepping into the bath. 'Your handwriting.'

'What do you hate most?' he asks as they lie in each other's arms in the warm water.

'What do you hate most?' she replies, turning the tables on him.

'Ownership,' he says. 'Being owned.'

She gets out and coldly tells him: 'When you leave you should forget me.'

When they next meet, Ralph's character says: 'I can't work, I can't sleep, I can still taste you.' They secretly make love in the scorching Cairo sun after she feigns a dizzy fit at the British troops' Christmas party – while just yards away her husband Geoffrey, with unfortunate irony, is playing at Father Christmas, handing out festive gifts to the soldiers.

Doom and desperation begin to gather over the lovers like a desert sandstorm. The smitten Almasy refuses to accept the inevitable but the strong-willed Clifton eventually succeeds in ending the affair. As she walks away, Almasy pathetically calls after her, 'Katharine, I just want you to know that I'm not missing you yet.'

Fast forward to the dying days of the war. It transpires that Caravaggio is trying to track down Almasy, believing he betrayed him to the Germans. And eventually the English patient (Almasy) admits as much, saying: 'I had to get back to the desert, the rest didn't matter.' But he insists, 'I wasn't a spy.'

A flashback summarizes the final events leading up to his 'betrayal'.

A desert camp. Clifton's husband – who now knows of the affair – has offered to collect Almasy. But he flies in low and the plane crashes, killing Clifton and leaving its passenger, Katharine, with a broken ankle, wrist and ribs. Almasy carries her to a cave, promising to return as soon as he has summoned help.

'You promise?' she asks weakly. 'I wouldn't want to die here.'

'Yes,' he replies. 'I promise I'll come back for you. I promise I'll never leave you.'

He walks for three days until he arrives at British lines without I.D. papers. Questioned by soldiers, and knowing the sands of time are running out for his beloved Katharine, he demands, 'Just give me a fucking car!' Put on a convict train, he escapes and does a deal with the Germans to get back to the cave – only to find a last letter from Katharine saying, 'My darling, I'm waiting for you.' He carries her into the sunlight, shaking with emotion.

'Yes, she died because of me,' the English patient tells Caravaggio. 'She died because I had the wrong name. But you can't kill me. I died years ago.' After Hana has granted his plea for a lethal injection of morphine, the film closes with a dream-like scene in which the silver bi-plane flies over the desert – echoing the film's opening.

In some ways, *The English Patient* was a thoroughly old-fashioned film, in others a modernist melodrama.

It was an erotically charged epic – with lush, desert settings and brilliant blue skies; stylish period fashions and beautiful bi-planes; spies, battles and sandstorms; and a passionate love affair set against the turmoil of the Second World War – conjuring up with intense nostalgia, the glamour of a bygone, somehow more heroic, age.

Above all, it was that rare thing, a big but intelligent film – abounding in startling images, looking at issues such as love, hate, passion, loyalty, betrayal, nationality, identity and possession. A film that refused to patronize its audience. A film that refused to accept the notion then common in Hollywood that a film had to conform to the lowest common denominator to triumph at the box office.

Cast and crew justifiably felt they had made a special film, though Scott Thomas jokingly complained, 'Ralph looked prettier than me – I'm never going to act opposite someone so beautiful again.'

Minghella, who broke his ankle a month into the shooting but was determined not to let the injury balk his dynamism, commented: 'It's hard to find material you can be so passionate about. Someone once wrote that I was as interested in the big picture as in the intricacies of human behaviour. That's what I aimed to do with *The English Patient*. To look at how extraordinary people are, look at the way they destroy each other and look at how they heal and bless each other. To look at how Almasy can throw away his life over his obsession with a woman.'

Furthermore, contrary to what sceptics were suggesting, he insisted Miramax's involvement did not undermine his freedom of manœuvre, saying; 'I shot the film and cut it the way I wanted.'

As for Fiennes, who reportedly pocketed around $1.5 million for his starring role, he showed how difficult it was for a closed-off, abrupt man such as Almasy to lose himself in the grip of an erotic fever – and evolved into a very different character as the person in the later stages of the film: a wittier, warmer, wiser man.

Several weeks before *The English Patient* opened in the US, the movie magazine *Première* – which prides itself on supposedly having its finger on Hollywood's pulse – predicted: 'The word is the story loses something in the translation from the book and *In Love and War* may steal some of its wartime love-affair thunder.'

In fact, its American release, in November 1996, was accompanied by the sort of reviews that movie-makers everywhere pray for but seldom receive.

'It's completely intoxicating,' raved the *Washington Post*. 'As all great films must, *The English Patient* transports us to another time and place.' The *New York Times* called it 'a fiercely romantic, mesmerizing tour de force, a cinematic triumph.' And *Time* commented, 'This you realize, with a gasp of joy, is what movies can do. It's a ravishing film which gets all the rapture right, with a mystery and majesty rarely dared by film-makers since the days of David Lean.'

Fiennes, who sent the pulses of women racing as soon as he appeared minus his burns, won particular acclaim. *Rolling Stone* commented, 'Ralph Fiennes gives a performance of probing intelligence and passionate heart.' While *Time* argued, 'Fiennes hasn't been this good since *Schindler's List*.'

Others shrewdly observed that in the kind of subtropic attire associated with enduring heart-throbs such as Trevor Howard and David Niven, Fiennes represented a type of character that had long been threatened with extinction – the British romantic lead.

Such acclaim helped the film to become an unexpected smash-hit in America, grossing more than $30 million by the year's end and proving beyond doubt that a picture could reach both 'the arthouse crowd and the popcorn patrons' regardless of whether or not it starred apparently bankable stars such as Demi Moore (whose most recent film, *Striptease*, had in fact been a box office disaster).

The picture got a further fillip as 1996 drew to a close, when three leading US publications – the *New York Times*, the *Los Angeles Times* and *Time* magazine – voted it the film of the year.

In January 1997, it garnered a Golden Globe award for best dramatic picture. And then, on 11 February, *The English Patient* received a record twelve Oscar nominations – beating the previous British best, *Ghandi*, which had eleven nominations in 1982, (but falling short of *Gone with the Wind*'s thirteen in 1939, and Bette Davis's *All About Eve* which attracted fourteen in 1950). Among those nominated were Fiennes for the Best Actor category, Scott Thomas for Best Actress, Binoche for Best Supporting Actress and Minghella for Best Director.

The front page of the next day's *Times* splashed on a photograph showing an unusually smiling Ralph, hearing of his nomination. Sixteen years after *Chariots of Fire* screenwriter Colin Welland had warned Hollywood 'the British are coming', it looked as if his prediction was finally coming true.

The next few weeks saw Britain gripped by the sort of movie mania that had not accompanied the release of a home-grown picture in years, even though *The English Patient* would not be domestically released until 14 March – ten days before the Academy Awards ceremony.

When it finally opened in the UK the ensuing critical fanfare proved every bit as positively frenetic as it had been in the States the previous year.

The *Daily Telegraph* hailed it as 'an extraordinary film' and applauded Ralph's ability to play what it called 'a dashing explorer and a living corpse' by 'acting with his eyes' over-riding the experiences of the patient's heavy make-up. And the *Evening Standard* thought it a 'resplendent, sensuous, intelligent, superbly photographed, edited and deeply literary work'.

The *Sunday Times* dubbed it, '*Lawrence of Arabia* and *Brief Encounter* rolled into one' and described it as 'a rapturous piece of film-making' and 'utterly unique'. *Empire* claimed it was 'truly a wonder', adding that both Fiennes and Scott Thomas were 'stand-outs'. And the *Guardian* reckoned, 'Minghella has given us an intelligent, tense and satisfying drama that's epic in scale but intimate in its study of character.'

The newspapers' one – arguably justifiable – gripe was that, at nearly three hours, the film was too long.

Much of the credit for the film's success was attributed to Fiennes and Scott Thomas and their extraordinary handling of the love scenes. 'They are essentially two of a kind,' explained Minghella, 'both pulsating, complex, strange creatures – and there was a powerful erotic charge between them.'

Yet Scott Thomas, while admitting the heart-throb actor was 'a very nice kisser', revealed that their on-screen chemistry ended as soon as the cameras stopped rolling. 'We really didn't hang out a lot together,' insists the married mother-of-two. 'Ralph's a bit of a loner and would just disappear off into the desert between scenes. He's quite mysterious.'

The film's British première took place at the Curzon Mayfair cinema, where Ralph was joined by his glamorous co-stars, Kristin Scott Thomas and Juliette Binoche. But within days he was jetting out to Los Angeles for the 1997 Academy Awards ceremony, accompanied by Francesca Annis.

The cast had a feeling that this was going to be *The English Patient*'s year. It was up against one big-budget Hollywood movie, *Jerry Maguire*, starring Tom Cruise, and three smaller, independently produced pictures: *Shine*, *Fargo* and Mike Leigh's thoroughly modern slice of London life, *Secrets and Lies*.

As before, Ralph – whose challengers for the Best Actor category were Tom Cruise, Woody Harrelson, Geoffrey Rush and Billy Bob Thornton – found it impossible not to get caught up in the excitement that infected Tinseltown as countdown to the Oscars got underway.

He had just missed glory when he was nominated for Best Supporting Actor in *Schindler's List*. Family and friends now hoped it would be a case of second time lucky. He was now indeed the odds-on favourite to scoop the award but, as one Hollywood veteran cautioned, 'Academy voters like the idea of a landslide, but not a total landslide, especially if the film in question isn't even American.'

On the big night itself, Ralph turned up at the star-studded ceremony in a limousine – an essential accoutrement for any self-respecting Academy Award nominee. Cameras and television reporters made a beeline for him as soon as he appeared with Annis, who looked stunning in a slinky, fluid, brown dress. He appeared relaxed and in good spirits, politely fielding the typically banal questions. Would he win? 'We'll just have to wait and see,' he said with a smile.

It soon looked as if predictions about *The English Patient* were set to be spectacularly fulfilled – as it accumulated gongs for cinematography, art direction, sound, original dramatic score, costume design and film editing. To the surprise of many, Binoche secured the Best Supporting Actress award – expected to go to Lauren Bacall for her incisive performance in Barbra Streisand's *The Mirror Has Two Faces*.

But the Best Actress award went to *Fargo*'s Frances McDormand for her splendid performance as a small-town police chief in the throes of pregnancy. However much this particular actress deserved to prosper, it was not a good omen. Then Susan Sarandon mounted the stage, ripped open the gold envelope and declared: 'The Best Actor award goes to ... Geoffrey Shine.'

The auditorium erupted in applause. Hiding his disappointment, Ralph clapped along and Annis squeezed his hand in consolation.

However, *The English Patient* went on to scoop the all-important Best Picture and Best Director categories, bringing its final tally to nine statuettes – the best result for a single movie since Bernardo Bertolucci's 1987 epic *The Last Emperor*, which also won nine Oscars. Only *West Side Story* with ten and *Ben Hur* with eleven have achieved greater glory.

One of the few other British winners that night, Andrew Lloyd-Webber – who picked up a gong for Best Original Song from the movie *Evita* – summed up the feeling of many in the audience who felt Minghella's movie was unbeatable when he joked, 'Thank heavens there wasn't a song in *The English Patient*.'

As he was leaving for an exclusive party at the Mondrian Hotel in Sunset Boulevard, Ralph said, 'This is the greatest night of my life'. He professed not to mind about missing out on a gong: 'Awards can't make you happy; only the knowledge of a job well done can do that.' Other celebrities at the grand festivities included Glenn Close, Kenneth Branagh and Winona Ryder. And when LA's strict licensing laws brought the flow of champagne to an end at 2 a.m., Ralph, Francesca, and the rest of the guests headed for the 12th-floor penthouse where the party went on through the night.

As the sun rose over the City of the Angels, a bleary-eyed Fiennes made his way back to his hotel room, the previous night's applause still ringing in his ears. The much-fêted star may not have received his very own personal statuette but, as everyone present knew, *The English Patient* would not have been the remarkable film it was but for him. In recognition of this, one of the producers, clutching the Best Picture award to his bosom as if it was a new-born baby, announced, 'Without you, Ralph, we wouldn't be here. You were, are and always will be the English Patient in the eyes of the world.'

All who saw *The English Patient* were entranced by the actor's portrayal of the mysterious Count Laszlo de Almasy – little knowing that he had led a considerably more ambivalent life than the complex hero portrayed in both Ondaatje's book and Minghella's celluloid story.

A precocious child, he was sent to school in Britain, where he picked up fluent English, and later flew with the Hungarian Air Force in the First World War. After hearing stories of the British expeditions on the trail of a lost city in the Sahara, he headed for North Africa where, with the patronage of the Egyptian Royal Family, he set out to uncover this mythical civilization buried beneath the desert's ever-shifting sands.

On his third attempt to find the city, he discovered the prehistoric cave paintings – thought to be over 15,000 years old – depicted in the film. By this stage, Almasy, Lawrence-like, had developed an obsession with the desert, and chose to spend much of his life among the Bedouins, riding a camel and living in a tent. But several revealing factors about him are conveniently glossed over in both book and film.

Firstly, he wasn't a genuine count. For, despite being born in 1895 in northern Hungary a member of a minor noble family, the title of 'count', which he liberally used in his later life in Egypt, was never officially recognized in his homeland.

Secondly, there is little doubt that Almasy became a Nazi spy by choice, not by any unfortunate accidental circumstance. His map-drawing expertise, encyclopaedic knowledge of the Sahara and fluency in German as well as Arabic, French and Italian made him a valuable Nazi asset during the struggle for control of North Africa. And, while a reserve lieutenant in the Hungarian Army in 1941, he insisted on being seconded to the Afrika Korps where he became a key Rommel aide.

Mystery surrounds much of his wartime activity but it is known that in 1942 he smuggled German spies – including the infamous Hans Eppler – behind the British lines in Egypt in a secret mission code-named Operation Salaam. So highly were his services regarded that in 1943 he was awarded an Iron Cross.

Thirdly, and somewhat ironically, given Ralph's portrait of him as a dashing romantic lead – the tall, slightly stooped Almasy was homosexual and his illicit love affair with a young German officer was intimately described in a cache of letters in the possession of Kurt Meyer, son of the Austrian film-maker Rudi who made a documentary about one of his early desert expeditions.

The *Daily Express* even claimed that Almasy (who died in 1951) had been the legendary Desert Fox's gay lover. 'He was a well-known homosexual in Budapest before the war,' a relative told the newspaper. 'And there were strong rumours that he had a relationship with Rommel.'

Nevertheless, the sanitized screen story of his life, which subsequently won three BAFTA awards – though once again Ralph lost out in the race for best actor – was one of the most successful 'British' (albeit financed by American money and based on a Canadian book) films of all time.

By the summer of 1997 it had grossed more than $225 million (about £150 million) around the world, performing spectacularly well just about everywhere. In total, it took more than $75 million at the US box office, about £13 million ($20m) in the UK and Germany, and substantial amounts in territories as far-flung as Australia, Scandinavia and Japan.

For a while it seemed as if the entire world was caught up in *English Patient* fever. Michael Ondaatje's original novel shot up the best-seller lists, where it was to remain for months. And Penguin even published a new edition of works by the Greek historian Herodotus because Ralph's character carried a copy with him in the film.

Perhaps inevitably, the picture's blanket critical approbation from all corners of the world triggered off a backlash.

'Frankly, I found it languid to the point of inertia, pretentious, self-indulgent and with all the authenticity of *The Wizard of Oz*,' pronounced the best-selling author Frederick Forsyth. 'I don't think I've ever been so bored,' bitched the maverick art critic Brian Sewell. 'It went on too long, it was too shallow and most of the acting was cardboard. I have never seen an actor with so little expression as Ralph Fiennes. He was better when he was half-dead. There was more expression in his bandages.'

Others also cavilled. Dr Jonathan Miller condemned it as 'perfumed piffle; a mixture of Biggles and Barbara Cartland.' And film-maker Donovan Winter claimed the film was 'a monstrous piece of meretricious nonsense'.

It's easy to be cynical in today's sometimes despairing world. But for all the hype, *The English Patient* is likely to remain, as one American critic put it, 'a film for the ages'.

CHAPTER EIGHTEEN
Chekhov's Hamlet

After the success of his stage *Hamlet*, it was no great surprise when Ralph Fiennes announced his intention to return to the theatre once again. But his choice of material was more of a shock. For he forsook a leading role in an acknowledged classic for the lead in an early, little-known Chekhov play, *Ivanov*.

The famous Russian dramatist eventually enjoyed an almost Tolstoyan dominance of his country's literature, thanks to the success of his three most famous plays – *Uncle Vanya* (1899), *The Three Sisters* (1901) and *The Cherry Orchard* (1904).

However, his first play, *Ivanov*, written in two weeks in 1887, has long been denigrated by critics. It favoured the use of monologue and direct address, featured a hero who made conspicuously long speeches and lacked the subtlety with which the writer later satirized Russian society. It has consequently been regarded by many academics as a mere blueprint for Chekhov's later, maturer work and has been dismissed as the first, unsteady stumblings of an apprentice wordsmith.

When it was commissioned by Moscow's Korth Theatre, which specialized in farce, Chekhov was primarily known as a comic short story writer. The theatre was therefore surprised by the seriousness of the play. Its scanty rehearsal time resulted in a disastrous début performance.

One of the actors stumbled over his lines in the first act, while the 'drunken' party guests were stumbling too. They really *were* drunk in the second act; even knocking over the stage furniture. A furious Chekhov vowed to have nothing more to do with the theatre again.

Two years later, though, he rewrote much of the play, including the ending, after the Alexandrine Theatre in St Petersburg expressed a desire to stage it. This time, despite the author's doubts, it was a resounding success. Nevertheless, it has remained one of his lesser-known plays – partly because he expressed disdain for it in his private correspondence.

Fiennes had had a sentimental attitude to the play ever since taking the lead role in a RADA production when he was 22 and 'far too young'. He also felt that the critics had never accorded the drama – about a Russian landowner who rejects his wife and is crushed by his inability to find happiness – the recognition it deserved.

The play's troubled central character, Ivanov, is cut from the same cloth as *Hamlet*'s tragic hero – and in fact is sometimes dubbed 'Chekhov's Hamlet'. Despite recognizing the similarities, Fiennes is quick to point out that 'Hamlet is more spiritually dynamic while Ivanov is in the grip of the bleakest suicidal despair.'

But the story also appealed to something deep within his psyche. 'I like things that are not clear-cut and have ambiguity running through them,' he explained. 'I also felt that at 34 I was just the right age. As far as I know, everyone else who has tackled the part over the last thirty years has been a generation older.'

The Russian playwright's ambivalent persona, embodying shades of light and dark not unlike Ralph's, only heightened the actor's interest in the play. Born in 1860 in Taganog, Russia, Anton Chekhov was one of six children, was famously attractive to women and was the product of an over-close family. He was also a habitual visitor of prostitutes and died in 1904 of tuberculosis aged just 44.

One night Fiennes suggested to the Almeida Theatre's Jonathan Kent – with whom he had collaborated on *Hamlet* two years earlier – that they collaborate on a new stage version of the play. Kent needed little persuading but he pointed out that *Ivanov* had not had a particularly happy British history.

Following its première in Barnes, south-west London in 1925, John Gielgud had starred in his own production of *Ivanov* at the Phoenix Theatre in 1965, and distinguished actors such as Derek Jacobi and Alan Bates had also tackled the part. But, as one theatrical commentator put it, it had never been 'a must-see play'.

The solution, according to Fiennes and Kent, lay in a new translation of the text – and who better to turn to than the director's old friend, David Hare, the critically acclaimed playwright perhaps best known for the 1985 production of *Pravda*, the story of a megalomaniac media mogul brilliantly played by Anthony Hopkins at the National Theatre.

He had also penned the screenplays for the films *Wetherby*, *Plenty* and *Damage*. But just as importantly, Hare had already adapted Pirandello's *The Rules of the Game* as well as Brecht's *The Life of Galileo* and *Mother Courage and Her Children* for Kent.

The Cambridge-educated dramatist shared Ralph's feelings that Chekhov's early work had long been undervalued.

'Perhaps we can allow that the absurdly long *Platonov* is indeed a sort of young man's mess,' says Hare. 'And admit that *The Wood Demon* is only a sketch for the much more satisfying *Uncle Vanya*. But we are overlooking something really valuable if we regard the brilliant rogue play, *Ivanov*, simply as the staging-post of a writer on his way to greater things.

'Unless we see that *Ivanov* is not a lesser play but simply different to the rest of his work, then we will miss the versatility of a playwright who can still surprise us by the variety of his styles – and there are ways in which it provides an infinitely richer experience for the audience than many a cooler, supposedly more mature play.'

Another of the play's virtues, in Hare's mind, was that it gave a 'singular insight' into a younger, more robust Chekhov, sometimes anarchic and blustering, who was willing to address the ugliness of Russian anti-semitism with head-on courage yet referred to a Jewish girlfriend as 'Efros the Nose'.

The trio of Fiennes, Kent and Hare recognized that the play's dominant theme was honesty: the implications of which it explored via the contrast between the self-confident Dr Lvov (who thought honesty involved speaking the truth, no matter how offensive) and the more cautious Ivanov (who argued that one could only acquire honesty if one also had the self-knowledge to examine one's own motives).

'It's hard to see how Chekhov could have written a play which asks what real honesty is, and just as importantly, what its price is, without being willing to let a little more of his feelings show,' says Hare. 'There is little doubt where his sympathies lie but his achievement is to provide Ivanov with an opponent who is, in an odd way, as compelling as the hero.'

Furthermore, Hare refuted the oft-repeated criticism that in Ivanov, Chekhov had created an excessively self-pitying hero. 'He portrays a character who is actually horrified by the idea of depression and who is repelled to find himself its victim,' argues the dramatist. 'Far from indulging in that melancholy, as perhaps some of the weaker characters in Chekhov's later plays do, Ivanov fights it. The play is a portrait of a man who will do anything rather than falsely dramatize his feelings.'

Some of the reporters who covered the news of Ralph's return to the stage gave the impression they had never heard of *Ivanov*, let alone knew the way in which the play's name should be pronounced. But it would not take them long to draw parallels between the drama's central character and its actor – men who had both turned their backs on their wives.

Aware that *Ivanov* was unlikely to have the same sort of public appeal as *Hamlet*, Fiennes and Kent opted to stage the play at the Almeida itself.

The Upper Street building that it called home had opened its doors in 1837 as the Islington Literary and Scientific Institution, the premises originally comprising a lecture theatre, library, museum and laboratory. Over the ensuing years it had been everything from a music hall to a Salvation Army citadel, at one point even becoming a factory for carnival novelties.

In 1989 it was taken over by two actors, Ian McDiarmid and Jonathan Kent, who installed 300 seats, christened it the Almeida and against all odds turned it into *the* theatre success story of the decade.

Its 1992 production of *No Man's Land* won the late, much-loved Paul Eddington (who starred in *The Good Life* and *Yes, Minister*) a best actor award. While its production of *Medea* won former *Avengers* star Diana Rigg a best actress award. The following year saw the Almeida score a double whammy again – winning *Ever Decreasing Circles* star Penelope Wilton a best actress award for her role in *The Deep Blue Sea* and the veteran actor Ian Holm a best actor award for his role in *Moonlight*.

In 1995, it enjoyed a further triumph with Ralph winning a Tony award for his Broadway *Hamlet*. And in 1996 it notched up yet another success – when Diana Rigg walked away with another best actress award, this time for her performance in the theatre's revival of *Who's Afraid of Virginia Woolf?*

How had McDiarmid and Kent been able to coax such high-profile actors into appearing in London N1 for next to nothing? The secret, according to Wilton, is that 'it's run by two actors. It's not a directors' theatre, it's an actors' theatre.'

The big question was could Fiennes repeat the success with *Ivanov*? Ralph thought Hare's vigorous new version of *Ivanov* struck just the right balance. 'What David has tried to do is tease out the struggle inside Ivanov,' he said. And rehearsals began in earnest at the start of January 1997.

Tickets for *Ivanov*'s six-week run, costing up to £19.50, all but sold out before the first performance – even though Fiennes gave just one interview to publicize the play, and that to a local weekly newspaper, the *Hampstead and Highgate Gazette*. It was a glowing testament to the actor's pulling power.

The bulk of the press were fascinated by the fact that Fiennes would be earning the extraordinarily low 'standard' actor's fee of £200 a week during its run. After deductions for tax, national insurance and his agent's 10 per cent, he would be left with just £135 a week, the sort of wage he might have pocketed from working in a fast food outlet. 'You wouldn't find Daniel Day-Lewis appearing in an off-West End-revue for that money,' quipped the *Mail on Sunday*.

As the first night approached, Fiennes expressed confidence in both the production and the players. His only concern, he said in a moment of self-doubt, was that the audience might find his interpretation of Ivanov too 'self-lacerating'.

The opening night, Wednesday 19 February, saw a host of stars turn up to show their support – including Sean Connery, actresses Zoe Wanamaker and Janet Suzman, Miramax Films chief Herbie Weinstein, writer-director Christopher Hampton, movie director Karel Reisz and Ralph's partner, Francesca.

The play opened in the garden of Ivanov's estate with Fiennes sitting alone reading. His peace is shattered by his drunken, 'pug-ugly' estate manager Borkin (played by Anthony O'Donnell), bearing down on him with a gun. 'My God, what on earth are you doing?' he says, shocked.

But the audience, accustomed to Ralph as the clean-shaven matineé idol, was also somewhat shocked by the Lech Walesa-style drooping moustache he had grown for the part which the *Sun* declared made him into a dead ringer for England goalkeeper David Seaman.

Like so many other people Fiennes has played, Ivanov is a character in crisis. At 35, he is bankrupt, he has fallen out of love with his tubercular Jewish wife, Anna Petrovna (Harriet Walter), and is seeking nightly solace in the arms of his debtors' nubile daughter Sasha (played by 21-year-old newcomer Justine Waddell). Furthermore, his callous behaviour towards his wife – at one point he screams that she is a 'dirty Jew' – is sending her to an early grave, Dr Lvov (Colin Tierney) insists.

'She's a wonderful woman, an extraordinary woman,' says a shabbily dressed Ralph in words that could have perhaps been spoken about his real wife, Alex. 'Any sacrifice I required she was ready to make ... She gave up the name she was born with ... On my side, I have sacrificed precisely nothing. I married her because I loved her passionately and I swore to love her for ever but ... all right ... Five years have gone by, she is still in love, and I ...'

If Kingston had been in the audience on that night, the real-life overtones in the drama would surely have sent her fleeing the auditorium.

He further informs Lvov that even though he is aware that Anna is dying, he feels neither love nor pity, 'just a terrible kind of emptiness' – and that however much he attempts to 'unfreeze' this numbness, however much guilt he senses in his subconscious, he is powerless.

'Don't take on the world,' he tells Lvov. 'Don't tilt at windmills. Don't waste your time bashing your head against brick walls ... Just pull your little shell over your head and get on with your life. It's the only way. I did the other thing and it has destroyed me. My life? A story of unceasing error and absurdity!'

The righteous doctor is unmoved by this display of self-pity. 'A woman is dying,' he says. 'Yet you prance around like a pigeon boasting of your ... despair. You are a man who is detestable.' Ralph's character concurs with the assessment. 'Perhaps,' he says (and you could not help but wonder whether the real Ralph was simultaneously speaking for himself and the way the world perceived his treatment of Alex) 'you see me from the outside.'

Later on, Anna beseeches Ivanov not to leave her alone in their rambling, decaying mansion.

Ivanov: Anna, my sweet one ... I need this selfishness.
Anna: I don't understand. What changed you?
Ivanov: I don't know ... All right, let me say it ... I begin not to love you. Yes. That's why I run.

His mind made up, he takes his leave – leaving the stricken Anna to ask, 'Why is not love answered with love? Why is truth always answered with lies?' But nothing can prevent her tormented husband – who bitterly compares himself to Hamlet, and like the Prince, has come to see the world as 'weary, stale, flat and unprofitable' – from travelling towards a tragic ending.

By Act Two he is telling Sasha: 'It's an extraordinary irony. I used to think and work all the time and I never felt tired. Now I do nothing and I'm completely exhausted. And all because of my conscience. Hour after hour, eating away at me. All the time I feel guilty ...'

The idealistic young Sasha believes she has the answer to Ivanov's troubles. 'You are unhappy because you are lonely,' she tells him consolingly. 'Love alone can help you.'

But the cynical, world-weary landowner believes nothing can cure him of his woes. 'Love?' asks Ralph's character, shoulders stooped and eyes downcast. 'Does love help? Does it? Really? I promise you, I could endure everything I'm experiencing – the poverty, the depression, the loss of my wife, the loneliness, my own useless decay – but the one thing I cannot endure is the contempt I feel for myself. I'm half dead with the shame of it ...'

Nearly three hours after it had begun, the play – which also cast a critical eye on the socially stagnating Russia of the time – ended in an ultimate moment of high and devastating drama with Ivanov announcing 'Let me be free!' before putting a gun to his head and taking his own life.

The production was a *tour de force* with Fiennes – who visibly wilted as his character sank ever deeper into despair – on top form. 'If a begrudging few thought his Hamlet had not been tormented enough,' one observer commented, 'he has now successfully tackled a role that, psychologically speaking, takes him into the catacombs and torture chambers of Elsinore.'

It was a role that Fiennes, with his predilection for tortured intellectual figures, seemed tailor-made to tackle. Yet Ivanov was a torturous figure by even his standards, and a role that exercised all his dramatic skills. 'The problem is he starts off in despair and you have to find the gradations by which he comes to the point of shooting himself,' said the actor. 'You cannot fully enter into that state of mind.'

But *Ivanov*'s success was also a tribute to its stellar supporting cast – which included Bill Paterson, Oliver Ford Davies, Rosemary McHale and Diane Bull, as well as Walter, Tierney and O'Donnell.

The audience gave a standing ovation as the actors, led by Ralph, took a bow after the curtain went down. Someone threw three red roses at his feet and in gentlemanly manner he picked them up and handed them to his three female co-stars: Walter, Waddell and Bull.

Afterwards, the celebrities in the audience lavished praise on the production. Christopher Hampton said, 'I loved the mix of farce and tragedy and in Ralph Fiennes it had a wonderful actor.' Karel Reisz said: 'It was bolder than I expected – more like Gogol than Chekhov.' Janet Suzman also gave it the thumbs up, adding, 'As for Ralph, I have never seen him *not* give a good performance.'

This time the critics were all but unanimous in their praise. 'It is one of those evenings when you want to salute the entire cast, particularly Fiennes who gives a remarkable performance,' said the *Daily Telegraph*. 'Anyone who has had any experience of clinical depression will recognize the listlessness of his voice, the sudden bursts of pettish temper, the restlessness and the self-contempt.'

The *Observer* hailed it as 'a magnificent, raucous revival with a gallery of glorious grotesques' which made for 'a truly exhilarating evening' and it praised Ralph's 'brilliant performance'. The *Sunday Times* congratulated Kent on his 'energetic production' and proclaimed Fiennes 'the perfect nineteenth century existential hero'. While the *Guardian* thought that Ralph had got closer to Hamlet in *Ivanov* than he did playing the Danish prince at the Hackney Empire.

The *Mail on Sunday* agreed that Fiennes was 'superbly cast' as Ivanov. 'As tortured souls go, few can touch him,' it declared. 'His eyes simultaneously freeze and blaze, seethe with arrogance and self-disgust, harden pitilessly, then well up with self-pity. Knowing what we know about him, though, it's hard not to speculate which auto-biographical chapter he's drawn on to convey a character with such a detailed and forcible reality.'

Only one newspaper, the *Evening Standard*, voiced reservations: while admiring Ralph for scaling 'the heights of fury', it branded the production 'surprisingly heavy-handed' and concluded that 'it fell several feet away from triumph'.

Despite the play's official sell-out, each day sixteen tickets were set aside and sold to the lucky few who turned up early enough to buy them at the door.

Some diehards spent the night shivering on the pavement outside to ensure a ticket for a performance. While one female Fiennes fan from America – where else? – flew to Britain on the off-chance of catching her idol in action. Landing at Heathrow at 5a.m., she got a taxi straight to the Almeida, joined the back of the queue and struck lucky. Could there be greater proof that *Ivanov* was indeed the hottest ticket in town?

The icing on the Chekhovian cake was an invitation extended to the Almeida to perform *Ivanov* at Russia's oldest theatre, The Maly, which had not staged the play for more than thirty-five years. It was a cultural risk but how could anyone forgo the chance to make history by becoming the first British company to bring a Chekhov play to Moscow?

In late April, Ralph and the rest of the cast flew out to the Russian capital to give three performances of the play at the 150-year-old theatre – a trip sponsored to the tune of £80,000 by the British Council which promotes British culture abroad. 'It's extraordinarily exciting,' said the actor before leaving.

There was an element of risk about a British theatrical company performing Chekhov in a city where even taxi drivers could quote their literary luminary hero faultlessly. But Fiennes remained unfazed, remarking: 'We'll get the response that we get.'

Just twenty-four hours before the actors were due to take the stage there was an unexpected hitch. It was discovered that the revolving set from London would not fit the stage of the Maly – even though the theatre auditorium seated more than three times as many people as the Almeida – forcing the technical crew to work round the clock to make it function.

All the tickets had sold out by 24 April – the date of the first performance. And 150,000-rouble (about £20) tickets were changing hands for ten times their cover price, as well-dressed Russians, along with a spattering of British, American and European expatriates, filed into the theatre half-an-hour before the performance was due to begin.

The audience took their seats in the lavish red and gold auditorium and the more Fiennes beat his brow, the more the Russian section of the audience murmured its approval. When the curtain finally went down, the audience spontaneously leapt to its feet with shouts of 'Bravo!' Bouquets of flowers bombarded the stage and the frenzied applause lasted more than ten minutes.

The mood was one of elation at the after-show party. And while the champagne flowed and the guests tucked into cinnamon pears, a flushed, happy-looking Ralph posed for photographs with Russian fans and signed autographs. The partying continued at the actors' hotel where the cast sat around singing Beatles' songs until the early hours.

Over the next few days, he got to see the Kremlin and the Red Square. 'Moscow is much more interesting than I was led to expect and the Russian humour has a fine irony that I like,' he said. But the undoubted highlight of his whistlestop sightseeing tour was visiting Chekhov's modest grave in Moscow's Novodevichi Convent Cemetery. 'That was a significant moment for me,' he confessed. 'I was able to stop and think about what we were doing.'

All too soon, the third and final night approached. 'This has been the happiest company I have ever worked with,' said Ralph, shortly before his curtain call. 'When it's over I think we will all feel a great sense of loss.' The best of it was that the actor could reflect that his Ivanov had been a resounding triumph in Britain *and* Russia. And not only had he rescued the play from obscurity in his homeland, he had won it new fans throughout the world.

CHAPTER NINETEEN
A Star Without Question

For all his star status and Hollywood clout, Fiennes remained defiantly unconventional in outlook, turning down job offers unless he could commit himself 100 per cent to a project. So when *The English Patient* wrapped, he began work on another big screen version of a Booker prize-winning novel close to his heart – Peter Carey's *Oscar and Lucinda*.

It was a complex story of chance and fate centred on the figures of Oscar Hopkins, an Oxford seminarian with a love of gambling, and Lucinda Leplastrier, a Sydney heiress with a passion for glass. The two meet on a ship travelling to Australia, where Oscar is heading to spread God's word. They immediately fall in love. Both are gamblers but in a strange way also innocents – their love, and fates, sealed with a wager over a grand folly, a church made from glass that can be packed flat and taken into the Australian outback.

This Sydney-based author's unusually structured, 110-chapter novel attracted critical acclaim upon publication in 1988. The *Financial Times* hailed it as 'the most original novel to appear in the English language for many years' and the *Guardian* called it 'a novel of extraordinary richness, complexity and strength'.

A wide-screen version had spent years in studio development, with numerous 'names' including Winona Ryder's and director John Schlesinger's attached to the enterprise. The long-dormant project was finally resuscitated by Australia's Film Finance Corporation – and a heavyweight Hollywood partner, in the shape of Fox

Searchlight, was found to help underwrite the costs. When Ralph was offered the male lead, he felt unable to turn it down. 'He's a long-time fan of the book and finds Oscar a curiously compelling character,' says a friend.

Shooting on the £10 million movie started in early September 1996, and went on until mid-December. Scenes were shot in Cornwall, Portsmouth and Oxford before the cast and crew headed Down Under. Besides donning period costume, Ralph was also required to dye his hair orange. 'Not everyone felt it suited him,' observes a crew member.

The film is unlikely to set the box office alight on its 1998 release. But now Fiennes is a star he can afford the indulgence of appearing in something that is close to his heart but appeals to arthouse rather than mainstream movie audiences. Having said that, before it was released sceptics dismissed *The English Patient* as an arthouse movie ...

In February 1997 Ralph and Francesca made their first public appearance together, at the *Evening Standard* film awards in London's West End (prompting one tabloid to dub the event 'The Fiennes and Francesca Film Awards'.)

Relaxed and confident, they posed outside the Savoy Hotel for photographers, Fiennes sporting the moustache he had grown for his *Ivanov* role and Annis looking radiant in a low-cut black and silver gown. 'For all their age difference, they made a supremely elegant couple,' says one onlooker.

By now, the actor was living in a fabulous four-floor Victorian house he had bought in Ladbroke Grove, one of the main thoroughfares in London's fashionable and cosmopolitan Notting Hill.

The urbanization of the area to the north of Holland Park Avenue began in the first half of the nineteenth century with the laying out of the leafy avenues and majestic crescent of the exclusive Norland and Ladbroke estates. Gradually, the area went downhill and by the 1950s it was described as 'a massive slum, full of multi-occupier houses, crawling with rats and rubbish'. Its cheap accommodation was a magnet for West Indian migrants and local white prejudice engendered Britain's first race riots in 1958.

This proved to be the nadir in Notting Hill's fortunes. Nowadays the area – which is dotted with fashionable restaurants and bars but retains a gritty multicultural urbanism – is the place in London to live if you're young and famous, and work in the arts or media. Actor Alan Rickman, Blur star Damon Albam and his rock singer girlfriend Justine Frischmann, Labour politician Peter Mandelson and magazine publisher Nicholas Coleridge are among those calling it home. Notting Hill is also the first choice of American stars – such as Uma Thurman – looking for a temporary London base. It's even been immortalized in Martin Amis's cult novel *London Fields*.

Despite being up-and-coming, Ladbroke Grove, like much of the area, is notable for its startling social contrasts and while the southern end of the street is lined by palatial villas, the northern end – with its shabby terraces and rundown council estates – has a very different atmosphere and has at times been seen as something of an urban ghetto.

As one might expect, Ralph's house lies in an exclusive segment of the street, though only just qualifying for this delineation. The property – about halfway along Ladbroke Grove – would be swathed in scaffolding for much of 1997 as he set about transforming it into his dream home. It reputedly cost more than £1 million but that was small change to the now wealthy actor.

Friends said he and Francesca were 'very much in love' as was obvious to anyone seeing their public displays of affection – when they held hands, kissed and touched each other with tenderness. However, perhaps in a bid not to rub salt into their former partners' wounds, they kept separate houses – Annis living in Addison Road, Shepherd's Bush, about a mile away.

Occasionally, a tabloid photographer would lie in wait and snatch a picture of Fiennes jumping over the wall of her home or waiting outside his house in a dressing gown for her to arrive.

And for all that they say about life imitating art, the pair seemed determined to prove the reverse true. First, Fiennes had played a husband who turned his back on his wife in *Ivanov*. Then, in early 1997, his lover appeared in a television series in which she played an older woman who embarks on a passionate affair with a young doctor (played by *Soldier, Soldier* star Robson Green).

The gripping drama – described as a cross between *Fatal Attraction* and *The Graduate* – was made all the more compelling by the knowledge that Annis had also swapped a middle-aged partner for a handsome young lover in real life. Though, intriguingly, she only agreed to play the part after the writers turned the doctor from a toy boy in his twenties to a more sensible mid-thirties 'relationship man'.

The name of the series – *Reckless* – couldn't have been more fitting in many people's eyes.

The favourable word-of-mouth surrounding *The English Patient* helped Ralph clinch the lead role in a big screen remake of *The Avengers* before the desert epic was even released. He had been in the running to play John Steed – the series' suave special agent who was never seen without his trademark curly-brimmed bowler-hat and cane-handled umbrella – ever since the preliminary discussions about the project.

Originally, *Strange Days'* poor box-office performance had led some Hollywood executives to question whether Fiennes had the necessary box-office appeal to carry the movie. 'There were those who thought he was just another Brit who should never be let out of period costume,' says one movie industry source. And at one point Mel Gibson, Jeremy Irons and Hugh Grant were all being considered for the part.

However, the upper-crust Ralph eventually signed on to play the upper-crust Steel. His fee? A reported $3 million (£2m). To celebrate, his agent bought him a bowler hat exactly like the character-full John Steed's.

The series started life in 1960 as *Police Surgeon* starring the late Ian Hendry, before evolving into *The Avengers* the following year, initially with Hendry as the star, and Patrick Macnee playing second fiddle.

But the series, as the world remembers it, began when Hendry was replaced by the statuesque, husky-voiced Honor Blackman who played anthropologist Cathy Gale. She became the first of the show's famous action girls. Her costumes regularly split under the stress of all the karate kicking – so leather cat suits were introduced to preserve her dignity. Overnight both the ratings, and the temperatures of male viewers, shot up.

In 1965 Diana Rigg replaced Blackman to become Steed's new

sidekick – Emma Peel – inaugurating the show's glory years.

The Swinging Sixties were well and truly under way. Britain was the epicentre of a hip, happening youth revolution, spearheaded by the Beatles and Rolling Stones. With the appearance of Emma Peel – who kept Gale's leather catsuit but gave it a sexy new skin-tight look – it was as if *The Avengers* was carrying the revolution into the then rather unadventurous world of television too.

Set in a psychedelic Little England, dotted with abandoned RAF bases and sinister country houses, the series was clever, witty, tongue-in-cheek and in the words of one critic, 'exquisitely absurd'. Macnee hammed it up as the unflappable aristocrat who never carried a gun but outfoxed a succession of fiendish masterminds and glamorous villains. And the palpably feline Rigg rescued him from many a tight spot, karate kicking bad guys into oblivion and putting 'girl power' into practice long before the Spice Girls had even been conceived.

In 1967, Rigg handed over to Linda Thorson who played Tara King until 1969 when the series folded. Six years later, there was an ill-advised resurrection, *The New Avengers* – starring Joanna Lumley as Purdey – but it never recaptured the show's earlier success.

By the mid-1990s, a string of hit television series – including *Batman*, *Mission Impossible* and *The Saint* – had been turned into movies, albeit of variable quality. So it was only natural that Hollywood moguls would eventually turn their attention to *The Avengers*. Having grown up in the 1960s and 1970s, Fiennes was familiar with the show. In fact, he was more than familiar, he was a fan.

At first, the media appeared surprised by Ralph's casting as Steed – a role that was unlikely to stretch him intellectually. Wasn't Fiennes the desperately serious actor who specialized in playing tormented souls? 'I just saw it as an opportunity to do something enjoyable without having to tear my guts out or contemplate suicide,' explained Ralph, who pursued a rigorous programme of abdominal training in preparation for the part at the Lambton Place gym in west London, and brushed up on his fencing skills. 'In addition, the screenplay indicated a style that appealed to me.' There was also speculation that 'getting to sit behind the wheel of a classic Jaguar SS100' may have influenced his decision.

By the time cameras on the £40 million film were ready to roll, it had an all-star cast. Both Nicole Kidman and Gwyneth Paltrow were initially in the running to play Steed's sidekick, Emma Peel. But Kidman's husband, Tom Cruise, wanted to get back to America, having already shot two films – *Mission Impossible* and *Event Horizon* – in the UK. Similarly, Brad Pitt wanted his fiancée, Paltrow, beside him in the States, not on the other side of the Atlantic. (Ironically, the duo split up shortly after Paltrow passed on *The Avengers.*)

The role therefore went to Uma Thurman, the waif-like blonde best known for her starring roles in *Pulp Fiction* and 1997's *Batman and Robin*. Cult comic Eddie Izzard was given a minor part as a baddie, and Shaun Ryder, lead singer of the rock group Black Grape, got to make his movie début as a villain called Bully Boy. Even Macnee was promised a small cameo role.

But the film's biggest coup was in persuading Sean Connery – with the help of a £4 million cheque – to play the part of the diabolical mastermind Sir August de Wynter, who attempts to conquer the world by manipulating the weather.

The opening credits – shot at a disused air base in Gloucestershire – showed Uma Thurman, dressed in a leather catsuit every bit as tight as Rigg's, slapping an 'out-of-order' sign on an old-fashioned telephone box before disappearing Avengers-style through a secret trap door. The rest of the film – directed by Jeremiah Chechik, who the previous year had given the 1955 French classic, *Diabolique*, a Hollywood make-over – was shot, over the course of the summer, at Pinewood Studios in Buckinghamshire and on location in London.

The following weeks saw paparazzi-style photographers grab several sneak pictures of Ralph, in bowler hat and three-piece suit, during location shoots on the capital's streets.

The *Daily Telegraph* subsequently carried a rather pompous article claiming that Fiennes's bowler hat made him look more like 'a surly Oxford porter' or '1930s bank clerk' than the dashing Steed of the television series. 'The problem is that he's wearing the wrong kind of bowler hat,' claimed the newspaper. 'There is only one solution – filming has to stop and Fiennes must be persuaded to don a more rakish hat.'

But the shape of Ralph's bowler hat was just one of the problems that dogged producers during the first weeks of filming.

Permission to take over Trafalgar Square for a day and smother it in fake snow, for one sequence, was refused. Then a controlled explosion on the set of the film at Pinewood went disastrously wrong when sparks shot up in the air, setting the roof alight. Sixty fire fighters were called in to tackle the blaze which resulted in thousands of pounds worth of damage. 'It's a serious blow but the Avengers can handle anything,' insisted producer Jerry Weintraub, playing down the incident.

It can only be hoped that such incidents are not a portent of an even bigger disaster: namely, a dud movie. Because doubts remain – despite its top-drawer cast.

Stepping into Steed's shoes was never going to be easy. Before filming started, Fiennes contacted Macnee for advice on playing the part. The 75-year-old gave his blessing to his casting, saying: 'He's a wonderful actor and I hope the film's a success.' Nevertheless Macnee was the definitive Steed in the eyes of many *Avengers* purists and it remains to be seen whether Ralph can shake off his long shadow.

Others wondered whether Ralph could bring the necessary lightness of touch to Steed's role. Brian Clemens, creator of the original series, said sceptically, '*The Avengers* is hardly *Schindler's List*. Fiennes is too sardonic ... he lacks warmth.'

The actor himself admits he can seem terribly serious. 'I'm often accused of that by my girlfriend who says I'm over-intense,' he said in 1992. 'I think she's probably right.' But Estelle Kohler, who worked alongside him in the RSC, insists, 'People have this idea that Ralph is always terribly serious but he's got a lively sense of humour – as anyone who's worked with him will testify.'

Furthermore, despite Weintraub's pledge that *The Avengers* 'will be true to the TV series', it looks as if it's going to be pitched as a kitschy, tongue-in-cheek James Bond-style adventure comedy. That's fine so long as meddling Hollywood executives don't turn it into a *Saint*-style travesty of the original. Having said that, Ralph's track record inspires the hope that it will be several cuts above the usual big budget Tinseltown movie.

In June, 1997, *Première* published a list of the movie world's Top

Fifty stars. It may have been unscientific and subjective but it shed a useful light on actors' standing in Hollywood.

Top of the list was Tom Cruise who, along with Mel Gibson, Tom Hanks, Arnold Schwarzenegger, Harrison Ford and John Travolta was branded an 'A+' superstar. The next section – the 'A' list stars – included Clint Eastwood, Brad Pitt, Kevin Costner, Jim Carrey, Sly Stallone, Michael Douglas, Sean Connery, Jodie Foster and Demi Moore.

Bubbbling under were borderline 'A' list actors such as Robert De Niro and … Ralph Fiennes. To be even a borderline 'A' list actor was a fantastic achievement for someone whose name would have scored a 'zero' recognition Tinseltown rating just a few years earlier.

He is already one of just a handful of British actors – including Anthony Hopkins, Daniel Day-Lewis and Connery – whose involvement in a project will almost certainly guarantee a seal of approval from a major studio. And if *The Avengers* performs anywhere near as well as Warners hope, it will catapult Ralph up this particular ratings list.

Few movie moguls doubt that he is one of the finest acting talents to emerge from these shores in a long time – despite being a very different actor from the conventional American product. 'He's a polar opposite of someone like Tom Hanks, who just doesn't have that dark side,' observes one Hollywood executive. 'But that dark side is fascinating to watch and it's what gives Ralph his unusual quality as an actor.'

Possible future projects include providing the voice of Jesus in an animated film called *The Jesus Story*, set for a 1998/9 release; starring in and co-producing *The Child in Time*, based on a novel by Ian McEwan about a man who tries to hold his marriage together following his daughter's kidnapping; and playing the lead in a big-screen version of Sebastian Faulk's *Birdsong*, the story of a passionate romance set against the First World War. And it has been rumoured he might star in a film based on Alexander Pushkin's novel in verse, *Yevgeny Onegin*, to be directed by his sister Martha.

Yet he has anchored himself very firmly in the British theatre and after naming his price for the project of his choice he will be able to return to the Almeida for £250 a week if he chooses. 'He's also aware that Hollywood stardom can evaporate,' says his friend and former

RADA tutor Bill Homewood. 'One day you're a name to drop, the next you've been dropped. Deep-shoring of a career is essential.'

For all his fame, Fiennes still has a rare passion for the acting process. 'Mine is a clinical, methodical approach,' he says. 'I always try to be as prepared as anyone possibly could for a role, because only then can you free yourself. There are too many bad actors around already for the world to need another who hasn't bothered to learn his craft. By the end of my marriage I felt very rootless, and it was only in acting that I could find a centre.'

Mark Fiennes views his son's success with a degree of objectivity unusual in a typical proud parent. 'So much in life is being in the right place at the right time,' he reflects. 'It just happened that Ralph was seen in *Wuthering Heights* by Steven Spielberg who was casting a movie of immense importance. There are lots and lots of talented actors out there who did not have that incredible break. It's like winning on the horses.' Publicly, Fiennes isn't inclined to argue. 'This is a weird business and if *Schindler's List* had not been so successful, nothing would have changed for me,' he says modestly.

Like another seemingly moody, upper-middle-class actor, Daniel Day-Lewis, Fiennes exhibits an ambivalent, peculiarly English attitude towards stardom, becoming incensed when people ask him personal questions. 'I did not become an actor because I wanted to be in magazines,' he once said contemptuously. 'I became an actor because I love the theatre, because I love language, I love painting. I love all art forms.'

That may well be the most important issue, but fame didn't come knocking on his door. He, like any actor who becomes a star, actively sought it out. And despite the apparently fatalistic attitude he expressed about his career in interviews, Fiennes is 'fiercely ambitious' claims his ex-wife Alex.

Achieving fame and fortune may have 'never been something Mark or Jini Fiennes encouraged him to think important' but his bohemian, unorthodox upper-middle-class parents dreamt big dreams, giving him the confidence to believe that he could reach for the stars. Mark and Jini weren't the sort of parents to suppress ambition in their children, no matter how fatalistic the dream. They were givers, not dashers, of hope, they were not prisoners of respectability or class. Furthermore, a knowledge of what his forbears achieved and a desire to emulate their success propelled him to ever-greater heights. 'He always had a sense of his own purpose,' says his sister Martha.

But isn't any actor who accepts millions of pounds to appear in a movie to some extent entering into a kind of Faustian pact with the Devil? Part of the reason he is paid so much in the first place is because Hollywood's marketing men have turned him into a 'satisfaction guaranteed' brand name. When people fork out a fiver to see a Ralph Fiennes film, they're not just going to see the picture, they are going to see its star.

Isn't a relative loss of privacy the price a movie star has to pay in return for the great dividends – financial and otherwise – he reaps?

To show such an uncompromising attitude – almost an arrogance – at so early a stage in his career is the only foreseeable factor that could hold back his rise up the 'A' list (other than a string of box office flops – in which case he could always return to the theatre). There again, if the pressures of fame became too unbearable, he could always follow the example of his hero, T.E. Lawrence, adopt a pseudonym and seek anonymity. Somehow, though, that doesn't seem likely just yet.

Several old friends believe he is only playing at being the reluctant star anyway, and maintain that his 'shyness' is nothing more than a posture – a performance by which he escapes media intrusion. 'He was never as painfully withdrawn at school as he now seems in television interviews,' comments one Bishop Wordsworth's contemporary. 'I therefore find it hard to buy his "shy boy" routine.'

All might be well in Ralph's professional life but what of his private life? His former wife, Alex, found fame in 1996 in the bodice-ripping costume drama *Moll Flanders* – in which she had sex seventeen times, married five husbands and gave birth to six children – before landing a £500,000 deal to star opposite George Clooney in the hit American TV hospital drama *E.R.*

But time does not seem to have healed the wounds left by the acrimonious split. She deliberately cut off all communication with her ex-husband and there were even rumours that she had gone back to Fiennes seeking a bigger divorce settlement.

'There's no way I could simply have a friendship with Ralph

because I've worked so hard to let the pain fly away,' she said. 'I'm scared that the pain may just be superficially buried and that, if he re-entered my life, all the old wounds would be reopened. To be honest, I don't think I would want him back now.'

In contrast, Ralph seems to have put Alex behind him. He and Annis seem happy to enjoy the here and now. 'I don't expect everybody's approval but you have to bite the bullet and get on with it,' says Francesca defiantly, speaking for them both. But her mother, Marquita, voiced the unspoken thoughts of many when she reflected, 'He is a young man who may want children and Francesca is not a young woman any more – how can it work out?'

His behaviour towards his wife might have been branded 'callous' by one newspaper, but the reading tour he embarked upon to publicize his late mother's last novel, *Blood Ties* – about a family who take in a foster-child (as the Fiennes family did) – inspired nothing but admiration. Even now he visibly softens when talking about Jini, who, he credits with teaching him to 'appreciate art, love and poetry'.

He gave readings at book shops in London and Dublin and travelled to the Hay-on-Wye Literary Festival in Wales in May 1997, an event which is rather well-regarded, but nonetheless – by its considerable distance from London – is inevitably labelled 'provincial'. After his talk he skilfully fielded questions about the bleak nature of the novel's characters, which one inquisitor linked to the film roles he had played.

It is a tribute to Jini and Mark that all but one of their children has opted for a career in the arts – forming what's been dubbed 'a mini-dynasty of the performing arts'. Joseph, like Ralph, is an actor; Magnus is a composer; Martha is a film director and Sophie a theatrical designer. Only Jake has trodden a different path, becoming a gamekeeper. (Their foster brother, Michael Emery, is an archaeologist.)

But their mother's legacy also had its dark side. Indeed, Martha Fiennes suspects her mother's volatility had a formative impact on her elder brother. 'We all witnessed Jini's derangement at times and I'm sure Ralph absorbed it,' she says. 'I think Ralph has a dark side; he has an innate understanding of it, a very true understanding of human nature at the nether-nether region. He understands great distress and sadness and the fact that there is a strange beauty in tragedy.'

His other sister, Sophie, agrees: 'He is not so emotional as my mother was but he has a lot of understanding of darkness, of pain, of the twisted, darker recesses of the human psyche.' But for this awareness of life's dark side and what Fiennes calls 'the flip side, the B-side of people', he very likely would be a lesser actor and, dare one say it, human being.

Like other truly great actors, he has an uncanny, osmosis-like ability to absorb a character's qualities. But like them, it 'sometimes seems as if he's only half a person, only real when he's acting,' according to his ex-wife Alex. Could this be because, as Jonathan Kent reveals, 'Ralph actually said to me once that there are areas of his self that he only reveals when he's acting'? Shadier areas, where like the archetypal Hitchcock hero, he's drawn to look at evil and wonder at its awful seductions?

Fiennes, who has consistently played down his family's illustrious background, is undeniably more secretive than most. 'He's this beautiful house, but there are a couple of rooms that are locked and you can't go in,' observes his *Strange Days* co-star Angela Bassett. Kingston must have asked how well she had really known her husband, following their split. How well does Francesca Annis know the real Ralph now?

In the final analysis, the Capricorn-born actor – who once admitted 'Capricorns are ambitious, obsessive, solitary and moody' – is an enigma. This is how he likes it: he has a horror of being pigeon-holed and served up for public consumption, once contemptuously asking, 'How can people possibly judge me when I can't even judge myself?' How indeed?

Theatre

Theatr Clwyd

Night & Day (1985)
Theatr Clwyd, Mold, Wales
Starring: Keith Barlett, Caroline Lagerfelt, Jonathan Burn, Ralph
Fiennes and Simon Clark. Directed by Toby Robertson.

Coliseum Theatre, Oldham

Me Mam Sez (1986)
Starring: Judith Barker, Carl Forgione, Ralph Fiennes, Diane
Whitley, Michelle Holmes and Ian Marr. Directed by John Retallack.

The Mad Adventures of a Knight (1986)
Starring: Barry McGinn, Stuart Golland, Malcolm Scates, Renata
Allen, Christine Cox and Ralph Fiennes. Directed by John
Retallack.

Cloud Nine (1986)
Starring: Stuart Golland, Malcolm Scates, Chris Barnes, Christine
Cox, Diane Whitley, Liz Rothschild and Ralph Fiennes. Directed by
Barry McGinn.

Open Air Threatre, Regent's Park

Romeo & Juliet (1986)
Starring: Ralph Fiennes, Sarah Woodward, Peter Wyatt and David
O'Hara. Directed by Declan Donnellan.

A Midsummer Night's Dream (1986)
Starring: Ralph Fiennes, Beverly Hills, Ben Cole, Carolyn Backhouse, Andrew Collins, Philip Bowen and Diane Fletcher. Directed by David Conville and Emma Freud.

National Theatre

Six Characters in Search of an Author (1987)
Starring: Richard Pasco, Barbara Jefford, Ralph Fiennes and Lesley Sharp. Directed by Michael Rudman.

Fathers and Sons (1987)
Starring: Robert Glenister, Ralph Fiennes, Alec McCowen, Richard Paslo and Robin Bailey. Directed by Michael Rudman.

Ting Tang Mine (1987)
Starring: Lesley Sharp, Peter Halliday, Ralph Fiennes, Jay Villiers and Caroline Wildi. Directed by Michael Rudman.

The Royal Shakespeare Company

Much Ado About Nothing (1988)
Starring: Maggie Steed, Clive Merrison, Julia Ford, Ralph Fiennes and David Waller. Directed by Di Trevis.

King John (1988)
Starring: Nicholas Woodeson, Julia Ford, Susan Engel, David Lyon, Ralph Fiennes and Antony Brown. Directed by Deborah Warner.

The Plantagenets (1988)
Starring: Ralph Fiennes, Penny Downie, David Waller, David Calder, Anton Lesser and Ken Bones. Directed by Adrian Noble.

The Man Who Came to Dinner (1989)
Starring: John Wood, Estelle Kohler, Maureen Beattie, Ralph Fiennes and Barrie Ingham. Directed by Gene Saks.

Playing With Trains (1989)
Starring: Michael Pennington, Lesley Sharp, Ralph Fiennes and Simon Russell Beale. Directed by Ron Daniels.

Troilus and Cressida (1990)
Starring: Ralph Fiennes, Amanda Root, Sally Dexter and Simon Russell Beale. Directed by Sam Mendes.

King Lear (1990)
Starring: John Wood, Estelle Kohler, Ralph Fiennes, Sally Dexter and Alex Kingston. Directed by Nicholas Hytner.

Love's Labour's Lost (1990)
Starring: Ralph Fiennes, Simon Russell Beale, Carol Royle, Amanda Root and Alex Kingston. Directed by Terry Hands.

Hackney Empire, London/Belasco Theatre, New York

Hamlet (1995)
Starring: Ralph Fiennes, Francesca Annis, Tara Fitzgerald, James Laurenson, Peter Eyre and Damian Lewis. Directed by Jonathan Kent.

Almeida Theatre, Islington

Ivanov (1997)
Starring: Ralph Fiennes, Harriet Walter, Colin Tierney, Anthony O'Donnell, Oliver Ford Davies, Bill Paterson and Justine Waddell. Directed by Jonathan Kent.

Television

Prime Suspect (1991)
Starring: Helen Mirren, Tom Bell, Craig Fairbrass, Jack Ellis and Ralph Fiennes. Directed by Christopher Menaul.

Lawrence After Arabia: A Dangerous Man [TV movie] (1992)
Starring: Ralph Fiennes, Denis Quilley and Paul Freeman. Directed by Christopher Menaul.

The Cormorant (1993)
Starring: Ralph Fiennes, Helen Schlesinger and Karl Francis. Directed by Peter Markham.

Filmography

Wuthering Heights (1992)
Starring: Juliette Binoche, Ralph Fiennes, Janet McTeer, Sophie Ward, Simon Shepherd, Jeremy Northam and Simon Ward. Directed by Peter Kosminsky.

The Baby of Macon (1993)
Starring: Julia Ormond, Ralph Fiennes, Philip Stone, Jonathan Lacey and Don Henderson. Directed by Peter Greenaway.

Schindler's List (1994)
Starring: Liam Neeson, Ben Kingsley and Ralph Fiennes. Directed by Steven Spielberg.

Quiz Show (1995)
Starring: John Turturro, Rob Morrow and Ralph Fiennes. Directed by Robert Redford.

Strange Days (1996)
Starring: Ralph Fiennes, Angela Bassett, Juliette Lewis and Tom Sizemore. Directed by Kathryn Bigelow.

The English Patient (1997)
Starring: Ralph Fiennes, Kristin Scott Thomas, Juliette Binoche, Willem Dafoe, Naveen Andrews, Colin Firth and Kevin Whately. Directed by Anthony Minghella.

Forthcoming releases:

Oscar and Lucinda (1998)
Starring: Ralph Fiennes, Cate Blanchett, Ciaran Hands and Tom Wilkinson. Directed by Gillian Armstrong.

The Avengers (1998)
Starring: Ralph Fiennes, Sean Connery, Uma Thurman, Eddie Izzard, Shaun Ryder and Patrick Macnee. Directed by Jeremiah Chechik.